THE
EVERYTHING®
GUIDE TO
DIGITAL HOME
RECORDING

Dear Reader,

Much has changed in the field of digital home recording since *The Everything® Home Recording Book* came out in 2004. Home recording has literally exploded in the past few years thanks to the increasing power of computers and reduced prices of home recording equipment. The year 2009 brought a slowing global economy, and more and more of us are turning to our art and our music to express ourselves within our own homes. Recording in a professional studio is just no longer an option for many of us. I wanted this book to be a great overview of all the things you're going to encounter as you start setting up your own home studio. While I work as a professional engineer, I often find myself happiest creating music in my own home studio. I've been at it since 1997 when the home recording market looked very different than it does today. I hope that this book helps you create music that satisfies your soul—we can sure use it nowadays. Good luck on your journey. If you post your music online, Google me and send me a note. I'd love to hear what you've created.

Musically,

Marc Schonbrun

Welcome to the EVERYTHING® Series!

These handy, accessible books give you all you need to tackle a difficult project, gain a new hobby, comprehend a fascinating topic, prepare for an exam, or even brush up on something you learned back in school but have since forgotten.

You can choose to read an *Everything®* book from cover to cover or just pick out the information you want from our four useful boxes: e-questions, e-facts, e-alerts, and e-ssentials.

We give you everything you need to know on the subject, but throw in a lot of fun stuff along the way, too.

We now have more than 400 *Everything®* books in print, spanning such wide-ranging categories as weddings, pregnancy, cooking, music instruction, foreign language, crafts, pets, New Age, and so much more. When you're done reading them all, you can finally say you know *Everything®*!

QUESTION

Answers to
common questions

FACT

Important snippets
of information

ALERT

Urgent
warnings

ESSENTIAL

Quick
handy tips

PUBLISHER Karen Cooper

DIRECTOR OF ACQUISITIONS AND INNOVATION Paula Munier

MANAGING EDITOR, EVERYTHING® SERIES Lisa Laing

COPY CHIEF Casey Ebert

ACQUISITIONS EDITOR Lisa Laing

DEVELOPMENT EDITOR Elizabeth Kassab

EDITORIAL ASSISTANT Hillary Thompson

EVERYTHING® SERIES COVER DESIGNER Erin Alexander

LAYOUT DESIGNERS Colleen Cunningham, Elisabeth Lariviere, Ashley Vierra, Denise Wallace

Visit the entire Everything® series at *www.everything.com*

THE
EVERYTHING®
GUIDE TO DIGITAL HOME RECORDING

Tips, tools, and techniques
for studio sound at home

Marc Schonbrun

Author of *The Everything® Music
Theory Book with CD*

Aadamsmedia
Avon, Massachusetts

This book is dedicated to Les Paul, who
made so much of this book possible and truly
changed the world.

———————————

An Everything® Series Book.
Everything® and everything.com® are registered trademarks of F+W Media, Inc.

Published by Adams Media, a division of F+W Media, Inc.
57 Littlefield Street, Avon, MA 02322 U.S.A.
www.adamsmedia.com

ISBN 10: 1-60550-164-6

ISBN 13: 978-1-60550-164-2

Printed in the United States of America.

J   I   H   G   F   E   D   C   B   A

Library of Congress Cataloging-in-Publication Data
is available from the publisher.

Pictures of M-Audio, Sibelius, Digidesign and Avid products are Courtesy of
Avid Technology, Inc.

All other trademarks are property of their respective holders.

This book is available at quantity discounts for bulk purchases.
For information, please call 1-800-289-0963.

Contents

Acknowledgments

I have to start by thanking Kevin Anker, whose help went far beyond the call of duty. This book wasn't possible without your time and effort. Also thanks to Lisa Speegle, Scott Chruch, David Das, Tobias Thon, Dave Hill, Jr., Jeff Horton, Kyle Ritland, Jeff Cross, Brian McConnon, Dr. B.J. Buchalter and all at Metric Halo, Orren Metron, Barry Diament, and countless others who've contributed to my knowledge of digital audio over the years.

The Top Ten Reasons
to Record at Home

1. It's cheaper than going to the studio.

2. No more watching the clock waiting for the "perfect take."

3. It's a blast!

4. You can work when you want to.

5. You can produce high-quality music yourself.

6. You've always wanted to.

7. You can form new musical collaborations and record them.

8. Your computer is wasting away surfing the web—put it to work.

9. You can sound as good as the pros do, and you can do it yourself.

10. You can sell your music on iTunes.

Introduction

IF YOU'RE READING THIS book, then making music is an important part of your life. Furthermore, whether you're making music just to have fun or to pursue a serious interest, you would like to get into home recording. Where do you start? Maybe you've gone to a music store and left more confused than when you walked in. All those choices! Analog versus digital, microphones, cables, rack gear, microphone preamplifiers, mixing boards, computer interfaces, recording software, MIDI . . . the list goes on and on. Even worse, you may have picked up a book on home recording and on page six read about hi passing 200Hz to eliminate some rumble from a bass-heavy cardioid microphone to battle proximity effect. Proximity . . . what? Maybe all those terms were scary, with so little real-world instruction on where to start and what to do.

The Everything® Guide to Digital Home Recording is written for someone who has little or no experience in the field of recording. The only prerequisite? Having music in your soul that you wish to record. That's all. This book is designed to take you through digital home recording step by step. From getting the gear to setting it up and recording properly, you don't need a technical background to use this book successfully. If you're somewhat familiar with recording, you may want to skip directly to some of the meatier chapters later in the book. Even so, you might want to look through each chapter to make sure you haven't missed anything vital.

The field of recording is rooted in math and physics, so there's no denying the academic link and why it's important. There's no way to avoid talking about hertz and kilohertz, just as there's no way around decibels and ratios. That's because we have the daunting task of explaining sound. Warm, muddy, clear, and boomy are all terms to explain characteristics of sounds; so are 20Hz and 10kHz. Don't be scared of the math side of things; it's just one way of looking at it. You'll be pleased to find that this book explains both sides of the fence: some theory and a lot of application. No one learns this in a vacuum. No matter how many books you read, or how much physics you understand, there is no substitute for twiddling knobs to see what happens. That's really the only way to learn. Special attention is paid to the common mistakes beginners make. Topics like which microphones to use and setting proper input levels are covered in great detail here. While these topics might not be as glamorous as getting that Pink Floyd sound, these are the foundations of your recordings.

This book gives you clear information on where to start and how to sharpen your skills. But your experimentation and drive to create will teach you more than any text. Get ready to learn just about "everything" about home studio recording! Let's go!

CHAPTER 1

Recording Basics

The technology for recording sound has been around for just a little more than a hundred years. But it has come a long way since it began. This chapter covers recording history and the development of an industry that was once exclusive and expensive and is now an affordable and practical alternative for home and semiprofessional musicians.

How It All Began

From cave paintings to the Dead Sea Scrolls, information has been written down and preserved for all to see for centuries. But recording sound has been around only since the late 1800s. Sadly, much of the history of sound itself has been lost because it occurred before it was possible to record it. Imagine being able to hear Mozart play his own piano pieces, or to hear Abraham Lincoln speak. These memories survive only through written words and recollections of the events. Recording sound has served not only as an important historical tool, but also as a way for music to be preserved and enjoyed.

A Brief History

In 1877, a man working in New Jersey single-handedly invented recording, the art and science of capturing sound. Thomas Edison recorded the tune "Mary Had a Little Lamb" on a tin cylinder and played it back. Edison's system recorded sound as indentations on a rotating tin cylinder, and the sound was then played back via a needle that felt the indented grooves and replayed the sound. This was the beginning of sound recording as we know it. However, tin was not a durable medium to record sound because it deteriorated upon playback. Tin cylinders were also limited to three minutes of recording time. The fidelity of the sound wasn't exactly beautiful either, but it was a start.

Edison was not the only inventor working on sound recording; he just got there first. In the late 1800s, others saw the commercial potential in sound recording and sought to make improvements on Edison's work. Other inventors devised different disks and cylinders made of various materials to improve sound quality, recording time, and durability.

The Art of Recording Improves

Edison pioneered the first audio recordings and brought them into people's homes. Edison's work on the disk phonograph in 1914 was one of his most significant achievements as an inventor. His disks were more durable, produced immeasurably better sound quality, and could record longer pieces than anything else available. After mass-production of phonographs began, their price fell and they became widely available. Record companies started popping up everywhere! This was the beginning of the revolution of bringing recorded sound into the home. Unfortunately, making recordings was an expensive and time-consuming operation, and very few companies had the capital or the equipment to do so.

Recording Defined

What exactly is recording? Recording is the transmittal of sound waves onto a device capable of preserving and reproducing that sound. Several components are necessary to make a music recording today. First, a sound source is needed—this can be an acoustic instrument, an electronic one, or, in the case of a computer-based synthesizer, a virtual one. Then, the sound needs to be transferred into the recording device. For acoustic instruments, a microphone is needed to convert the acoustic information into electrical signals.

FACT

The first microphone was invented in 1876 for Alexander Graham Bell's telephone system, which received a patent that same year. Bell's microphone picked up sound and converted it to electricity that could be transmitted and reproduced. Chronologically, the microphone predates all recording by one year!

Electronic instruments, such as keyboards, interface directly with the recorder, bypassing the need for a microphone, although it's also possible to use an amplifier and then record the sound conventionally. Because all electronic keyboards output their sound as an electrical signal, recording directly this way and bypassing the amplifier ensures the purest signal.

Now that we have generated and captured the sound, we need somewhere to store it. Today, sound is stored in either of two ways: as an analog signal (a continuous periodic signal) or as a digital representation of an analog signal. A continuous periodic signal is like a wave in its periodic nature. Like waves breaking on the beach, first comes the crest of a wave, followed by a trough, then another crest, then another trough, and so on. Analog media stores the waves themselves as a continuous electrical charge. Magnetic tape is the most common analog medium.

Digital media store a numerical representation of the wave using a code consisting of only zeroes and ones, called binary code. In the early days of digital recording, the common way to store this binary information was on magnetic tape. Digital audiotape, unlike traditional analog media, recorded only digital information—there was no sound on digital audiotape. Today, an audio interface converts analog signals to a digital representation, called encoding, on the way into the computer and converts the digital representation to analog signals, called decoding, on the way out. These two processes are commonly called A/D and D/A conversions. A/D is read as "A to D" or "analog to digital;" D/A means digital to analog.

FACT

Analog tape recording has been around since the 1950s and is still favored by many artists and producers for its warm, rich sound. A reel of 2-inch tape retails for nearly $300. The same amount of information can be recorded to a computer hard drive or CD for a fraction of the cost.

Traditional analog tape is very expensive and hard to get, more so now than ever. Because of the tremendous size of modern hard drives and their low cost, they are a great choice for storing music. The format you ultimately use is unimportant; every recording format does the same basic job of recording sounds.

The final step in recording is playing back the recorded sound. Both analog and digital media must convert information to electrical signals, which are rendered as audible sound waves by speakers, called monitors, or through headphones.

Early Recording Techniques

When tape recording first gained prominence, all recordings were done live, as opposed to recording in a studio. All the sources converged onto one track of a magnetic tape. Because there was only one track, there was no way to adjust the individual levels of the recorded instruments after the initial recording. If you didn't get the balance right the first time, you had to record the entire track again. Overdubbing, the process of adding live tracks after the initial recording, was impossible because of the mechanics of early tape recorders. As time went on, though, tape recorders divided the width of the tape into multiple tracks. In time, it became possible to record four or eight tracks, allowing each of the tracks to be manipulated individually.

Les Paul's Innovations

Before jazz guitarist Les Paul came on the scene, overdubbing was virtually impossible. To understand the difficulty in overdubbing at that time, you first need to understand how the analog tape machine works. In an analog tape machine, three electric heads—the record head, playback head, and erase head—handle the recording process. The record head magnetizes the tape that flows beneath it, transferring information to the tape; the playback head picks up the information from the tape and sends it out to the speakers; and the erase head erases the tape when necessary. The three heads are set up one after another, so that as the record head writes, the playback head picks up tape farther along in the recording. Because each head is reading a different part of the tape, they aren't synchronized. For overdubbing to work (such as layering guitar sounds one on top of another), the artist needs to listen to the previously recorded track to know when to start, when to pick up the tempo, etc. Unfortunately, since the playback head is in a different spot than the record head, the recorded signal will be out of sync; it plays back later than the artist played it.

ESSENTIAL

Les Paul revolutionized the art of recording music, but he also had a profound impact on music itself. His design for a solid-body electric guitar was so impressive that Gibson began producing it with Paul's permission in the 1950s. The Gibson Les Paul is one of the classic electric guitars.

Les Paul was a very innovative man. Not only did he invent the solid body electric guitar as we know it today, he also made overdubbing and multitrack recording possible. Paul had the idea to combine the record head and the playback head into one unit, allowing artists to overdub in real time with no delay. Les Paul died just before the completion of this book in 2009. His legacy as one of the most important innovators in music will live on.

FACT

Les Paul's first multitrack guitar recording was the song "Lover," which was released by Capitol Records in 1947. It featured eight tracks of guitar, painstakingly overdubbed one track at a time. This was the first multitrack recording in history. The rest of the music industry quickly picked up on the technique.

Paul's records were revolutionary; no one had ever heard such a thick, lush sound. Based on Paul's discovery, the company Ampex released a four-track recorder with Sel-Sync (Selective Synchronization) in 1955. However, while this innovation made overdubs possible, most bands still recorded live and used overdubs to add solos, harmony parts, or additional vocals.

How Multitrack Changed the World

Multitrack recording was the single most important innovation in audio recording. The ability to record instruments on individual tracks, have control of separate volume levels, and add other parts after the original recording changed the recording process forever. No longer did you have to settle for an imperfect live take. If the singer were off key or off tempo, you could go back and rerecord individual parts. Guitar players could layer acoustic guitar backgrounds with electric guitar rhythm parts. The possibilities were endless.

The number of tracks available increased over time. At first, the four-track was common. The Beatles, for example, recorded "Strawberry Fields Forever" on two separate four-track tape machines, for a total of eight tracks. Modern recordings can be twenty-four, forty-eight, or, with the help of computers, several hundred tracks. For the home-based musician, this process allows you to slowly build up arrangements one track at a time. You can start with a bass line, add a guitar part, and track some vocals later—all by your lonesome. The finished product will sound like one large, live band even though you played it all yourself.

But home studio owners aren't the only ones who work this way; Trent Reznor of Nine Inch Nails always multitracks. He records alone in his home studio, multitracking to build songs. Tom Scholz of the group Boston records the same way, playing each instrument one at a time.

Modern-Day Developments

We live in the digital age. Everywhere around us, technology is changing the way we work, play, and communicate. The computer has become a fixture in the home, and it's hard to imagine life without one. The need to create coupled with advancements in technology are allowing even the average hobbyist the chance to create and share quality music without going into considerable debt.

The Advancement of Technology

Analog multitrack recorders capable of recording twenty-four or more tracks can cost a lot of money. Even now, though they are less popular, it is easy to spend $30,000 to $50,000 on a good one. Their prohibitive cost meant that for a while, home studios were available only to rich, successful musicians. Digital technology has brought the cost down considerably. Digital tape machines such as the ADAT, while not cheap, were nowhere near as expensive as multitrack analog tape machines. When they were introduced in 1992, Alesis ADATs cost about $3,500. These modular tape machines started showing up in professional studios, and more and more home studios were being equipped with digital recorders.

Recording on Personal Computers

Software provides an interface for laying out tracks and editing them visually in ways that were impossible in the analog or digital tape world. Unlike a tape-based machine, on which you record at a specific point in the tape, digital audio can be placed anywhere. This is impossible to accomplish with analog tape unless you physically cut out a section of tape and splice it somewhere else.

Using computers in studios came with its own problems. Early personal computers were not able to handle the tremendous computing power that digital audio required. To those computers, digital audio was very complex to work with. The solution was to use add-on digital signal processing (DSP) cards inside the computer to help process the digital audio signal. One of the most successful products is Digidesign's Pro Tools.

Professional Pro Tools setups are still very expensive. It's easy to spend $30,000 to $50,000 on a nice Pro Tools rig. Pro Tools was one of the first proprietary systems available, a combination of software and hardware for recording music in a computer. Today, Pro Tools is the standard in recording studios around the world. Other systems are available, but none with the popularity and compatibility of Pro Tools.

How Technology Made the Home Studio Possible

The home studio has followed a path similar to that of professional recording studios. In 1979, TASCAM invented the Portastudio, a four-track recorder that used standard audiotapes. It was priced around $1,000, which was very inexpensive for a unit of its type. It caused a revolution and created the home studio market in one step. The unit was small and compact and could be taken anywhere. Four tracks could be recorded and mixed separately in the unit and later mixed down to a final stereo cassette. Musicians quickly began using the Portastudio for creating their own music and making demos. The Portastudio line by TASCAM is still around today in the form of standalone digital multitrack recorders.

FACT

Recording signals come in two forms: monophonic and stereophonic. A monophonic signal can be reproduced using only one speaker. Old radios with one speaker are monophonic. All of the modern music we listen to now is mixed for stereophonic sound, which uses two speakers: left and right.

In the digital world, the hard disk began showing up as part of standalone recorders in the 1990s, greatly increasing the quality of recorded sound. Because hard disks were able to hold more data, they became a viable solution to storing digital audio. Digital audio files are very large: each monophonic CD-quality track takes 5 megabytes (MB) of memory per minute. A typical ten-minute song consisting of eight tracks requires 400 MB of storage space. By today's standards that's not very much, but in the early 1990s most home computers shipped with hard drives of 500 MB, total! As the computer grew in popularity and power, it became feasible for a computer with a simple audio interface to handle the demands of digital audio without the need for additional DSP cards. Computer recording software such as Cubase, Digital Performer, Sonar and Logic answered the call by providing musical instrument digital interface (MIDI) and digital audio in one package. These programs exist to this day, alongside other popular recording programs like Nuendo, GarageBand, and Live. Computer recording software is immensely popular because it's easy to use, relatively inexpensive, and quite powerful for a system requiring just a home computer and an audio interface.

Your Home Studio

What does all this history mean for you and your home studio? Being able to layer track upon track is a critical part of the home studio experience, especially if you work alone. Many bands record albums one layer at a time for greater control.

Elements of a Professional Recording

As a home studio owner, you should be aware of how the professional studios operate and what techniques they employ. In the end, we are all trying to do the same thing: get sound onto a recording device, spice it up, and mix it to a final product. We all want to get the best sound possible. The differences in techniques directly affect the quality of the final product.

Why Your Favorite Recordings Sound So Good

Cue up your favorite recording, one that you think is recorded well. Sit back and listen closely. Notice how all the instruments blend together, how no instrument sticks out of the mix more than it should. All the instruments sound present, the drums don't sound far away, and the overall effect puts you in the same room as the band. Notice the lack of background noise. The recording has a smooth and polished sound to it, without harshness. These are all qualities of good engineering, good mixing, and good mastering.

When you listen to a professional recording, realize that you are listening to months, if not years, of hard work recording and mixing the music. Big studios also have access to the finest equipment, the best microphones, acoustically perfect rooms, and most important of all, experienced engineers to run the sessions. Does this mean your home studio masterpiece will sound bad? No, not at all! With some basic equipment, a little knowledge, and your inspired music, you can make professional-sounding recordings.

ALERT

Professional recording studios can charge up to several thousand dollars an hour for recording services! For the cost of one session in a professional studio, you could take that money and invest it in your own studio and work whenever you want to.

Recording sessions are broken up into three main components: preproduction, production and engineering, and postproduction. Each component plays an important part in the quality of the finished product.

Preproduction

Preproduction involves everything that happens before the actual recording session. This can include selecting the right material to record, rehearsing the band, and getting ready for the recording sessions. For the home studio owner, it involves working out your material so that you can record it. It also might include purchasing gear to facilitate a particular project, such as a second vocal microphone to record a vocal duet for a new song. Basically, preproduction is anything you can do in advance to make your recordings go more smoothly.

Production and Engineering

Production involves the actual recording sessions. At the sessions, the engineer runs the recording show. It's up to the engineer and any assistants she might have to set up and place the microphones for optimum sound, get proper recording levels, run the mixing board, operate the recording device, and make sure everything sounds good. The engineer is the most important link in the chain (besides the musicians themselves) in getting a great-sounding recording. Engineering, like any other skill, requires a certain level of artistry and practice. An experienced engineer will be able to identify problems and quickly find solutions.

QUESTION

How can I learn more about studio engineering?
Many colleges offer courses in recording techniques. Check the colleges in your area to see if they have anything that fits your schedule. You could also volunteer your services at a local studio in order to gain experience and learn the business from the inside.

Editing and overdubbing might take place in subsequent sessions, but it's still considered production. In your studio, you will most likely be wearing all of the various hats needed to make a recording. It will be up to you to properly set up your equipment and the microphones, run the recording device, and engineer the recording. This can be a tall order to do all at once, but this book will show you how to get started easily. With a little practice, you'll be off and running!

Postproduction

Postproduction includes anything that happens after the recording sessions. Most often, postproduction involves mixing the tracks to a polished, uniform sound. Mixing involves several key elements:

- **Track levels:** Loudness of each track
- **Panning:** Side-to-side placement of instruments and voices in the mix
- **Equalization:** Boosting or cutting certain frequencies in the mix
- **Effects:** Adding signal processing such as reverb, delay, and compression in order to achieve a polished sound
- **Mix down:** Mixing all the tracks into a single stereo pair suitable for distribution or mastering

Even the most basic studio has the capability to do all these things. Remember that the basic sequence of events is always the same: sound capture, recording, and playback. Now that we explained a little about the history of the recording process and got you thinking about some concepts, it's time to shift gears and move into your home studio to find out what you need to get started.

CHAPTER 2

So You Want to Cut a Record . . .

You're ready to make the leap from weekend warrior to home recording studio owner—but how do you do it? What do you need? It's easy to become overwhelmed with all the choices when you're getting started. This chapter serves as a primer and guide to getting you started on your home recording odyssey. Let your creative juices flow!

Bringing It Home

So just what *can* you do in a home studio? What is it, exactly, that you will be able to do once you have your studio set up? Even if you have no recording experience, you'll find that your natural talent and years of listening to well-produced music have given you more tools than you thought you had. It's all about listening.

Recording

The most obvious thing you can do in a home studio is to record sound into your computer. Whether you are learning to use microphones effectively or just plugging in a keyboard, recording covers the whole spectrum of capturing sound. For those who have never recorded before, the process can be very rewarding. Having the ability to come home from work and spend a few hours in your studio creating music is very freeing, and the icing on the cake is that you have total control. Whether you are making an elaborate multitrack masterpiece or simply singing and playing guitar, you need to know how to get a good sound. This is where you learn the basics of engineering: setting levels, choosing and placing the correct microphones for the best sound, and mixing tracks. For the keyboard players out there, using MIDI, an electronic standard used for the transmission of digital music, is an important part of the recording process. All these elements fall under the umbrella of recording.

Mixing

Mixing is generally done after the initial recording sessions. Mixing is the art of setting the loudness and sound color of each instrument that you record. Mixing is a learned art, and like any other skill, it takes practice. Using faders to control the volume of tracks helps the instruments sound more cohesive and balanced. Equalization (EQ) is the process of boosting or lowering certain frequencies. Using EQ you can clarify the sound of a muddy bass, or create a round, warm sound from a thin, lifeless guitar.

Effects are also a major component of mixing; they can help you achieve a more polished final sound. For instance, you can add reverb to give the illusion of having recorded in a large space or use compression to even out sudden changes in volume.

All of the things discussed here will be covered in more detail later in this book. Don't be worried if it sounds like a lot to learn! Chapter 17 discusses mixing in more detail, and effects are covered in Chapters 15 and 16.

Editing

Look at music editing as the ability to cut, copy, paste, and whiteout your sound. In the world of editing, you can cut a section and rerecord it, or you can go back and fix a note that sounds bad.

Imagine you are recording a song with the structure: chorus, solo, chorus. Suppose the choruses are exactly the same, and when you recorded the piece, the second chorus sounds better. Computer software gives you the ability to cut the first chorus and copy the second in its place. You don't even have to play repeat sections twice; you can just loop together small repeating bars of music. You can even click and drag sections of music around with your mouse. Did you decide after the fact that you want to record an introduction to your masterpiece? Just drag the original audio to the right, make room for the new, and paste it all together. This is just the tip of a very large iceberg—so how do you get started? First, you've got to determine what your needs are.

Assessing Your Needs

You've scoured the Internet. You get every music gear catalog known to mankind. You've been to the local music store countless times. You know it's time to start doing some home recording, but the myriad choices and lack of concrete how-to instructions is getting to you. Have no fear! You're in the right place now.

"Home recording" is a broad term—musicians have different needs and ideas about what the studio is going to provide. For some, home recording is a sketchpad for small ideas that might be taken to a professional studio later. For others, their home studios are used to flesh out ideas so they can present them to members of their bands. Still others use home recording as a way to save money. Because professional recording studios can be very costly, they invest in a home studio and can make demo recordings as frequently as they want. And finally, some musicians use their home studio as a creative tool to write, produce, and ultimately sell their own music. Some home studio owners enjoy the process so much that they eventually upgrade their equipment and open their studios to the public. What you do with your studio is as personal as the music you create. The sky is the limit and, with modern technology at your side, you will be armed with all the tools to make recordings that sound great.

Start Simple

It's very easy to go overboard in this field. There is plenty of equipment out there, and you could spend lots of money on it. Everyone fantasizes about the professional studio with a 10-foot-wide mixing board and floor-to-ceiling rack equipment. Some musicians do need all that stuff, but what do *you* need? The first step is assessing your needs. Ask yourself these questions before you start buying gear:

- How many instruments do I need to record at the same time?
- Are the instruments electric or acoustic?
- Will I use MIDI or sequenced instruments?
- Do I need portability?
- Do I plan to distribute or sell the music recordings I make?

Keep the answers to these questions in the back of your mind as you read this book. The theme you'll see repeated throughout is: Make the most of what you have. Expensive gear won't necessarily make anything better. What really matters is what you do with what you have. Too many studio owners get caught in the trap of having the nicest toys without understanding or utilizing their gear to the fullest. Imagine Grandma driving a Ferrari to church once a week. Bit of a waste, eh?

Have a Goal

Having a goal seems like a simple idea. However, many people jump on the home studio bandwagon without even considering a goal. Ask yourself, "What do I want to do with a home studio?" The result you're looking for—be it demo tapes to send to local clubs, or recordings to sell after a show—will help you determine what you need in a home studio. More often than not, at first you'll want to start small. You can always upgrade as you become more skilled at the process. Remember, home recording is a skill like any other, and it takes a while to get really good at it.

Seek Advice from Others

More than likely, you know other musicians. It's safe to assume that a percentage of them will also own home studios, in one form or another. Spend some time talking with them and, if possible, get hands-on demonstrations of the equipment they use. Find out how they use it and listen to how their final product sounds.

FACT

The recordings of the 1950s and 1960s were recorded with equipment that would be considered limiting nowadays. You'd be amazed at how many major recordings that you know and love were done by a highly skilled recording engineer on very basic equipment. Rudy Van Gelder's 1950s and 1960s Blue Note jazz sessions come to mind, as do George Martin and the Beatles.

Another invaluable resource is your local music store. Many of these stores are staffed with very talented musicians. Many of them, in addition to knowing a great deal about the equipment they sell, have home studios of their own. Ask them what they use, and what they use it for. They might even let you listen to a CD of their work. There are also many magazines and online sources devoted to recording. Popular recording and technology publications include:

- *Mix Magazine*
- *EQ Magazine*
- *Keyboard Magazine*
- *Tape OP*

In the online world, you'll find many resources and bulletin boards where you can exchange ideas with other home studio owners. Many professional engineers frequent these sites and you can learn a lot by listening, reading, and posting. For general recording tips, check these websites and forums:

- *www.bigbluelounge.com*
- *www.homerecording.com*
- *www.harmonycentral.com*
- *www.audioforums.com*
- *www.recording.org*
- *www.tapeop.com*
- *www.kvraudio.com*

Shopping for Gear

Okay. Now you're really excited. You're ready to start. You've thought through the whole process. You've talked to other studio owners. You've looked around on the web.

Start Shopping

Depending on where you live, you might have access to music stores that carry a lot of recording equipment. Your best bet is to buy from a store, instead of online. There are a bunch of good reasons you should buy from a store. For starters, you'll get to see, touch, and even use some of the gear you are planning to purchase before you spend your money. You'll also be able to get advice from the salesperson on what might suit you best. Developing rapport with an individual salesperson is important because, as you keep going back to the same person for all your gear, not only do you develop a nice business relationship (which might result in discounts), you might also get honest, real-world advice.

But there's nothing wrong with buying gear online, either. If you live in a remote area, this might be your only option. If you purchase online, returning gear you don't like is a pain. But then again, there are some great deals online. If you shop around, you can get a great price. Many stores also price-match, so even if you've found a better deal somewhere else, bring the information to the attention of your salesperson. Many stores will accommodate you in an effort to keep you as a loyal customer. You can also find some great deals in the used-gear market; check out eBay.

ALERT

Don't feel pressured into buying more than you need at first. You can always upgrade as you go. Certain components, such as cables and microphone stands, don't change from setup to setup, so you won't waste money upgrading those items.

Creating a Budget

Here comes everyone's least favorite subject—spending money. You work hard for it, and the last thing you want to do is squander it on equipment that isn't suitable for you or doesn't get the job done. The good news is that there is a studio to be had at almost every price level, and you can get started with a basic studio for around $250—maybe even less, depending on your configuration and what you already own. The bad news is that there's a lot of equipment available, and you can easily get carried away and spend many thousands of dollars on all the various gear out there. Figure out exactly what you can spend at first. Your budget should take into consideration the following:

- What is the maximum you can spend?
- Do you want the ability to record more than one track at a time?
- How many microphones do you need?
- How many interconnecting cables does your setup require?
- Do you need computer recording software?
- Do you need a computer recording interface?
- Does your computer need to be upgraded to handle the demands of working with large music files?
- What signal effects do you need?

- Do you need a separate mixer? (This is becoming less necessary these days.)
- How do you plan on listening to your work—headphones or speakers?

As you can see, these are important issues. You must take all these points into consideration when planning your budget. Since every studio is different, this book talks about general setups, and you can modify the setup that is closest to your needs.

What You Will Really Spend

You've already learned the three elements necessary for recording sound: something to capture the sound, something to store it and play it back, and something to enable you to hear it played back. First, you need a sound and a device capable of capturing that sound, usually a microphone. Some instruments interface directly via cables; keyboards and amplifier line-out jacks are examples of direct instruments. Next, you need a recorder capable of recording the sound and playing it back later. Last, you need something to hear the recording with—either speakers or headphones. These elements are commonly found in all studios, regardless of price or quality.

Capturing Sound

Microphones are typically used for sound input. Prices of microphones range widely; you can pay around $60 for a starter variety, $200 for a good one, and $500 and above for a top-of-the-line model. Figure out how many you'll need. You will probably need one microphone for each acoustic instrument or vocalist, and two to four for a drum kit, depending on how you set up the kit. If you are recording one instrument at a time, you can get away with fewer microphones. You might pool the money you save by doing this and buy one or two higher quality microphones.

Instruments such as keyboards, drum machines, and guitar effects processors plug directly into an audio interface. Also, many amplifiers feature direct outputs and bypass the need for a microphone; all you need is a cable. Cables are cheap, thank goodness! You might also need a direct box to change the impedance of certain instruments to match the input of the recorder. We'll discuss that more in Chapter 11. Direct boxes range from $20 to $400.

Since the majority of recording systems are based around computers, why would you consider a dedicated hardware recording system? Dedicated hardware recording systems can be perfect for those who need a simple setup and who rely on portability. Computers are expensive, and only laptops are easily portable. Computers can also be susceptible to viruses and crashes. You won't encounter those issues with a dedicated hardware recording system.

Finding a Recorder

For quick and simple recording, there are many portable digital recorders on the market. Some of these offer features like built-in stereo microphones, onboard digital effects, and overdubbing capabilities. Many are small enough to fit in your hand. Portable digital recorders can run as little as $150 to as much as $900.

You can also record with a computer, though you'll need software, which ranges from free to $1,000. You'll also need a computer interface that accepts audio and possibly MIDI if you plan to use that. Depending on how many sources you need to record at once, computer audio interfaces can range from $100 to more than $1,000. MIDI interfaces are less expensive, and you pay more depending on how many MIDI inputs, or separate instruments, you need to use at the same time. Expect to spend between $30 for a simple one-input/one-output MIDI interface and up to $550 for eight MIDI devices.

Playing the Music Back

In order to play back the recorded sound, most home studio owners start with a pair of decent headphones. Headphones range from $30 to $200. If you choose to use professional speakers, called monitor speakers, you can expect to pay anywhere from $100 to $800 or more for a set. Some monitors are self-powered and don't require additional amplifiers to run; others need an amplifier, which will cost you money as well! Your best bet is to go for self-powered monitors. There are some great ones in the $200–$300 range. A low-tech solution is to monitor through your home stereo. It's not the optimal way to go, but it might tide you over until you can afford dedicated monitors.

Don't Get Carried Away

It's so easy to get carried away in a music store. You go in for one thing and walk out with five things you didn't need. This is known as Gear Acquisition Syndrome (GAS). This ailment affects many musicians who fall victim to the grandeur of a music store that has "everything." Out of the three elements of your studio, it's important to balance the quality of each part. The result is only as good as all the equipment you use. Add one weak link and the chain will break. For example, if you blow all your cash on a top-of-the-line audio interface and you plug a cheap, noisy microphone into it, your computer will play back a noisy signal, in perfect digital quality. See the problem? We address the issue of Garbage In, Garbage Out (GIGO) later in this book. Go into this process with a clear understanding of your needs and your means. Try your best to choose components that work together to deliver a quality result.

Typical Setups

Let's take a look at some typical setups for various types of recording systems so you can get an idea of what equipment is commonly used. Chapter 4 goes into much greater detail on this subject, but for now you can get an idea of how some people work.

For Working Alone

Many "solo" engineers and players own just a few microphones, usually one all-purpose and one specialized microphone. They focus on quality purchases over quantity. For example, it wouldn't make sense to have eight average-sounding channels in an audio interface when two great ones cost about the same and will be enough for your needs. A lot depends on what instruments you plan to record. Many studios use MIDI to control drum machines and keyboards. While standalone sequencers and standalone recorders do exist, they are rarely used anymore as computers have all but replaced their functionality at a lower cost with added flexibility. The solo home studio owner doesn't require huge amounts of space, and usually a corner of a room or a desk area is enough to get anyone started. Since the computer is the modern recording standard, many home studios are built around computer workstations and desks.

For Working in Groups

If you're in a group or you plan to record a lot at one time, you have some choices on how to proceed. For live groups, multitrack recording isn't a necessity, although it's nice to have. A good-quality portable digital recorder can do a great job. If the recorder includes a stereo microphone, you can place the unit in the center of the group and get above-average results. If the portable digital recorder doesn't include a stereo microphone, you'll need a mixer. Figure 2-1 illustrates what a compact mixer looks like.

A mixer allows several sources of sound to be mixed together into one stereo output. You can connect eight or more microphones to the mixer, which will output one stereo sound to your recorder. The nice part about this system is that it's not all that expensive; however, there are some serious drawbacks to it.

Figure 2-1: Compact mixing board *Courtesy of Avid Technology, Inc.*

First, the balance of the group has to be set in the mixer before the recording takes place. Since you're not multitrack recording, you can only record the single output of the mixer. Also, you have very little opportunity to add individual effects, except again through the mixer at the time of recording. If you set up the microphones, digital interfaces, and effects carefully, you can get a good sound, but it's very difficult. If, after you're done, you realize the snare drum is too loud, for example, there's little you can do. Even so, you'd be surprised to know how many albums—especially jazz records— have been recorded this way.

Those who step up to multitrack recording do so in much the same way the solo artist does. However, there are specific concerns that need to be addressed, such as the number of instruments that are going to be recorded at once. Having the right number of simultaneous inputs is crucial to be able to mix the sounds after the fact. By placing individual instruments on individual tracks, you have greater control over their relative timbre and volume levels. When you are limited to a few inputs, you have no choice but to place multiple instruments on the same track, thereby losing the ability to balance them after you record. Typically these setups use a lot of microphones. You'll need one input for every microphone you use. Your needs as a multitracker really depend on what you're recording and how much control you want.

Portable Setups

If you are doing a lot of your recording at gigs, you'll need a setup that is portable and easy to move. Portable stereo recorders are great for this. If your live gig has a soundperson, you can benefit from her gear as well. You can get a stereo mix from the soundperson and plug into your portable stereo recorder and you are good to go. (That is, of course, assuming that the mix off the board sounds good.)

If you have a laptop and an audio interface, you can take this setup with you to record gigs. With this kind of setup, you could record the stereo mix from the soundperson, or set up your own microphones and direct boxes and multitrack record the gig; if you have enough inputs on your audio interface, you can do both.

What's been missing in all this discussion about gear, options, and budgets is the creative spark. That is the spark that only you can provide.

Recordings can't make things magically appear. No matter what kind of gear you have, if you don't bring your creativity into play, nothing happens. We've all heard good players playing cheap instruments who still sound great. We've also experienced amateurs playing expensive gear and sounding terrible. Keep that in mind as you go through this book. You make it happen.

CHAPTER 3

Elements of a Home Studio

Now that you understand the basics of recording, it's time to explore in greater detail the elements that go into a studio. As you start to make choices about what to include in your studio, a thorough understanding of the equipment will help you make informed decisions and get you past the advertising rhetoric.

The Center of It All—The Recorder

The recording device is the center of any studio. No matter what you record, all the magic happens at the recorder. Picking the best one for you and your needs is important, so be sure to do your homework and get it right. These days, the computer is your most capable digital recording tool. The best news: you probably already own one suitable for recording!

If you own a computer, especially one that's fairly new, you may already own a recording device just waiting to serve you. (Chapter 6 covers computer setups in much greater detail.) Why would you want to use a computer? Well, for one thing, if you already have one, there's less to buy. At this point, the alternatives to computers all utilize digital technology just like a computer. Lastly, and most importantly, most of the amazing innovation happening in digital home recording technology is centered on the computer. One such innovation is the lowered cost of home recording—a computer is just plain cheaper in the long run.

FACT

Digital recordings are stored as binary information. Music going into the recorder goes through a complicated analog-to-digital conversion that turns sound into binary information for storage. So it's important to buy the correct conversion equipment and compatible recording software for your machine. Every software manufacturer has minimum system requirements; it's up to you, the educated consumer, to make sure your machine qualifies. Software is usually not returnable.

So what kind of computer makes a good recording computer? It's difficult to answer that question because technology changes so quickly; what was current six months ago is considered old news today. There are two main types of computers based on the operating system they use: Microsoft Windows or Apple Mac. Many people swear by whichever they use, and great music can be made on each. Traditionally, professional music studios have relied on Apple computers, but Windows-based systems are becoming more and more popular, especially in home studios.

The computer debate can get very silly and many people get carried away with numbers and current trends. The basic rule of thumb is age:

If your computer is less than two years old, you'll be in good shape. But here's the problem: While current computers work well now, they do so only because the current software is optimized for the current technology. When newer, faster computers arrive, software manufacturers change their software to work with the enhancements of new processors. When you try to run new software on old processors, you can run into problems.

What's So Great about a Computer Anyway?

Computers are simply tools that help you get a job done. Let's talk about the pros and cons of using a computer for music. On the pro side, here are several advantages to recording music with a computer:

- You may already own a suitable machine.
- Computers have increased sound processing quality.
- You can edit on a large screen using a mouse.
- You can take advantage of powerful music software.
- It's easy to turn your music into MP3s and share them online.
- It's easy to burn and label CDs of your music.
- You can easily sell your music online—even through iTunes.

On the con side, there are several disadvantages to recording music with a computer:

- Computers crash (and often at the worst possible times).
- Except for laptops, you can't easily take computers anywhere.
- The price of software and hardware can be steep.
- New software has a learning curve.
- It can be difficult to keep up with changes in technology.
- Computers are susceptible to viruses.

If You Don't Have a Computer

What if you don't have a computer? Or maybe you have one, but it's impossible to get your family away from it at the times you want to work. If you fall into one of these categories, you still have many options. There are plenty of standalone recorders. The playing field consists of digital hard-disk recorders, digital multitrack tape machines, and studio-in-a-box solutions. You can even find applications for your iPhone or iPod Touch to record ideas anywhere! The standalone solutions are portable, which makes it easier for you to move around. While the editing is superior on a computer, more and more of these recorders have the ability to interface with a computer so you can do complex editing and sound manipulation later, giving you the best of both worlds.

The studio-in-a-box is another type of standalone recorder. It features inputs, some microphone preamps, recording, integrated effects, integrated mixing, and mastering. Many include CD burners so you can burn your final product. If portability is crucial when you're just starting out and don't own any mixers or effects, a studio-in-a-box is a great way to go.

FACT

The all-in-one studio has brought digital studio quality to the masses. Before the advent of digital recording technology, cassette tape recorders lacked the sound quality and fidelity of professional studios. But now anyone can make a recording that sounds great without spending a fortune.

Roland was one of the first companies to introduce the studio-in-a-box concept. Their VS-880 was a revolutionary product because it incorporated a recorder, mixer, editor, and effects processor in one small tabletop unit. It was small, portable, and, considering all you got in one package, surprisingly affordable for the time.

There are some downsides to these units, though, so you need to make sure the unit you select can handle what you have in mind. The number of tracks you can record at the same time can be limited, as is the quality of the effects—and they usually can't be upgraded. Some units allow the use of external effects through an insert jack, but not all of them do. Many units of this type store music on either a hard drive or, more recently, on Compact-Flash or SmartMedia cards. When the drive is full, you have to stop recording. Some devices let you burn the data tracks as a backup, and some don't; you have to mix, finish, and delete before you can do anything else. Disadvantages aside, these units are very popular and sell very well.

Capturing Sound

The next step is getting sound into the recording device. Sound gets into a recorder either by being plugged directly into the recorder with a cable, or by using a microphone to pick up the sound.

Microphones

If you're recording an acoustic instrument or vocals, a microphone is necessary to convert the sound waves into electrical signals. What makes one microphone different from any other microphone? As a budding sound engineer, you should understand why engineers choose different microphones for different purposes.

Every microphone "hears" sound differently. Unidirectional microphones only hear what's directly in front of them, while omnidirectional microphones pick up everything from all sides. And figure eight microphones hear sound on two distinct sides. If you were trying to use one microphone to record a room full of sound coming from all sides, you would choose a microphone that hears sounds from all sides, the omnidirectional microphone. If you were trying to zero in on just one instrument without picking up other sounds, you would want to use a unidirectional microphone pointed right at the sound source.

ALERT

Knowing what direction a microphone hears is usually the determining factor in choosing which microphone to use. You must choose the one that works best for what you're trying to record. See Chapter 9 for more information about different microphones and how to use them.

Some microphones also are more sensitive to certain frequencies of sound than others. This is called frequency response. You wouldn't want to use a microphone that can't hear very high signals clearly on a high-pitched instrument, or low signals on a low-pitched one. Microphones also color the sound they transmit; this is tied into frequency response. These colorations are what give microphones their distinct sound—"warm," "clean," or "clear" are terms commonly used to describe sound colorations. Because of construction differences between microphone manufacturers, every model sounds unique. With some training and experience, you'll be able to pick the right microphone(s) for your setup. Getting the right type of microphone is more important than buying a particular brand.

Microphone Preamps

Microphones don't produce much signal by themselves. If you plugged one directly into a recorder, the sound level wouldn't be high enough to register a signal on your recording device. You could try to compensate by turning up the entire track, but unfortunately you'd turn everything up, including the noise. You need a preamplifier to raise the output of the microphone enough to make the signal clear and strong.

QUESTION

How many microphone preamps will I need?
You will need one preamp for each microphone you record at a time. If you don't record live groups, you might need only a few microphones, recording one or two tracks at a time.

Preamps are commonly built into mixing boards, studios-in-a-box, and computer interfaces, so you might not need to purchase these separately. You can also buy individual microphone preamps if your device has none or you need more. The number of microphone preamps that your mixer or other recording device has is a critical factor in determining if the gear is right for you. This is the time for you to evaluate how many microphones you plan to use simultaneously.

Direct Inputs

An instrument that plugs directly into the recorder is called a direct input. Microphones aren't necessary in these cases. Keyboards, synthesizers, drum machines, and certain guitar and bass amplifiers are equipped with "line outs" that can be plugged directly into a mixer or a recording device. A guitar or bass plugged in directly via a cable won't be line level, however; that is, its signal won't have enough juice to be heard. It also has the wrong impedance, which is an electronics term referring to how much force the signal has due to the way it impedes the outward flow of electricity.

Guitar and bass are very high impedance sources and generate very low output levels. Even though it appears that you can connect a guitar or bass directly to a recorder, you'll need a direct box, or DI, if you want to record a guitar or bass without an amp. A direct box simply takes a signal that is unbalanced or has the wrong impedance, and converts it to a perfectly balanced output suitable for plugging into a mixer. It's a common misconception that a DI box is all you need for guitar and bass. It's not. After the DI takes care of the impedance, you'll still need preamplification of some sort. This can either be a mixer or a computer recording interface.

Direct boxes come in two flavors: passive and active. Passive DIs don't require extra power to run; active DIs do. Active direct boxes require power for changing impedance and outputting balanced signals, while passive DIs do all their work through transformers. Every studio should have at least one direct box.

Another nice benefit of a direct box is that it can isolate nasty buzzes that studios encounter from time to time via a button called a ground lift. Even if your amplifier or keyboard has a line out, if you are getting buzzing that's driving you crazy, try a direct box between the output and the recorder's input, and flip the ground switch. Many times this will do the trick. Anyone who has played on stage has encountered a direct box; it's indispensable. If you plan to record bass, guitar, or certain keyboards that aren't line level, you will need a few direct boxes.

To Mix or Not to Mix

No piece of gear is more closely associated with the recording studio than the mixing board. Historically, that's where the engineer spends most of her time working. A mixing board is simply a device that takes many individual audio channels and mixes them to a stereo left and right output. (Many mixing boards have more than a single stereo output, but for a general description, think of a mixer as a device that sums many signals to a pair of outputs.) Mixing boards also allow you to preamplify microphones and adjust equalization (EQ). EQ is further explained in Chapter 15. Despite all this, mixing boards are no longer a necessity for everyone. Who needs one? And how do you benefit from having one?

Why You Might Want a Mixer

If you have a standalone recorder, you need a mixer. Standalone recorders only record and play back. They don't set levels or provide EQ; they just capture sound. So you need a mixer to control audio levels. This is why the mixer is so closely associated with the recording studio. Only in recent years, with the studio-in-a-box and computer software, have mixerless setups become possible. Traditionally, every recording device was a simple record and playback machine; the mixer wasn't optional. Even as computer systems become more commonplace, some engineers still like having the control a traditional mixer provides, instead of mixing with a mouse.

Let's say you need to record three microphones and you only have two inputs on your recorder. You might use a mixer to help you overcome this limitation. As an example, one input could be used for one of the microphones and you could combine the other two microphones through the mixer. However, you lose the ability to control the volume of the individual microphone signals, so if you're going to do this, be very careful to get a great-sounding mix of those channels before you record anything for real.

ESSENTIAL

If you're going to combine your microphones, be sure you trial record each track to get the best sound before you commit to the final recording. Once it's recorded, you can't change it. This is why it's important to get the right number of inputs on your recording device so you can avoid these difficult compromises.

You may want to use a mixer if you've had experience with one and feel comfortable with it. You might also want a mixer if your recording device has limited inputs. Suppose that you have an eight-input recording device;

you can record a maximum of eight channels at once. (You can overdub more than eight, but eight signals at once is your limit for recording.)

If you're recording a live band and need more than eight signals, you might want to use a mixer to pare down some of them. For instance, instead of a drum kit taking up six valuable available inputs, you can use a mixer for the drum tracks. You can take those six drum microphones and mix them down to four tracks so they take up fewer inputs. Maybe you can combine the tom toms into a single track and save a channel. The only downside to this is that whatever gets mixed into one channel is there for good. Using the tom toms as an example, if you decide later that the right tom is too loud, there's no way to change the balance—you can't unbake a cake!

Why You Might Not Want a Mixer

If you're going the route of the computer-based studio, you likely won't need a mixer. You may find that USB and FireWire interfaces sporting eight or more inputs give you enough simultaneous inputs. In fact, most home recording studios rarely need to record more than eight signals at once. Computers also sport amazing virtual mixers for controlling levels after recording. You can even use a control surface if you enjoy mixing by moving knobs and faders rather than a mouse. There's more on these in Chapter 17.

Achieving Portability

In the past, the terms "recording studio" and "portable" were rarely used in the same sentence. But with the miniaturization of technology, studios can be tucked under your arm and taken wherever you want. Even the iPhone and iPod Touch are part of the portable recording game! This is also great news for those with small apartments where space is at a premium.

Laptops

In the last few years the laptop has gone from a convenience to a power-house. Desktop computers aren't selling as well as laptop computers, especially with younger students. The term "desktop replacement" is now used in laptop advertisements. If you are computer recording, the laptop is a very attractive choice because you can take it anywhere. The speed and disk size of current machines make them more than adequate for tackling even complex recordings. Pick up any recording magazine and you'll find some article explaining how your favorite artist's record was recorded live on a laptop at a gig. And with USB and FireWire audio interfaces dropping in price and increasing their features, laptops are a great choice.

The laptops themselves can be more expensive than a desktop, so that is a drawback for some. With desktop LCD flat panel displays typically sporting between 20 and 30 inches of screen real estate, a laptop's typical 13- to 15-inch screen may seem paltry; with recording software, you have a lot to look at.

Standalone Units

Standalone recorders such as ADATs, DA-88s, and hard-disk systems by Alesis and Mackie can be thrown in a rack carrier and taken from place to place. Add in the necessary mixer, additional microphone preamps or other extras, and the weight starts to add up. But it is possible to get very high-quality results from these standalone recorders, making them good portable solutions. You'll find that many engineers who specialize in live recording still rely on standalone recorders, even though computers are more popular.

Pocket Recording

If you are trying to record live sounds like the sound of the ocean, kids playing at a park, or a noisy city street for some added effects, you can do so easily with one of the new CompactFlash-based recorders like the M-Audio MicroTrack II, as seen in Figure 3-1.

The sound quality of these cell phone-sized recorders will amaze you. This setup

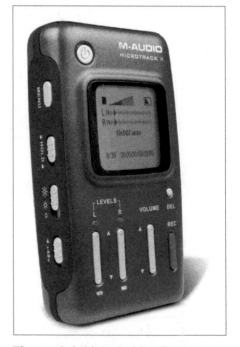

Figure 3-1: M-Audio MicroTrack II handheld recorder *Courtesy of Avid Technology, Inc.*

can be great for picking up an acoustic orchestra or band that doesn't require multitracking; most orchestral recording is done with one set of stereo microphones in front of the group. You can even record a live gig this way. Many of the CompactFlash-based recorders allow microphone inputs from studio-quality microphones, so you can make studio-quality recordings anywhere. They even provide power for the microphones through their internal batteries! You can truly go anywhere.

Setting Up a Space

Having a comfortable work space is critical to working efficiently. If your gear isn't readily available, you aren't going to be as likely to use it, so don't cram yourself into a corner someplace or exile yourself to a basement.

Being comfortable is vital to working efficiently. You can either make do with the tables and chairs you already own or invest in studio furniture. Yes, they make furniture just for this kind of thing! But before you furnish your studio, establish your main focus. For most people, easy access to their primary instrument is their greatest concern. Then comes placement of the recording device or mixer. If you use a computer, do yourself a favor and put the computer on the floor if you can. This will free up much-needed desk space. Figure 3-2 shows a well-organized recording space.

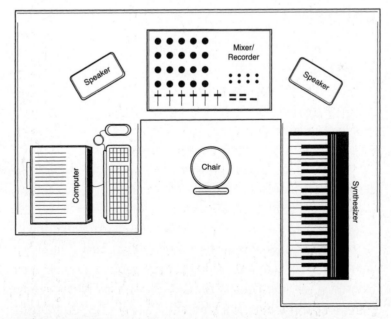

Figure 3-2: Setting up a good space

You need a place where you can get work done. Your music requires concentration. Selecting a spot for your studio might not always be in your complete control, but you should take a few things into account when setting up your space. To record with microphones you will need a quiet place. Microphones have this pesky little way of hearing things you don't want them to hear: dogs barking, doors shutting, and phones ringing, just to name a few. If you plan to work late at night, you'll want to be someplace out of the way so you don't disturb anyone.

Instruments

The discussion so far has emphasized equipment, but you can't forget about the instruments you're going to play. They're pretty important to this process because, no matter how good your recording gear is, your instruments need to sound good. It stands to reason that any problems you have with your instruments are going to get worse when you record them. There's a widely used phrase in the recording world: Garbage In, Garbage Out. Make sure you have decent-sounding equipment. It's a myth that "you can fix it in the mix."

Experiment

Adding new sounds to your music is one of the fun parts about home recording. Even if you only play guitar, adding several different-sounding guitars on different tracks can widen the scope of your music. Experimentation is the name of the game here; you'd be amazed at what sounds good together. Keyboard players can really go to town with different sounds, layers of instruments, and even drum kits from the keyboard.

Drum machines have always been useful to nondrummers and home studio musicians alike. Acoustic drums can be difficult to record well and can be too loud for many apartments and houses. Sample-based drum programs such as Battery from Native Instruments and EZdrummer from Toontrack sound so realistic it's uncanny. Their quality is so high because samples are actual recordings of drums, not synthetic versions. That's right, someone recorded each drum one by one at different volume levels and the sampler plays them back for you!

Another option if you're not going to play individual drums, is premade drum loops. These loops are professionally recorded in studios and are every bit as real as having the drummer with you. They're well mixed, and they sound very cool, so they're definitely worth checking into. To utilize loops, you use a computer and recording software. Loops come as pre-mixed audio files; you simply add them into your recording program on an empty track and voilà, instant drums!

All recording software works with loops. From Apple's highly intuitive GarageBand to the über-powerful Pro Tools 8 software from Digidesign, loops are a common way for musicians to work.

Collaborate

Just because you can lay down eight or more tracks of yourself playing each instrument one pass at a time doesn't mean that you should. Why use a sampled drum when a real drummer is close by? By getting to know other musicians and home studio owners, you can collaborate with each other and utilize the combined power of all your talents. Maybe you'll even make a record together. Who knows what could happen. The possibilities are endless.

CHAPTER 4

Recording Equipment

The number of options in the home recording market is staggering and, for many, a bit scary. Finding the gear that's right for you can be a tall order. This chapter covers noncomputer equipment from the simplest to the most extravagant. What you will not find are specific recommendations on brands and models. Instead, you'll learn about the available options so that you'll have the information you need to decide what will work best for you.

What the Right Gear Can Do for You

There are many pieces of gear available, some fancy and some basic. Finding the gear that's right for you can mean the difference between creating music and creating frustration.

It's only in recent years that the sound quality and low prices of home recording equipment have made recording professional-sounding music at home possible. The early tape-based studios lacked the quality that professional studios could produce. With tape, it was easy to tell a homespun demo from a demo recorded in a professional studio. Digital gear has blurred that line substantially. The noisy recordings and tape hiss that plagued home studios are now a thing of the past. Twenty years ago, even an experienced engineer couldn't make a budget home studio sound truly professional; now, anything is possible.

It's not true that good recording equipment can make musicians sound better. Great gear can't improve musicianship, songwriting, or your general skill on an instrument. While signal processing can enhance your sound, the quality of the final product will primarily depend on two factors, no matter how much you spend on equipment. The first, and most important, is the quality of the sound you are recording. Unrehearsed, badly organized music and music played on poor-sounding instruments will sound lousy every time, no matter how expensive the recording gear is. The second factor is the knowledge and skill of the recording engineer. The art of microphone placements, EQ, and all the effects settings contribute to the quality of the sound. You get out what you put in.

ESSENTIAL

Just as buying a Ferrari won't necessarily make you a better driver, buying top-level equipment won't instantly make your music sound better. In fact, the better your gear, the more accurately it records and plays back, including both the good *and* the not so good.

It's time to break down gear into categories based on price, which is the determining factor for many people. Remember that prices might change over time, but the ideas behind the return on investment for any piece of equipment should remain the same. Every piece of home recording gear is trying to imitate the features of a professional recording studio on a smaller scale. While technological advancements might allow more features, the goal is still the same: achieve at home the quality that the professionals get in a studio.

The Four-Track Tape Recorder

Thirty years after its initial introduction, the four-track cassette recorder (shown in Figure 4-1) refuses to go away without a fight. Many home studio owners got their start with machines like these. Nowadays, this is one of the least expensive ways to get into home recording. If you are just getting started and money is at a premium, you can do very well with a tape multitrack.

Today, cassette multitracks, which are no longer in production, go for about $100 or less. eBay is a great place to find a cassette multitracker. The most basic machines allow one track at a time to be recorded. However, a maximum of four separate tracks can be played back at once. You can control each

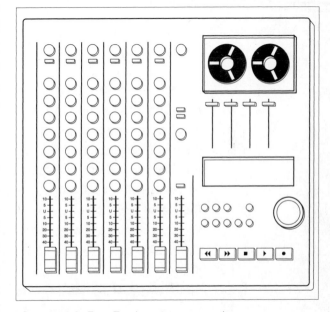

Figure 4-1: Four-Track cassette recorder

track's level (volume) and the pan (left to right balance), but that's all the control you get. After you find a blend you like, you can output the recording to another two-track "normal" cassette deck to capture the final mix. As for the quality, don't expect miracles. Even so, these recorders work well for documenting ideas and rough sketches, and they are very portable.

Slightly better machines allow you to record two inputs at once. You still only get four tracks to work with, which might be plenty of tracks for you. Many of these machines offer no EQ or sound manipulation other than volume and pan.

When you get into higher-quality machines, the feature set really spikes. Four inputs can be used at once and the units add high and low EQ. You also get the option of using effects processors plugged into auxiliary channels. Don't know what an auxiliary channel is? Take a peek at Chapter 10 to learn how to utilize auxiliary channels.

The best four-track cassettes feature eight inputs, which can be used simultaneously, and all four tracks can be recorded at the same time. High, middle, and low EQ are included for better control of the sound. The standard volume fader and pan knobs are found along with auxiliary inputs for effects.

Transition to Digital

Not too many years ago the cassette was the format of choice for home recording. But at the time of this writing, there are no longer any four-track cassette recorders in production. It's likely the number of four-track recorders on the used market will diminish over the coming years; digital technology is so common and inexpensive that few people will see the value in trying to sell their old four-track. Now that digital technology is here to stay, the era of the cassette tape has passed. In spite of that, a four-track cassette recorder is a great learning tool and can be used as a creative sketchpad for years to come.

Low End Digital Multitrack Recorders

Small multitrack recording devices proved to be so successful that it was only natural that more powerful digital recorders would replace the cassette four-track recorder, especially as digital recording technology became cheaper. While computer-based recording is still the most powerful method of recording today, there is still a good selection of inexpensive digital multitrack studios-in-a-box. When you enter the digital multitrack recorder market you instantly gain some nifty features compared to the old four-track cassette machines. Built-in effects such as reverb, delay, and even guitar amplifier simulators are standard. Today's digital recorders record on CompactFlash or SmartMedia cards. CompactFlash and SmartMedia are the memory modules originally used in digital cameras. They have now found their way into the home recording market.

For between $200 and $400 you can purchase a digital recorder from manufacturers such as TASCAM, Boss, Alesis, or Fostex. These low-end digital recorders let you play back between three and eight tracks at once. The built-in effects are a great addition, but they won't sound as good as external effects processors. And the number of simultaneous inputs is usually small in this range, so don't expect to record more than two sources at once. However, if you plan to record track by track, that won't pose a problem.

FACT

With digital technology, the size of the storage or memory media determines the length of your recordings. The more megabytes the unit has, the more music you'll be able to store, and even the least expensive recorders offer significant storage capabilities. Of course, there are some limitations to low-end digital recorders including fewer inputs than a similarly priced audio interface, fewer controls, and a smaller display screen for editing.

One really neat feature that you can find in these units is background drum and bass rhythm tracks. You pick the style and tempo you want, and the machine creates the background music for you. And many of these units can run on battery power, making them great for taking with you to capture spur-of-the-moment ideas. In addition, many offer a USB port for easy connectivity to a computer. You can use a USB cable to transfer the music to your computer and then burn a CD.

Mid-Range Solutions—Studio-in-a-Box

The next step on the ladder will take you up in price. Every jump in price will add something to the previous level, usually more inputs, better quality effects, and more support for multiple channel recordings. Hard-drive storage begins at around the $550 mark and tops off at $1,000. At this level you start gaining more control over your sounds. You'll be able to play back at least eight tracks, and some models will let you play back as many as sixteen. You also get into editing features at this level: the ability to move music around, cut and paste, and easily rearrange tracks. Many units also include a built-in CD burner so you can master to a CD when you have finished your sessions. Small LCD screens are standard for accessing effect settings and editing the tracks.

Mid-priced hard-disk recorders (shown in Figure 4-2) can be purchased from TASCAM, Fostex, Korg, Yamaha, and Boss. Pay particular attention to the size of the hard drives. The bigger the disk, the more music you can store. Since the hard disks are buried inside the unit, once it's full, you have to finish the process and get the music off in order to record more. Compare models to see what's available. You can achieve very high quality results in this price range.

Top-of-the-Line Solutions

Units that cost more than $1,000 can be considered top-of-the-line. This category consists of studios-in-a-box and standalone recorders.

What do you get in a top-of-the-line studio-in-a-box? More inputs, higher quality, larger hard drives, bigger LCD screens for editing, more tracks, and other fun toys. As you climb the price ladder, you get extra goodies, including motorized faders, external computer displays, mouse inputs for editing, and digital outputs for transferring to your computer.

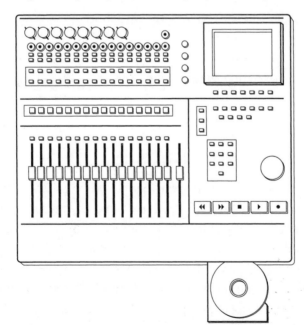

Figure 4-2: Studio-in-a-box

Top-of-the-line studios-in-a-box are serious systems, worthy of the name workstations. The quality of the internal effects, flexibility of editing, quantity of inputs, and support for more live tracks make these workstations "professional" quality. You can find high-end devices made by Yamaha, Roland, and Korg.

Standalone digital recorders, even the most expensive, only record audio. No mixing, no preamps, no effects—these units only record multitrack audio with professional quality. Why would you use these instead of an all-in-one studio? If you already own lots of outboard gear, tons of rack effects, and a mixer, then this might be for you. However, these systems are not for the first-time user! You will find these exact same units in professional studios all over the world. Popular units are made by TAS-CAM, Alesis, and Fostex. The quality of the recordings made on these is extremely high.

ESSENTIAL

Motorized faders let you record a mix as you go along. When you go to another part of the song, the fader remembers where the volume was at that point in the song and moves there. You can also "automate" a mix by recording the fader movements as you mix; they will play back by themselves.

Although top-of-the-line solutions are beyond the scope of most home recording studios, it's good to know they exist!

Microphones

Microphones are covered extensively in Chapter 9, but for now let's take a look at some of the basics. By themselves, microphones don't put out enough energy to be captured by the recorder; they require microphone preamps to boost their signal. Recorders tend to skimp on the number of supplied microphone preamps, so check the specifications carefully to make sure you have what you need. Based on the number of microphones you'll be using simultaneously, you may need an audio interface.

Let's say you find a great recorder at a great price, but it only has two inputs for microphones and you would like to record four microphones at once. Don't worry; you're not stuck. You have the option of buying external microphone preamps that can plug directly into the line inputs; most recording devices provide plenty of line inputs. Buying more microphone preamps means spending more money, so do your homework when you choose a recorder. The microphones themselves have a wide range of prices, from $50 to as high as several thousand dollars.

Headphones or Speakers?

When it comes to listening to your recordings, there are only two options: headphones or speakers (called monitors). Headphones are the least expensive solution, and many musicians prefer to mix on headphones. When selecting headphones (shown in Figure 4-3), make sure to buy headphones designed for audio mixing. Audio mixing headphones should have a flat response: They don't boost the bass or lower the treble like other "radio" headphones sometimes do. Headphones start around $20 and top off at about $150 or more.

Figure 4-3: Studio headphones *Courtesy of Avid Technology, Inc.*

If you want to listen without headphones, or you need to have several people hear the mix at the same time, you will want to go with stereo monitor speakers. Monitors resemble the speakers found on your stereo system. Like headphones, monitor speakers should have a flat response without any added coloration, so you can hear what's really going on with your music.

If the speakers unnaturally boost the bass or reproduce any part of the signal unfaithfully, you might decide to change the sound so it's balanced on those speakers. After you finish and mix down to a tape or CD and play it back on a good sound system, you might find that the bass is too low because your monitor speakers strongly emphasized the bass and you cut it during the mix to achieve a balanced sound. It's important to hear what's really there.

Figure 4-4: Studio monitor speakers *Courtesy of Avid Technology, Inc.*

Two monitors (left and right) are the standard way to mix, as you can see in Figure 4-4. There are two types of monitors: self-powered (active) and passive. Just like a microphone signal, the output from the recorder won't be loud enough to drive the monitor speakers: it needs to be amplified. Active monitors are slightly more expensive because they contain amplifiers built into the speakers. Passive monitors require a separate power amplifier between the recorder and the speakers. In a home studio, active monitors are usually easier to deal with. You can expect to spend $100 on the low end to $800 or more on the high end.

Accessories

It's the little things that can eat up your budget. You'll need cables for every input you plan to plug in, and there are different cables for every type of application. Chapter 8 covers in detail the different types of cables and what they are used for. You might need microphone preamps or direct boxes for your setup. If you plan to burn a lot of CDs, include blank CDs in your budget. Backup storage is a must, so you will want to have an extra hard drive or two. Adapters that take one type of cable and convert it to another can be very expensive.

Have some extra cash left over for emergencies. If you have ever done a do-it-yourself home repair project, you remember that you ran to the hardware store often. When you get started recording, you'll find yourself running to the music store often as well!

Keyboard Controllers

If you plan on using any virtual instruments, which are covered in Chapter 13, you will want some kind of a MIDI instrument controller. The most common kind of MIDI instrument controller is a keyboard controller. A MIDI keyboard controller (shown in Figure 4-5) allows you to play virtual instruments on your computer. That's not all, though; many MIDI keyboard controllers offer other features that can help you in other areas of recording!

ESSENTIAL

You can also use any MIDI keyboard as a MIDI keyboard controller. All you need is a simple USB to MIDI interface. Connect the MIDI OUT on your keyboard to the MIDI IN on the USB MIDI interface, and you're ready to rock!

MIDI keyboard controllers can be found with as few as 25 keys and as many as 88. There are three different kinds of keys: synthesizer keys, semi-weighted keys, and piano-weighted keys. Synthesizer keys are very light and easy to play. Semi-weighted keys play a little more like piano keys but are still very light. Piano-weighted keys play very much like a piano with a heavier action. Many piano-weighted keys even use hammers to simulate the feel of a piano. Today it's easier than ever to find a MIDI keyboard controller that is a size you want with the kind of keys you like. You can find keyboard controllers with as many as 76 synthesizer keys or as few as 49 piano-weighted keys.

Figure 4-5: A MIDI keyboard controller *Courtesy of Avid Technology, Inc.*

MIDI keyboard controllers, most of which connect directly to your computer with a USB cable, can include a variety of features. Many offer knobs and faders that you can assign to control parameters in your Digital Audio Workstation, or DAW. Software like Logic, Pro Tools, Cubase and Live are examples of DAWs. For example, you could assign knobs to control the pan knobs in your DAW, or the faders to control the volume of your tracks. Buttons can be assigned for controlling recording and playback, or for muting or soloing channels. Some MIDI keyboard controllers even offer audio interface capabilities with microphone inputs and speaker and headphone outputs.

Novation, Behringer, CME, Roland, E-MU, Edirol, Akai, Korg, Line 6, M-Audio, Studiologic, and Yamaha all offer keyboard controllers of different sizes and feature sets. You can expect to pay as little as $50 for a very simple keyboard controller or as much as $1,000 for "professional" keyboard controllers.

Studio Furniture

Now that you have your computer, your audio interface, your MIDI keyboard controller, your studio monitors, and so on, where are you going to put it? How can you organize this stuff? A spare desk, the top of your dresser, or even a card table will suffice, but if you want to give yourself a nice, dedicated workspace, you can get buy purpose-built studio furniture. There are many different kinds of studio furniture, from big rolling racks to three- and four-tier slide-out keyboard shelves, but for covering the most bases in the least amount of space, a studio desk does the trick.

A simple studio desk will have a tray for your computer keyboard, a desk area where you could put a MIDI keyboard controller, a mixing board, or some other larger piece of equipment, and a riser where you can put your computer monitor and your studio monitors. A simple studio desk will cost between $100 and $400. In the $500 to $1,000 range, you get added workspace, larger risers, and even built in rack mounting units. Many of these units can accommodate an 88-note keyboard. Higher-end studio desks have nicer looking wood veneers, more workspace, risers that can accommodate multiple computer monitors in addition to studio monitors, and even more rack mount spaces. High-end studio desks cost $1,000 and up.

Handheld Recorders

Handheld digital recorders are an emerging class of recording equipment worth considering. These units feature built in stereo microphones so you can just set the recorder down, press record, and start playing! They are perfect for catching ideas as inspiration comes, recording rehearsals and gigs, and even recording your songs. They are small enough to fit in your pocket, but offer features that are surprising for their size, such as multiple micro-phone or line inputs, overdubbing, and recording to MP3. Some even have multitrack recording functions and effects. Handheld digital recorders cost between $100 and $500. Sony, TASCAM, Line-6, Yamaha, M-Audio, Edirol, Marantz, and Korg all make handheld digital recorders that record to flash memory cards. Alesis and Belkin even offer handheld recorders that will record to your iPod!

CHAPTER 5

Recording on a Computer

In the 1990s, the personal computer began to enter the average home. Now, the computer is as standard as a couch and a TV. It's no surprise that the computer has been a valuable aid to music. In the past few years, the home studio owner has been able to reap the rewards of the love affair between technology and music. Luckily, computer prices have fallen so low that powerful machines are much more affordable than in years past.

Where Did It Start?

For the home studio user, computer music history started with the invention of the musical instrument digital interface (MIDI). MIDI is a standard language that allows electronic instruments and computers to communicate. The invention of MIDI led to the computer's ability to control a keyboard synthesizer. Unlike audio, MIDI does not have to be played in real time; it's a text file of commands, not sounds. Because MIDI data are just simple commands and not actual recorded audio, you can play MIDI parts one note at a time, at any tempo you choose.

MIDI, then, is a form of electronic composition; you write it one note at a time and the computers or instruments play it back. Since MIDI issues simple note-on/note-off commands to control the keyboard, editing and manipulating MIDI music is very simple. The sequencer was born from this marriage of MIDI and computers. Sequencers can either be physical machines or computer programs, although nowadays it's more common to use sequencing programs in your computer.

Sequencing

A sequencer functions much like a multitrack audio recorder. Tracks are recorded one on top of another and arrangements are built up one layer at a time. Since the sequencer doesn't actually make any music—all it does is control the keyboard, much like a player piano—the sequences can be substantially edited. Just like book publishers reveled in the idea of being able to cut, copy, and paste text in a word processor, the creation of sequencers gave MIDI-based musicians the same power. Whole sections of music can be rearranged with ease, and editing can be as precise as note-by-note changes. Since sequencing doesn't require a powerful machine to operate, computers of the 1980s could handle the job of sequencing MIDI. A great deal of the commercial music of the last twenty years has been a combination of sequenced and live music.

Sequencers continue to be a vital part of professional and home studios. For more about sequencers, check out Chapter 7 for details on specific programs.

Digital Music

Composers and musicians were delighted by the unbelievable editing power that MIDI sequencers afforded them. Sequencers answered the growing need for programs that made it easy to edit audio as easily as MIDI. In the past, editing audio with analog tape meant cutting and gluing tape together on a splicing block. This was a very difficult and arduous task, and inexperienced or careless splicers wound up with music that sounded like it had been hacked to pieces. The introduction of audio to the sequencer world made it possible to edit at high resolution of the computer screens.

However, the computers had a hard time dealing with the large file sizes of audio, nor were they very good at handling the complex processing needed to work with audio data. In time, multitrack computer audio became available and there is now an industry standard for multitrack audio: Digidesign Pro Tools. All of this technology came with a hefty price, however, which put it out of reach for most home studio owners. Recently, the power of the modern personal computer with its lower-cost, well-crafted software has allowed home musicians to join the party. Now, anyone can own a version of Pro Tools, and the democratization of recording technology has allowed other manufacturers to offer comparable recording tools at low prices.

What the Computer Can Do for Your Music

The computer has changed the way music is made. The flexibility and sound quality of current audio software has made the computer an indispensable tool. You might be asking, "This is all great, but what can it do for me?" Here is a short list of what a computer can help you accomplish:

- Integrate multitrack audio and MIDI
- Edit and move music around much like a word processor lets you edit words
- Easily burn to CD or distribute and sell your music online

In short, the computer can be whatever you want it to be. It can easily function as a recorder, sequencer, effects processor . . . you name it, a modern computer can handle the job. Now that you're convinced you want to use a computer in your home studio, you'll need to get the computer set up.

Processors and RAM

No matter how well your computer runs now, you'll need to tweak the setup for home studio use. Audio recording places special demands on the computer that are very different from the demands of surfing the web or checking your e-mail. The more power, the better when working with audio files.

Starting Fresh

In order to get your machine running smoothly, the best thing you can do is start over. If it's at all possible and you know how to do it (or can get someone who knows how to help you), back up your important data and reload a fresh copy of your operating system. While this might seem drastic, the majority of computers get lethargic and become prone to committing errors when there are old files hanging around the system. Generally speaking, spring cleaning like this will always help. Starting fresh can breathe new life into a machine when it begins to feel old and slow.

ESSENTIAL

Consider dedicating one computer to music alone. No e-mail, no instant messenger, no Internet—only music. In professional studios, a dedicated audio computer is standard. Think what would happen if a web-based program introduced a virus on the computer that holds all your music. You could lose everything!

Processor Speed

The processor, properly called the central processing unit or CPU, is the brain of the computer. The speed of your computer is measured by the frequency at which the processor is able to perform an instruction, called instructions per second (IPS). This number used to be stated in megahertz (MHz), which implied a million instructions per second or MIPS. Now that chips are faster than 999 MHz, the term gigahertz (GHz) is used for any chip that exceeds 1,000 MHz (1 GHz equals 1,024 MHz). The higher the number, the more tasks the computer can do at once and the faster it can do them.

However, we're getting into the multicore processor revolution. Imagine squeezing two chips into one; it creates a sort of dual brain. Multicore chips offer significant advances in speed, so don't look at just the number of gigahertz as your speed. Chips like the Intel CoreDuo set a new standard and give laptops almost unlimited power for audio production. More powerful processors are able to play more tracks, add more effects, and perform more elaborate edits. Unlike studios-in-a-box and analog tape machines, computers come with no guarantees on how many tracks and effects you can run in the software. The possibilities of what you can do with software are largely based on how fast your machine is. But many variables affect what the computer can do.

Different Types of Processors

It used to be that when you compared Macintosh computers with machines that run the Microsoft Windows operating system, the Mac processors had a lower stated speed when compared with the PCs. On the surface, this seems to indicate a decreased processing power, but this is no longer the case. Mac's processors (G3, G4, and G5) were very different from the Intel/AMD processors used in PCs, and they couldn't be compared simply by their processing speed. Now, Apple and almost all other companies use the same Intel chips in Mac computers (which was a significant switch for Apple), so you truly can compare apples to apples (no pun intended). You can choose your computer based on the available software and the quality of the OS, and not just the chip inside.

RAM

Random access memory, or RAM, is another vital system component of your computer and another number that should be high. RAM is a specialized area where data is stored temporarily while the computer is on. It is called volatile memory because it is gone when you turn off the computer. RAM is superfast and data can be written into it and read from it at much higher speeds than from the hard drive.

RAM holds important information that needs to be accessed quickly. RAM is measured by how much data it can store at one time. Having a lot of RAM will speed up a computer, no matter what speed the processor is. You could have the fastest processor on the market, but with only a small amount of RAM, the computer will crawl. Most software manufacturers suggest minimum and recommended RAM. For example, Digidesign's Pro Tools 8 requires 1 GB RAM and recommends 2 GB or more. Check out websites and call companies to see what they recommend. To run music-recording software, most computers need more RAM than what they typically come with. Installing RAM is not difficult, and the price of RAM chips has fallen dramatically. However, computers have limits on how many RAM chips can be installed, so your ability to increase RAM is not infinite. Pay attention to this when you are purchasing equipment.

FACT

Generally speaking, your computer should have at least half of the total RAM it can hold. If your machine can hold 4 gigabytes (GB) of RAM, 2 GB of RAM is a good starting point. The bare minimum for audio production is about 1 GB. Audio applications love RAM and will use more RAM if available.

Your magic number for RAM will depend upon what you do with the computer. If you plan on recording only a few tracks and you won't be going crazy with effects, filling your computer with RAM won't be necessary. However, if you plan to record a lot of tracks (sixteen or more) or do anything with samplers or virtual instruments (see Chapter 13), RAM is crucial. In this case, you can't have too much.

Hard Drives

There are a few attributes of hard drives to consider. The first and most obvious is the size. The larger the disk, the more music you'll be able to store. Like RAM, this number is expressed in GB or terabytes (TB). A terabyte is 1,000 GB. How big should your drive be? Buy as much hard drive as you can afford. More is definitely better.

The next critical factor in a hard disk is the rotation speed. A hard disk spins in the same way a CD does. The speed at which it spins is measured in revolutions per minute (RPM). The higher the speed, the faster the disk can access its data. Why is this important to you? Faster disks equal higher track counts in the software you use. If you have a fast CPU with tons of RAM, a slow hard drive will still limit you. The faster, the better. You will also find recommendations for hard drive speed listed on audio software manufacturers' lists of recommended hardware.

ESSENTIAL

Digital audio requires a good deal of storage space on your hard disk. Every minute of every track you record takes up many megabytes of space. As the quality of the recorded audio improves, file size increases as well. A typical five-minute song recorded in eight tracks with minimal effects can use 320 MB of storage space. This is why large hard drives are crucial.

The last factor is seek time. Seek time is how fast the data on the disk can be accessed. Seek time is measured in milliseconds. The lower the seek time, the better. You'll find that many drives average between 8-10ms of seek time. The lower, the better.

I'll Take Two

Chances are your computer came with only one hard drive, and this works fine. You can record and store files on a single hard drive. However, it's preferable to have a second hard drive dedicated to audio file storage. Why is this? Simply put, if you have one hard disk, the computer has to use the disk for running the operating system, running any open programs, and recording huge music files. This is a bit much to ask of just one disk. Your track count will always suffer by using one drive.

One Drive Can be Okay

You don't have to run out and buy a second hard drive right away, however. It's best to start out with one drive and see if you overtax the machine. Much depends on the number of tracks you work with and how many are audio versus MIDI. If you run into problems, use the advice from the previous section and get a second drive to increase performance and reliability.

Internal or External?

If you opt for the second drive, you have a choice: internal or external. Some computers won't accept a second internal drive, so that choice is made for you. Both get the job done, so it really comes down to personal preference and what your computer can handle. The only advantage of an external drive is that you can take it from computer to computer. If you collaborate with other home studio users, this could be a big plus. USB and FireWire are popular choices for external drives. Many users still swear that FireWire is more reliable for audio than USB, plus it's worthwhile to note that Digidesign does not recommend or support USB drives.

The Great Debate

Here we go . . . the big topic that has been debated and argued for years. Should you use a Macintosh or a PC running Microsoft Windows? Each side has its strengths and weaknesses, and each will let you run audio software. Let's consider the platforms separately.

Macintosh

Historically, Macs were the first computers to run music software, so more software was written to run on the Mac. Most professional studios still rely solely on Macs for audio. But Windows has caught up with the Mac. Even so, the Mac has a particular working style that appeals to some. If you're not used to it, you should spend some time using the Mac OS to see how different it is from Windows.

Apple is the only company that makes the Mac. Apple is the only game in town, and that's both good and bad. On the plus side, Macs rarely freeze or crash because the same company makes the operating system and hardware. Also, there is very little variation in the hardware, so software companies have an easy time making products that are compatible with Macs. On the downside, you can't select machines from different manufacturers. There may be some software differences that sway your decision. Some audio software is still Mac only, with no Windows version, so it's necessary to do your research. And Macs tend to be slightly more expensive than Windows computers, but that's becoming less of an issue as prices equalize.

Microsoft Windows

The majority of the desktop market is PC-based, and most of those computers run Microsoft Windows. Windows is perfectly capable of running music software as well as the Macs do. Lots of music software is now available for Windows. With Windows, the version of the operating system is critical for music applications. Windows Vista continues to be slowly adopted by audio manufacturers. Many musicians still rely on XP for audio tasks. As Microsoft has worked hard at Windows 7, it's promising to be a more stable and accepted release industry-wide. Only time will tell how fast users and the music industry will adopt the new Windows 7.

FACT

Since Macs now run with Intel processors, you can also run real copies of Windows on a Mac. Apple has a utility called Boot Camp that allows a Mac to dual-boot between different operating systems. There's even new virtualization software from companies like Parallels and VMWare that allow you to run OS X and Windows without ever leaving OS X.

No matter which version of Windows you choose to run, makers of software for Windows have the unique challenge of trying to be compatible with literally millions of different hardware combinations. Unlike Apple, many different companies make Windows-based PCs. Apple makes all its hardware, which is designed to run its exclusive operating system, whereas Microsoft Windows is a program run by computers made by a variety of different companies. Each computer running Windows uses different CPUs, different RAM . . . you get the idea. Sometimes software compatibility can be a problem on the Windows side because of this.

In the end, the choice is yours. Whatever you have, you'll be able to run some kind of music software. If you're thinking of buying a second computer just for audio, make sure to give both platforms a fair look. If possible, talk with other musicians who have experience with PC and Macintosh versions of the programs you're considering.

Interfaces

So now that we've covered the types of computer hardware that make a good audio system, let's focus on getting music in and out of the computer. It's time to talk about interfaces, those wonderful devices that connect music to an otherwise lifeless machine. Interfaces are pieces of hardware that connect to a computer to bring music in and out.

MIDI

MIDI interfaces are the simplest and least expensive interfaces for a computer. They come in many shapes and sizes, one for every need. You will want to get an interface that has one input for every piece of MIDI-enabled gear in your studio. The MIDI interface is shown in Figure 5-1.

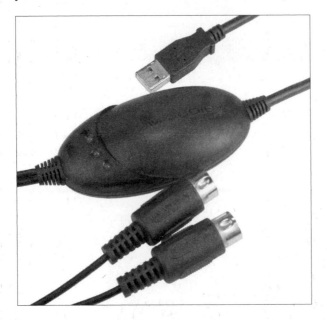

Figure 5-1: USB MIDI interface *Courtesy of Avid Technology, Inc.*

Prices for basic interfaces start around $35; an interface with more inputs will be more expensive. There are several types of MIDI interface connections:

- **PCIe/PCIx MIDI interface:** A card that sits inside the computer. Usually combines audio and MIDI.
- **USB MIDI interface:** A small rectangular port on the back or front of your computer. USB is on every computer now, so you'll find USB-based interfaces very easily.
- **FireWire MIDI interface:** FireWire, as it's known on the Mac, or IEEE 1394 as it's known in the Windows world, is a new connection that is becoming standard. FireWire interfaces usually combine audio and MIDI.

FACT

You will need a MIDI interface if you plan to record MIDI from keyboards, synthesizers, or drum machines that lack USB connections. More and more MIDI-capable instruments ship with USB connections, negating the need for a separate MIDI interface. If you plan to use the computer as an audio recorder only, a MIDI interface is not necessary.

Getting Audio In and Out

In terms of routing audio in and out of your computer, you have to make some hard decisions about how many instruments you can record at once. Simple interfaces that support one or two channels are relatively inexpensive. If you want to record eight simultaneous inputs, be prepared to pay more. Also key is the number of microphone inputs that the interfaces have. If you plan to record acoustic instruments such as piano, voice, or anything else that requires a microphone, you'll need a few microphone inputs (shown in Figure 5-2).

Just like MIDI interfaces, audio interfaces come in three basic forms and you can get started for around $200.

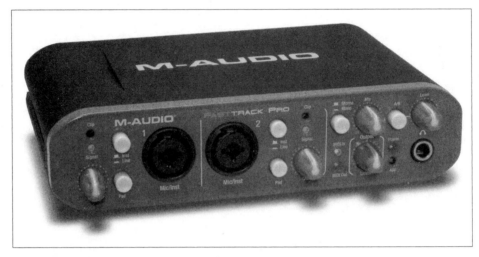

Figure 5-2: Computer recording interface *Courtesy of Avid Technology, Inc.*

- **PCIe/PCIx:** A card that sits inside your computer. A cable usually attaches from the card to a tabletop unit, called a breakout box, which contains the actual inputs.
- **USB:** USB is a popular choice for audio interfaces, especially after the advent of USB 2.0 made it faster and cleaned up some bugs. A large majority of audio interfaces are USB 2.0. You'll find great choices from Digidesign, M-Audio, TASCAM, Edirol, and Native Instruments.
- **FireWire:** FireWire is a great choice if your computer supports it. Most Macs and many PCs ship with FireWire. Digidesign, M-Audio, RME, and Metric Halo make some great FireWire interfaces.

Making It All Work

There are several things you can do to keep your audio computer running smoothly. First, unplug the Internet while you work. If you dial in or use broadband, the computer is always doing something Internet related in the background. This can take away from the power your music program needs. Log off or power down your DSL/cable modem. On the same theme, don't run other programs in the background while you are running music applications. Music applications ask a lot of the computer, so give it as much computing power as possible.

QUESTION

How will I know what equipment to use when there are so many choices?
Ask people, particularly music store employees and other home studio owners. You can even read the various Internet bulletin boards devoted to computer music. People aren't shy about opinions, but do keep in mind that many happy customers never post online and the customers with issues tend to scream the loudest.

There are many utilities to ensure that your disk is healthy and free of viruses and malware. You should also run these often to keep your disk in tiptop shape.

Always back up your work! You'll feel very bad if your hard work magically disappears or you catch a virus that wipes out all your data. You can back up by burning data to a CD or DVD. Both are cheap and very reliable. DVDs hold 4.7 gigabytes of information, while CDs hold 700 megabytes. You can even find places online to backup your software, and as the prices of hard disk drives continue to fall, you can just buy more external USB or FireWire drives for backup.

Computers are known for doing some strange things to your data, which is why backing up your files is crucial! Get in the habit of backing up your data as the last step after every work session. You'll be glad you did when disaster strikes. Hard drives are mechanical and they will fail. It's not if; it's when. Be prepared for the worst.

CHAPTER 6

Computer Recording Tools

Twenty-five years ago the personal computer was in its infancy. The last place you'd expect to see one was in a recording studio, unless it was used for billing and recordkeeping in the front office. When computers finally made their way into the audio world, they were considered the dreams of tomorrow. Tomorrow has finally come, thanks to powerful computers and groundbreaking software. What we have now is nothing short of a home studio revolution.

Power in a Box

While we could pay homage to the computer and its miraculous power, if it weren't for the evolution and development of software in the audio field, computers would be nothing more than glorified calculators. The software available today re-creates the recording studio inside a personal computer. Mixing, editing, instruments, and effects can all be achieved seamlessly in a virtual environment, mimicking a real recording studio and its hardware.

What makes computers so great? For many users, just the addition of recording software turns their ordinary home computer into a full-blown music studio. It also takes up little space, which is a big plus. Nowadays, the computer is becoming the central fixture of our life. Why not put our music studio there as well? Software manufacturers have answered the call with outrageous software for music production.

Advantages of Computer-Based Systems

Today's music software is state of the art and advances are made each year. Computers take up little space and can be upgraded as needed. Since even entry-level computers are so powerful these days, your current computer is probably already suitable for recording once you choose a recording application. Even today's laptops are more than capable of running cutting edge recording software, virtual instruments, and effects. If you're technical in nature, you might find the working style of computer music suits you very well. Many people feel that editing with a mouse on a screen is the best way to go.

Disadvantages of Software-Based Systems

Anyone who's worked with computers knows they are prone to crash, catch viruses, and eat files. And let's face it, some people are not tech savvy and just want to make music without worrying about the speed of their hard drive or the need to defrag their files. The mantra of "backup, backup, backup" becomes even more important when it comes to protecting your recordings from potential computer or hard drive failure. There's also a group of people who swear that digital recordings never sound as good as analog ones. The debate on that topic continues.

The Interface to Software

Computers are highly adaptable machines. They can handle almost anything you throw at them . . . that is, if you can get your information into the machine. In the case of music, you need a special interface to get sound and/or MIDI into the computer. In addition to the software component, the interface is just as important—and in many cases, it's more important. Let's break down the interfaces you will need in order to get sound and MIDI into your machine.

MIDI

Of all the interfaces, the MIDI interface is the simplest for the computer. MIDI format consists of simple data that can easily be streamed to a computer. You can get a simple MIDI interface inexpensively, and many companies make interfaces to work with every make and model of computer. The MIDI format is often included with the PCI Express, USB, and FireWire audio interfaces.

PCI Express

Peripheral component interconnect express or PCI Express (PCI-E) is a standard card that sits inside a desktop computer and adds audio functionality. PCI-E cards can range from simple one-input/one-output configurations to extensive audio options with many inputs and outputs. The cards with more extensive inputs and outputs usually plug into a box called a breakout box via a special cable. Unfortunately, laptops can't use PCI-E cards without an expensive expansion chassis. For desktop computers, PCI-E is a great option and there is a nice variety of these interfaces for every budget.

USB

Universal serial bus (USB) is a way to connect peripherals such as mice and joysticks to computers. One of the greatest benefits of USB is that it is compatible with desktop and laptop computers. USB is simply a kind of hardware port on computers that allows users to attach devices to the computer using a USB cable. USB is a standard found on all computers. USB devices simply plug into the computer; no work inside the machine is involved. This makes it possible for you to have a portable recording studio.

USB interfaces are reasonably priced. However, due to the way USB pushes data back and forth to the computer, don't expect a ton of inputs and outputs. USB is great for small setups and portable solutions. USB 2.0 is a newer form of USB that uses the same standard interface but transfers data at a much higher rate. Make sure your computer has a USB 2.0 port to take advantage of the greater speed it offers.

FireWire

FireWire or IEEE1394, as it's also known, is a high-speed interface that, like USB, no longer requires a card inside a computer. FireWire is another hardware port on the computer that allows devices to plug in directly using a FireWire cable. FireWire was originally conceived for digital video cameras to transfer large amounts of video data to a computer at high speeds. As an audio interface, FireWire is very popular because it can handle a large data flow and many simultaneous inputs and outputs. It's also ideal for laptop computers that need a powerful audio interface. FireWire is the standard for most audio interfaces offered today.

ESSENTIAL

No matter what interface you choose, make sure it offers the connectivity you need. Look especially hard at the number of microphone inputs your interface allows. The number of inputs you need is contingent on the number of microphones/audio sources you wish to record simultaneously.

Not all computers are equipped with FireWire ports, however, so it is important to know if your machine is equipped if you plan to buy a FireWire interface. Expansion cards for both desktop and laptop computers can give your computer FireWire capabilities. FireWire interfaces, connectors, and expansion cards are available in two speeds, FireWire 400 and FireWire 800. FireWire 800 allows you to transfer twice the information per second as FireWire 400. Look for FireWire S1600 and S3200 to enter the market in the coming year. Expect to see audio interfaces, external hard drives, and other peripherals taking advantage of these new FireWire standards in the coming years.

The Curse of Latency

Computer systems are great, but there is one catch: *latency.* When your guitar is plugged into an amplifier, you expect the sound to come out immediately after you play, right? You would expect the same from a recording system: You plug in and hear the signal in real time. But this is not necessarily the case with a computer.

Computers deal only with digital information, so they have to convert your audio (analog) signal to digital. The computer then has to store it somewhere and retrieve it to send it back out. Then it must convert the digital signal to audio again. The problem is that the process takes some time, on the order of a few milliseconds. One millisecond won't feel like much, but approach ten or more and it starts to feel lethargic. This has been a problem from day one, but it's getting better—that's the good news.

Computers are getting faster and can do all the conversions more quickly than they used to. Interface manufacturers have also smartened up and added features that give low or no latency monitoring, which cuts down greatly or eliminates latency. There is usually a catch with low-latency modes, however; you usually lose the effects from the computer. So if you're recording a vocal part and you want to monitor the signal with reverb, you have three options: you need a hardware reverb processor, you must sacrifice the reverb, or you must deal with the latency.

Types of Music Software

There are several categories of music software. But the lines between the categories are blurring, even as we work. In the last fifteen years or so, three main types of computer music software have been developed.

Audio Multitrack Software

Audio multitrack software attempts to re-create a multitrack recording and playback studio inside your computer. When recording software was first introduced, massive PCI cards and other hardware were needed to help the computer cope with all of the audio data. A good example is the professional Pro Tools audio software that still relies on PCI or PCI-E cards for computer power. Nowadays, software that deals exclusively with audio and not MIDI is very difficult to find, because most, if not all, studio software incorporates MIDI in some regard. But if you look hard enough, you might find some free or very cheap software on the Internet that deals with just audio.

MIDI Sequencing Applications

Before computer-based audio was even a dream, there was MIDI, which consists of small text commands to control the playing of synthesizers. Computers started to work with MIDI data around twenty-five years ago. A MIDI sequencer lets you record and manipulate many tracks of MIDI information, allowing the computer to play back long, complicated parts that might be unplayable by a single person. Editing and manipulation is possible on even the minutest of levels. You can create piano parts that are faster than anyone can play or program an entire orchestra to play back your music.

MIDI was the reason that the computer made its first appearance in the recording studio. Even today, you can still get MIDI-only sequencing programs. Some of the more famous programs that were the pillars of the MIDI sequencing world, such as Logic and Cubase, have grown up to include sophisticated audio features as well. So just like audio-only applications, it's hard to find just MIDI; most are integrated.

Integrated MIDI and Audio

Today, most recording software integrates MIDI with audio. As all of the programs grew up, an all-in-one solution became necessary. The software suites that dealt strictly with audio, such as Pro Tools, eventually adopted MIDI. Conversely, the MIDI-only camp grew audio wings. All the programs covered in this chapter allow you to record and edit MIDI and audio together in the same program. With audio programs, not only can you play and record, but you can process effects and perform exacting editing, which is what makes these programs special. On the audio side, nonlinear editing is the distinguishing factor that makes the computer more than just an emulation of a multitrack recorder. What's nonlinear editing? Read on!

What Nonlinear Editing Means to You

Let's start with linear editing. Think of a CD. Suppose you were recording a mix for your car's CD player. Later on you decide you'd prefer the track you placed first on the CD to be at the end of the CD. You would have to burn an entire new CD to rearrange the order of tracks. There is no way to just magically "move" that song. You can't do this because a CD is linear—it's read in a line and whatever appears first will be played first and so on.

Computer audio systems don't rely on linear data storage; instead they use hard drives that can read and write data in a nonlinear fashion. Although we hear this data as music, the computer processes and stores it like any other data, and that works in our favor. Audio data is stored on the hard disk in a nonlinear manner, which allows you to change the order of tracks and move whole sections of your song with ease. This is one of the main reasons computer audio took off. Editing is far superior on a computer system. It's easy to imagine that audio on a computer is processed much like text in a word processor—you're free to cut, copy, and paste as you wish. Audio data is treated the same way, and that's nothing short of revolutionary!

Audio-Editing Applications

Historically, the first audio recording on a computer was not multitrack audio but simply stereo files. These files were loaded into an audio-editing application that allowed nonlinear editing in high resolution. After the edits were completed, they were sent back to the tape they came from. This was the beginning. Even as multitrack grew up, audio-editing applications were still popular ways to edit in high detail. Nowadays, audio-editing programs like Wavelab are used for mastering and remastering because they don't deal with multitrack or mixing data, only the final stereo file. For many, audio-editing applications like these are the last step before burning or CD duplication. These programs are also handy if you work on a portable digital recorder and wish to transfer the final stereo output into the computer for editing and burning to CD.

Proprietary Audio Systems

Proprietary audio systems are audio software and hardware packaged together under a brand name and sold for use on a computer. Pro Tools LE is an example of such a system and is, in fact, one of the only proprietary systems on the market today that can be used in the home studio.

Unlike Pro Tools, almost all audio software and hardware systems are modular, meaning you can buy software and audio interfaces from different companies and they will work together. For example, you don't have to use Digital Performer with a MOTU interface just because they are made by the same company. So too, you can get standard drivers that allow you to use almost any piece of software with almost any piece of hardware, regardless of the manufacturer.

Pro Tools, as mentioned previously, is a proprietary system of hardware and software that works together on your home computer. Pro Tools M-Powered is designed for specific M-Audio hardware. Because the software is tied to the hardware, it's a self-contained system. This means you can't run Pro Tools LE or M-Powered software with any other hardware than what is supported, but you *can* use Pro Tools hardware with other applications. This is not a bad thing if you love Pro Tools and wish to spend all your time working with it. Many people get confused by this and think they can plug their sound card into Pro Tools.

Plug-In Formats

If you're working inside a digital audio workstation (DAW) and you want some nice reverb or maybe a compressor or two, you're going to need a plug-in. A plug-in is the software equivalent of a hardware effects processor or hardware instrument. Depending on what recording software you opt to run, you might need different types of plug-ins. Each recording program requires plug-ins to be written in a specific language that the host program will understand. Luckily, most plug-in manufacturers include multiple versions. Let's break down all the major formats so you can see what's around.

Virtual Studio Technology

Virtual studio technology (VST) is a plug-in standard format created by Steinberg, which also makes Cubase and Nuendo recording software. VST plug-ins work in Cubase, and other programs have adopted the use of VST plug-ins as well. VST plug-ins are available for both Macs and PCs. Because

VST has been around for a long time, there is a nice selection of VST plug-ins available.

Real-Time Audio Suite

Real-time audio suite (RTAS) is the only plug-in format that works inside Pro Tools. Because of the widespread use of Pro Tools systems, there are many RTAS plug-ins available on the market. Because Pro Tools runs on PCs and Macs, you can find RTAS for both. The British company FXpansion has created a VST-to-RTAS converter allowing the many VST plug-ins to be utilized inside Pro Tools.

DirectX

DirectX is a Windows-only plug-in format that is supported by FL Studio and a few other programs. DirectX was originally a multimedia language introduced by Microsoft to write games and other multimedia programs. Over the years, DirectX has fallen out of favor as the VST format now dominates Windows applications.

Audio Unit

Audio Unit is a plug-in format introduced by Apple as part of its remake of the Mac operating system version 10 (also known as OS X). The thought behind Audio Units was to create a system-level plug-in format that worked inside the operating system and could be available to any audio program on the system. Logic, Digital Performer, and Live all support Audio Units plug-ins. Apple's free recording software GarageBand utilizes Audio Unit plug-ins as well. Audio Unit plug-ins are available only on the Mac platform.

MOTU Audio System

MOTU audio system (MAS) is the plug-in standard written by MOTU for use in its Digital Performer application. Before Version 4 of Digital Performer, MAS was the only plug-in that could be used in Digital Performer; however, now Digital Performer uses MAS and Audio Units. Since Digital Performer is Mac only, no Windows versions of MAS plug-ins exist.

Wrappers

A wrapper is a program that converts plug-ins from one type to another. On the PC side, there are DirectX-to-VST wrappers that extend the choices of Windows plug-ins. FL Studio can act as a DirectX-to-VST converter. On the Mac side, there is a VST-to-Audio Unit wrapper that greatly improved the number of available plug-ins while OSX was just starting out, and it continues to be updated to this day.

Popular Software

There are countless programs available for making music on a computer. However, a few have emerged as top players, and those are the ones we'll focus on here. All of these programs basically do the same thing: they allow you to record MIDI and audio and to arrange and mix music, all on a computer system. The only differences are how they go about the task.

ESSENTIAL

Don't worry about spending a lot of money for Pro Tools and not knowing how to use it. Digidesign offers a vast support system, including classes, online resources, and its *DigiZine* magazine. You can choose from individualized study programs, in-person training classes, and online courses through Berklee College of Music.

Digidesign: Pro Tools

No other name is as synonymous with studio recording as Pro Tools. Until a few years ago, the only system you could get was its expensive TDM system, which went for well over $10,000. In 1998, Digidesign introduced Pro Tools digi001 and entered the home studio market. Currently, Digidesign markets a number of home studio products—the Mbox 2 family of USB audio interfaces; the 003 family FireWire interfaces, including the 003 Factory eighteen-input interface plus motorized control surface, and the 003 Rack, an eighteen-input FireWire interface; and the ProTools M-Powered capable series of interfaces from M-Audio. The Mbox 2 and 003 series ship with the same version of Pro Tools LE software, which is capable of playing back forty-eight audio tracks and unlimited MIDI tracks. ProTools M-Powered is available for compatible M-Audio interfaces, and features much of the same functionality of ProTools LE.

One of the biggest things Pro Tools has going for it is compatibility: Anything created on a Pro Tools home system can be taken to a larger professional version. This is great when you want to share your ideas or get expert mixing and mastering. As discussed earlier, Pro Tools is proprietary so you can run its software only with Digidesign hardware, or supported M-Audio interfaces. As a music tool, it's a mature product that works on both Mac and PC equally well. It's also completely portable because the current versions work on USB and FireWire formats—great for laptop use.

Figure 6-1: Digidesign Pro Tools 8

It's set up simply with two main windows—the mix and edit windows. The edit window shows you all your audio and MIDI data track by track, while the mix window shows the virtual mixing board and access to all your plug-in effects. Pro Tools 8 introduces new MIDI editing windows and a fabulous new score editor, powered by Sibelius. A nice selection of audio effects and virtual instruments are included with the package. You can always extend the system by adding RTAS plug-ins and other add-ons available from Digidesign and third party manufacturers.

Figure 6-1 gives you a look at what Pro Tools looks like in action.

Steinberg: Cubase

In the 1990s, Steinberg introduced Cubase VST, an integrated virtual studio for music making. It has grown over the years and remains a very popular choice on both the PC and Mac platforms. It can run with any computer audio interface you choose. Like all programs of this type, MIDI and audio are grouped together. Cubase is a fully featured studio capable of anything you throw at it. There are a large number of plug-ins available for Cubase in the VST format. Steinberg also includes a nice set of VST audio effect plug-ins to get you started.

Figure 6-2: Steinberg Cubase 5

Cubase is also a very capable MIDI editor. This is because Cubase started its life as a MIDI sequencer and added audio capabilities later. Because of its clean format and ease of use, Cubase remains a very popular application. It is also completely cross-platform, running identically on both Mac and PC, a feat matched only by Pro Tools. Cubase comes in three flavors: Cubase Essential, Cubase Studio, and Cubase. Cubase is their top-of-the line application. Figure 6-2 shows what the current version of Cubase, Cubase 5, looks like in action.

Mark of the Unicorn (MOTU): Digital Performer

On the Mac platform (sorry PC users), MOTU Digital Performer is a favorite among musicians. Originally a MIDI sequencer that added audio capabilities, Digital Performer (or DP, as users call it) is another robust and powerful audio and MIDI tool. It has a clean interface with great audio

Figure 6-3: MOTU Digital Performer

effects and powerful MIDI editing. You can find Digital Performer in many composing and film-scoring studios around the world. Digital Performer extends its power by adopting the Audio Units plug-in standard, greatly increasing the number of available plug-in effects. Of course, you get a nice starter set of audio effects from MOTU. Take a look at Digital Performer 6 in action in Figure 6-3.

Apple: Logic Studio

Logic, like many other programs, started its life as a MIDI sequencer and added audio later. Logic is currently produced only for the Mac platform, but at one time it was cross-platform. Logic is a very different program from the others covered so far. It is by far the most configurable and programmable software available for music making. It's almost a programming language wrapped in a music application. Don't let that put you off, though, because Logic is intuitive for basic MIDI and audio recording, and users who get into

Figure 6-4: Apple Logic Studio

the underlying layers will find great power and flexibility. Logic sports many different windows and views for editing information. It boasts some of the best MIDI editing around. It also includes score editing to view your MIDI as music notation. In addition to Logic, you also get Mainstage, a live performance program that allows you to take all the amazing Logic sounds out on the road!

Logic is a very popular program that is starting to show up in more professional studios due to its powerful mix of audio and MIDI adaptability to any situation. It's also one of the most fully featured virtual instruments and sampler hosts available, incorporating an impressive array of its own virtual instruments and the ability to host Audio Units plug-ins. For more on virtual instruments and samplers, refer to Chapter 13 for a full description. Logic comes in two versions: Logic Express and Logic Studio. Logic Express is the basic version and Logic Studio is the flagship application. What you gain with the Studio version are a suite of complementary applications, more plug-in effects, more virtual instruments and loop content, and generally more features. Figure 6-4 is a shot of Logic in action.

Cakewalk: Sonar

Sonar is an immensely popular workstation made only for PCs. Cakewalk has been making music programs for years and ease of use is a thread that runs through each of its products. A clean, uncluttered interface makes the connection between user and musician seamless and fun. Excelling at both MIDI and audio, Sonar is one of the best PC applications available, and it has a wide, loyal user base. You also get automation, a generous selection of plug-in effects, and a wide variety of MIDI editing techniques. Figure 6-5 is a shot of Sonar in action.

Figure 6-5: Cakewalk Sonar

Ableton: Live

Ableton Live is a unique piece of software. Originally, Live was conceived as a live performance tool geared toward improvisation and composition with prerecorded audio material. Essentially, it was a loop-based application on steroids. Over the years it has developed into a full-featured audio and MIDI production application and plug-in host, while

Figure 6-6: Ableton Live

staying true to its roots as a powerful performance tool. It is available for both Mac and PC, making it a good choice for those collaborating on projects on different platforms. On the PC, Live supports VST, and on the Mac it supports both Audio Units and VST. Figure 6-6 is a shot of Live 8 in action.

Which One Is for You?

The popular software products discussed in this section do the same basic job—they all allow you to manipulate MIDI alongside audio in a nonlinear manner. They differ only in presentation and organization. You owe it to yourself to look into each product. You'll find many demos are available online as well as at your local music store. Get some hands-on experience with the software before you purchase it. Ask around; ask friends. Online, there are dedicated support forums for each product. Read the entries and look into all the details. Buying a program is a major commitment, so do your homework.

If you plan to collaborate with other musicians or other people in your band, it makes sense for all of you to have the same system. (And if you buy a system that is also owned by someone you know, you might just be able to get a little tutorial from that person as well!) If you have aspirations of becoming a professional studio owner or attending engineering school, see what the current standard is—for most, it's still Pro Tools. Whatever you decide to get, you'll learn and do well with it!

CHAPTER 7

Loop-Based Software

Looping prerecorded audio has been around since the late 1960s. That's when classical music composers started experimenting with a technology called sampling, which allowed prerecorded audio to be repeated and manipulated. The digital home recording community has seen an explosion of loop-based recording software in recent years. If you record at home, loops will likely be a big part of your music-making experience.

What is a Loop?

A loop is a general term that has several definitions within audio software. The simplest explanation is that a loop is a piece of prerecorded information, one that can repeat over and over again. In the early days of looping, loops were digital audio samples that were meticulously edited to loop repeatedly. Some early loops were drum loops and were a mainstay of rap and hip hop music. The defining factor of a loop was that it could be repeated continuously without sacrificing sound quality.

FACT

Want to hear an early example of a loop? Check out the Beatles "Revolution 9" to hear looping in popular music. The Beatles used a technique called "tape loops" where audio was recorded onto a tape and repeated over and over again.

Looping was an art form that involved sampling an acoustic or electronic source, editing it for perfect symmetry, and utilizing it in audio software. Early looping and sampling required expensive equipment and a great deal of technical skill. Nowadays, loops come in both audio loops and MIDI loops and are very easy to insert into any composition. Loop-based software is becoming a staple of the recording industry. Programs like Pro Tools are embracing loop functionality, so everyone from home recording enthusiasts to professionals are utilizing loops as a mainstay of their compositions. One of the great benefits of loops is that they can act as a starting point for your own compositions and also allow a musician of limited skill and experience to use sophisticated prerecorded loops in a composition.

Popular Loop-Based Software

Looping hit the home recording market in 1998 with the introduction of a software program called ACID, then owned by Sonic Foundry and now owned by Sony. ACID was unique because it was extremely easy to use and provided a generous loop library. The user could simply drag and drop loops from the library onto audio tracks in ACID. ACID would take care of matching the tempo of the loops so that compositions always sounded smooth. Looping isn't new, but ACID's ability to understand the tempo of loops and make sure that they all worked together in a composition was nothing short of revolutionary. If a loop contained pitch information (don't think of loops as being exclusively for drums), ACID would make sure that the pitches transposed properly so that their keys would synchronize no matter what was combined on an audio track. This democratized music making and allowed home studio musicians to pump out professional-quality tracks. The ACID Loop was the native loop format for ACID and many third party companies offered additional loops that could be dropped into an ACID composition. ACID loop functionality is still available in ACID Pro 7, multitrack audio recording software for Windows PCs.

GarageBand

In 2004, Apple released GarageBand as part of its iLife suite. Apple had acquired Logic, a very popular DAW from the German company Emagic. GarageBand was a result of the combination of Emagic's history and skill with audio programs and Apple's understanding of consumer markets. GarageBand was a loop-based software that was designed for anyone and everyone. Its simple interface empowered any user (musician or not) to start making music. GarageBand '09 is shown in Figure 7-1.

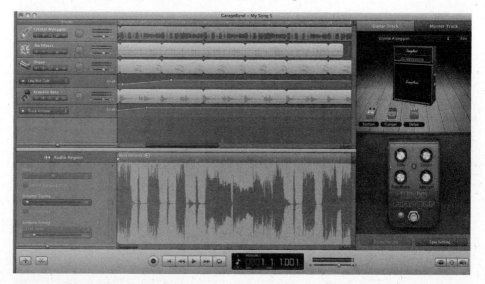

Figure 7-1: GarageBand '09

GarageBand was also an important step in that it worked with both audio loops and instrument loops. Behind the simplified skin, GarageBand was powered by Logic, so advanced users could record multitrack audio, mix and automate their music, and even add professional quality effects. Each year, GarageBand has grown, adding new features including guitar amplifier and effect simulation and keyboard and guitar lessons. Apple uses its own "Apple Loop" format, which has a healthy third party community of loop resellers in addition to Apple's own Jam Packs.

Other Looping Software

ACID and GarageBand are not the only software available that work with loops. Nearly every major DAW available includes some fashion of looping. Here are some software programs that include loop functionality:

- Pro Tools
- Cubase
- Sequel
- Sonar
- Recycle
- Fruity Loops
- Live
- Reason
- Session

When using loops with these software titles, check out the documentation to determine which types of loops are supported. There is more than one standard loop format, and not every loop format is compatible with every software program.

Audio Loops

An audio loop is any piece of digital audio that has been recorded and edited to facilitate looping without any additional help. Audio loops can be of any instrument, at any tempo and in any key. Looping relies on rhythmic accuracy in order to loop correctly. Figure 7-2 is a great example of an audio loop.

What makes the loop in Figure 7-2 so perfect? It's actually pretty hard to see in the picture, so here's a bit of help. Each vertical spike is a hard drum hit. The harder the hit, the louder the sound. Each spike is equally spread out, which shows a steady tempo. The end of the loop fits perfectly with the beginning of the loop to make it loop perfectly. A good loop has very little activity in the end of the loop; usually it's just decaying sound.

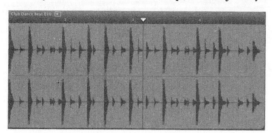

Figure 7-2: A perfect audio loop

Limitations of Audio Loops

Digital audio has some limitations. One of the biggest limitations is its inability to radically stretch the tempo and key of an audio loop without degradation. One of the mainstays of ACID and GarageBand (among others) is how the loops automatically conform to the key and tempo of your music when you drag and drop them. If the loop is 110 beats per minute (BPM) and your song is at 120 BPM, the loop will be stretched through a process call time stretching, so it conforms to exactly 120 BPM. This small 9 percent change will sound pretty transparent to the listener. But, if the loop had to be stretched more, the listener would likely hear some sonic degradation.

It's hard to explain on paper, but you'll know it when you hear it. If your loops suddenly sound odd, check out their original tempos. Too much of a stretch won't sound good. The same holds true for key changes. With more and more loops carrying melodic and harmonic information, loop programs have gotten smarter and allow loops to conform not only to tempo changes, but also to key changes, with the same limitations.

If you change the key of your loop too far up or down, it will start to sound funny! You can usually move a loop a third in either direction before experiencing any issues.

One of the other issues with audio loops is that you can't easily edit the audio. You basically get what you get. While it is possible to change the timing of an audio drum loop using Pro Tools' Elastic Time (a method for changing the timing of individual beats in an audio loop), it isn't available for every single DAW. For most home studio users, an audio loop is a pretty closed thing.

FACT

In your DAW, see if you have a Loop Browser like those in Logic and GarageBand. These browsers are searchable for keywords, tempo, and key, so you can find the best loop easily. And many of them include data filters, so you can narrow down your searches.

MIDI/Instrument Loops

The other kind of loop is a MIDI or instrument loop. MIDI loops don't contain any audio information. Just like MIDI data, a MIDI loop only contains instructions to play notes. The actual sound is produced from a plug-in synthesizer. When you add a MIDI loop to your composition, the accompanying instrument track (which will be played back by a virtual instrument of your choosing) is created for you. Remember that MIDI doesn't make sounds on its own! While MIDI loops often sound as natural and realistic as audio loops, they also have some pros and cons.

A MIDI loop is only as good as the plug-in that produces its sound. There are some great plug-ins that re-create instruments synthetically; there are also some bad ones. That's pretty much the only negative about MIDI loops. The biggest advantage to MIDI is that you can change the key and the tempo of a MIDI loop without consequence. Since a MIDI loop contains only instructions, there's no audio to stretch out; it just sends the command to play the note a bit later, or at a higher or lower pitch. MIDI loops are so much more malleable than audio loops. One really great thing about MIDI loops is that you can change them and make them your own. Take a look at this Apple Loop for GarageBand (Figure 7-3).

Figure 7-3: Apple Instrument Loop

Once you double-click on the loop, it launches in the editor, where you can make adjustments. You can change any note you want, raise or lower the pitches, and change the duration of any of the notes.

QUESTION

How do I know if my loop is audio or MIDI?
In GarageBand, for example, audio loops are blue and MIDI loops are green. Each software is different, but it should show you clearly which loops are audio and which are MIDI. Check your program's manual or help section for assistance if you're not sure.

It's not just GarageBand that lets you make these kinds of changes. Check your favorite DAW software and see what you can do to instrument loops.

How to Loop

Looping is actually very simple. Each program has its own interpretation of looping, but they all share the same idea: drag the right edge of the loop to extend it. In Pro Tools, for example, you choose the loop tool from the tool bar and then drag the right edge. Same idea, just a slightly different implementation. Let's take a look at GarageBand's implementation. Figure 7-4 shows a drum loop on an audio track in GarageBand.

Figure 7-4: A drum loop

If you bring your mouse over to the right edge of the loop, you'll notice the cursor changes to a loop symbol (see Figure 7-5).

Figure 7-5: Loop cursor

Figure 7-6: Loop repeat

In GarageBand, you get this cursor at the top right corner of the loop. Once you have that, click and drag to the right to extend the loop. At each repeat of the loop, you'll see a small divot (see Figure 7-6) signifying that the loop has started over from the start again.

You can even choose to loop only certain sections if you choose; just pull the loop out to a specific spot and release it.

QUESTION

Can I use my loops in a commercial project?
Most loop libraries are very clear about the royalty implications of using their material. Most loops are royalty free, while other companies let you do what you want without compensation, as long as you don't violate their rules. When in doubt, contact the loop maker for clarity.

Make Your Own

You can turn any audio or MIDI material into a loop. Simply record a few bars of music and using the trimming tools in your DAW, clean up the file so that the music starts and ends cleanly on downbeats. Then extend the loop. If all goes well, you'll have a great loop that you made yourself! With loop-based software, many other people may have the same loops as you do. While you can combine them in infinite ways, the building blocks are still a limitation. Making your own loops can really help you distinguish your music.

Making Loops Your Own

One of the greatest strengths of loops lies in their ability to empower musicians. For example, if you're not a drummer and you've always had a hard time programming drumbeats using a keyboard, a loop library of great drums can be a huge help. Many musicians use loops for styles of music and genres that they don't have a great deal of exposure to. They will take these loops and manipulate them to make them their own. Using effects is one of the best ways to personalize a preexisting loop.

GarageBand (and every other DAW) makes this easy. It doesn't matter if the loop is recorded audio or if a synthesizer in your computer plays it back. The end result is the same: audio comes out of your computer. In Garage-

Band, double-clicking on the track name will open up more information about the track. Figure 7-7 shows the track information page.

In the track information page, you have the option to insert audio effects. While effects are covered in greater detail in Chapters 15 and 16, some popular effects and what they can do to your loops include:

Figure 7-7: Track information

- **Delay:** Lets your loops echo and regenerate. Delay can yield some really great sounding effects.
- **EQ:** EQ filtering can radically change the quality of a loop, especially cool on drum loops when you sweep the frequency slowly over time.
- **Distortion:** Adds a hard-edged grit to your loops. When applied heavily, distortion can completely change the sonic character of your loops.

These are just some basic ideas of how you can manipulate your loops to make them unique. Make sure that you spend some time working with your loop library to make it your own.

Don't think that loops are just for electronic music and hobbyist musicians. Many professional musicians use loops as guide tracks, segments that will be replaced by real musicians eventually, but are needed to aid in the composition process.

Expanding your Loop Library

All of the loop-based DAWs ship with an included loop library. One of the great benefits of loops is that you can quickly expand your own library with third-party loops. These loops simply drag and drop into your software, greatly increasing its capabilities. Here is a list of some resources for third-party loops:

- **Apple**—If you use GarageBand, you can purchase five additional Jam Packs that give you more loops and more instrument sounds for

MIDI loops. Logic uses the same loops, and the most recent version of Logic Studio includes all of the Jam Packs.

- **Big Fish Audio:** Big Fish has a massive library of just about every instrument and style of audio loops you could ever want. Their titles include all three formats of loops (see below), so they're compatible with all the major DAWs.
- **Platinum Loops:** Another great loop provider with a massive catalog. They also ship their loops with all popular formats so they'll work in whichever DAW you're using.

There are so many more, including tons of free resources online. Go to Google and do a quick search for "free music loops" and you easily find some great content.

The three most popular loops formats are:

- Apple Loops—for use in GarageBand and Logic.
- REX/Reason—for use in Reason, Cubase, and others.
- WAV (also called Acidized WAV)—for use in ACID, Live, Sonar, Pro Tools, and many other software titles.

All of these formats include extra information that helps the loop software conform tempo and pitch, making it easy to use them in any composition.

CHAPTER 8

Setting It All Up

All that gear you have is worthless unless you know how to set it up. It's safe to say that every stage in the recording process is important and setting up your gear is no different. This is an essential step where many people make mistakes. But you can avoid those mistakes by following the techniques discussed in this chapter. You might even learn some tricks to simplify your life. A good setup goes a long way.

Cable Types Explained

There are a few types of cables that you'll have to deal with in your studio. You should know what each of them does; here is a breakdown.

Quarter-Inch Cables

The most common cable is the quarter-inch cable. It's the familiar "guitar cable" that we all know and love. These cables are used for connecting guitars and keyboards to amplifiers, amplifiers to mixers, and mixers to speakers, just to name a few. However, all quarter-inch cables are not created equal. There are specific types for specific uses. The most common is the instrument cable. The instrument cable is used for connecting instruments (guitars, keyboards, samplers) to amplifiers and other sources. The cable carries the mono (one-sided) signal to and from any source you choose.

ESSENTIAL

Instrument cables are also commonly referred to as tip sleeve cables. If you look at the connection end, you'll notice that the tip is separated from the rest of the connector with a plastic spacer. The spacer separates the hot side of the cable that carries the signal from the side that carries the ground.

The other type of quarter-inch cable is the speaker cable. Speaker cables are very different from instrument cables. A guitar or a keyboard puts out a very small amount of power. Because of the potential for noise, which no one likes to hear in recordings, instrument cables contain a shield inside the cable to help keep the noise down. But amplifiers push more power to speakers through their cables than instruments do. Because of this, speaker cables don't need a shield, due to something called signal-to-noise ratio.

Signal-to-noise ratio is critical to understand. The higher the level of a signal, the less you hear the noise that is present. This is why you should never record low levels. Noise, while it's annoying, can usually be covered up by a full, loud signal.

Speaker cables shouldn't be used for instruments and vice versa. The packages clearly state what the cables are used for. When in doubt, ask for help.

Figure 8-1 shows all the connector types: quarter-inch TR (Tip-Ring), quarter-inch TRS, XLR, MIDI, and RCA.

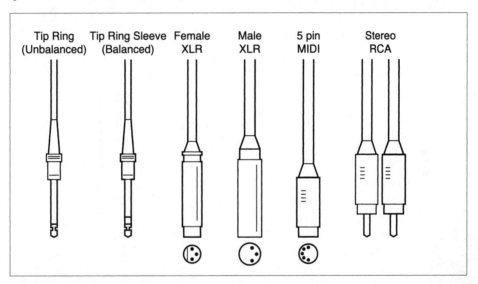

Figure 8-1: Audio cable types

Tip Ring Sleeve Cables

The tip ring sleeve (TRS) is a quarter-inch stereo cable. Pull out any pair of stereo headphones that you own and look at the plug. Notice how it was two plastic spacers? The quarter-inch tip sleeve (instrument) cable has only one. The extra spacer on the tip ring sleeve is there to accommodate another signal in the cable. Stereo cables carry two separate signals: left and right.

In a studio, a stereo cord is used for two purposes. First, it connects an effect processor into a mixer or recording device. This type of cable is called an "insert." Insert cables have the stereo connector on one side and two mono cables on the other side. The stereo cable splits the signal so that you can have an input and an output to an effects processor. In short, if you're going to use external effects, you'll need to own a few stereo insert cables.

The second use for a stereo quarter-inch cable is for a balanced signal. Balanced cables have a stereo plug on both sides. What does balanced mean? Basically, the cable copies one signal to the two internal wires and performs extra shielding and other electrical magic to cut down the noise. Balanced cables are used for microphones and whenever cord lengths are very long. This helps cut down on the noise that longer cables usually have.

XLR Cables

XLR is the standard microphone cable, and the letters stand for the three signals carried in the cable. X is for external, which is called the ground, L is for line, and R is for return. The connector is round and has three prongs on one side (the male side) and three sockets on the other (the female side). Microphone cables are always balanced. XLR cables are sometimes used for connecting mixers to recording devices, but their most common use is for microphones.

FACT

Balanced cables can be used only if your mixer or recording device supports them. It will be clearly stated in your manual if you can use a balanced signal. You find balanced connections on better recording equipment. Microphone inputs are *always* balanced.

RCA Cables

RCA cables, invented by the RCA Corporation, are another type of unbalanced cable. They are typically two mono cables that run together and split off into two ends with RCA plugs. RCA cables are commonly used in home stereo equipment. In the recording studio, RCA cables are used to hook up a tape machine to a mixer and recording interfaces to some computers.

Digital Cables

Digital audio cables fall into three categories:

- The S/PDIF digital cable carries one stereo signal digitally on an RCA cable.
- The AES/EBU cable carries the same stereo digital signal, this time on XLR cables.
- Fiber optic cables are used for audio.

Digital cables can transmit a stereo pair, or in the case of ADAT Light-pipe, eight signals at once! Digital connectors are very common on recording equipment today—even lower cost ones.

MIDI Cables

MIDI cables are simple, and there is only one type: the five-pin MIDI. You can't possibly buy the wrong one. If your MIDI interface has MIDI connector jacks, then you'll need one cable for each input and one cable for each output you want to use.

Patching, Levels, and Monitoring

There are some other vital areas to talk about that fall outside our main topics. These include essential gear like patch bays and important information about setting proper levels, setting up your studio monitors, and monitoring setup. Understanding these will help complete your knowledge of home studios and the components that go into them.

Patch Bays to the Rescue

If you have a lot of gear that you need to plug in often, you're going to love a patch bay. A patch bay (shown in Figure 8-2) doesn't look like much. But don't let looks fool you; this is one powerful piece of gear.

On the front panel are lots of input jacks; on the back panel are lots of matching jacks. Instead of crawling around the floor and repatching (reconnecting) all of your gear, you can leave it permanently plugged in to the back of the patch bay and use the front to make connections. Patch bays are also great for mixers that have rear connections because you're saved from the headache of crawling around or lifting up the mixer every time you need to patch something. If you have a small studio, you might never need one, but as you grow in size a patch bay is essential. You won't find a professional studio without several patch bays.

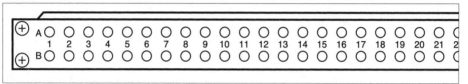

Figure 8-2: Audio patch bay

Understanding Input Levels

Setting a proper recording input level is essential. A full signal is best. You always want to record as loudly as possible without clipping (overloading the input, causing distortion) the input or preamp. Every recording device, even the cheap tape four-tracks, has a meter that shows you the level of an incoming signal. Figure 8-3 shows what a typical meter looks like.

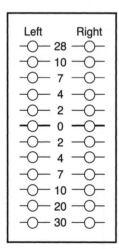

Figure 8-3: Mixer meter level

Usually the displays on a meter light up green at the bottom and red at the top. Just like a stop light, red on the meter means stop. Why? Because you're clipping, and you need to adjust the level. Your goal is to stay green most of the time and let your loudest parts stay away from the red, although it's okay to get close to it. By keeping the levels high when you record, you'll maximize the signal-to-noise ratio and drown out any extra, unwanted noise. If you record too softly, you'll have to boost the signal during mixing, and that boosts the noise along with it. No matter how loudly you record a signal, you can always turn it down later when you mix.

Setting Up Your Monitors

If you choose to monitor through headphones, setting up your monitors is as easy as plugging them in and placing them over your ears. If you're going to use monitor speakers, setting them up is almost as easy. First, place the monitors level with your ears; placing them on the floor just won't do. Face them slightly in toward each other so that both speakers focus their sound at the middle of your head. A line drawn from your head to one speaker to the other speaker and back to your head should form an equilateral triangle.

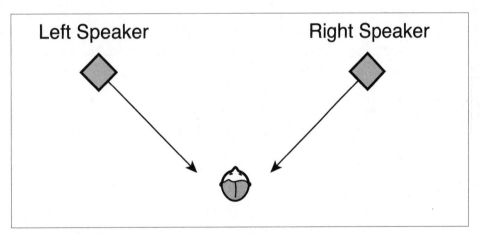

Figure 8-4: Monitor speaker triangle

Monitors are also referred to as "near field monitors" because they are designed to be used at close range, before room acoustics can color the sound. You should sit less than 5 feet away from your monitors and set up the monitors that same distance from each other as well. Use balanced cables, not instrument cables, to hook up your mixer or recording machine to your speakers.

Understanding the Signal Chain

The signal chain is the path your sound takes when it is recorded. Plugging your microphone into a mixer and plugging the mixer into a recording device is a common signal chain. Signal chains can be very simple or quite complicated depending on your setup. Here are two key elements to understanding signal chains:

- **Gain**. This is the recording engineer's term for the volume or loudness of a signal. Every time you turn up a guitar amplifier, move a mixer's slider up, or turn up your headphones, you're adjusting gain.
- **Gain stage.** This is any device that changes the volume of a device. Mixers, microphone preamplifiers, and input level controls are all gain stages.

Gain and gain stages are critical to recording great signals. Every time your signal passes through a gain stage, it is affected. Excessive gain stages can introduce noise in your signal. So, the fewer gain stages the signal passes through, the better.

Gain stages are used to set the level of an instrument to a proper, full level without distortion. Distortion is caused by adding too much gain, causing overloading. It's possible to clip a sound in one gain stage and turn it down in the next, resulting in a terrible signal—a low volume signal that clips.

There is a credo shared by many in the recording business: Garbage in, garbage out. If any part of your signal chain is weak, that weakness will come out in the recording. Bad microphones will still sound bad when played back on expensive recording systems. Noisy crackling cables will crackle on the recording. Clip an input and it will be clipped in the recording. Recording isn't a magic wand that magically cures problems. There certainly are some tricks of the trade, but you get what you put into it. Recording is very honest: Whatever you give it, it spits back at you.

Isolating Sources of Sound

Sound travels in waves, and it's always loudest directly in front of the sound source—the amplifier, the guitar's sound hole, the mouth of a singer, and so on. Once sound is released from its source, it can reflect and bounce all over a room. It's very hard to control where the sound goes.

Being able to separate sound is very important in recording. That's why isolation booths are a staple of recording studios. Being able to isolate sound is even more critical to the home studio owner because you don't have the luxury of using soundproofed rooms and isolated sources. So what can you do?

Banish It

Let's set up a scenario: You are recording a guitarist, and the amplifier is right next to the recording device. Unfortunately, because your room is small, you don't have much of a choice about placement. The guitar player, like most guitar players, loves to play his amplifier loud. You hook up a microphone and turn on your headphones, but all you hear is the roaring guitar amplifier 3 feet from you. How are you going to listen for microphone placement, clipping, or anything else for that matter? You need to get the offending sound (or player, whichever comes first) isolated so you can do your work.

ALERT

If you're just starting out or have never recorded before, your first recordings might depress you a bit; you might not sound as good as you think! Little problems in pitch and rhythm will be very clear when you listen to your recorded music. Recording is, in a word, honest. Many people find it a great tool for learning their strengths and weaknesses.

The easiest way to isolate the sound is to put the amplifier in another room and close the door. The guitarist can monitor his sound through headphones along with you. This way you'll be able to hear what the recorder is hearing and not what the amplifier is forcing you to hear. Closets work well for this because they are small and clothes will also absorb some of the sound. The bathroom can isolate sources pretty well, too! And it's also a great place to record sources, especially acoustic guitars, acoustic instruments, and vocals. Since most bathrooms are tiled, the sound is very reflective and live, which can be really good for adding some ambience and reverb to your recordings. You'd be amazed at how many home studios rely on the acoustics of a bathroom for recording sources.

Using Baffles

A baffle is an object that blocks sound. It's also referred to as a gobo. If you don't have the option of isolating sound to another room, a baffle might do the trick.

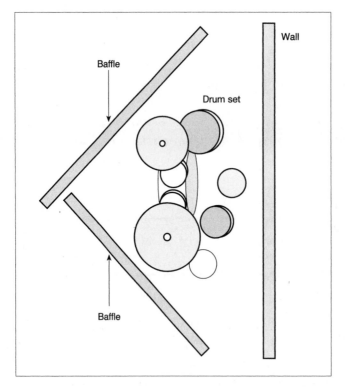

Figure 8-5: Drum set baffle

Baffles are often used onstage around drum sets (see Figure 8-5), and are typically made of Plexiglas. These help to keep the drum sound from traveling out on the stage and getting picked up by other microphones. If you plan on recording a live band performance and you wish to retain any hope of mixing signals separately, you'll need baffles because sound has a nasty habit of flying everywhere if you don't control it. The drums will bleed into the guitar microphone and so on, making it hard to separate sounds and mix independently. Putting baffles between instruments can do the trick.

Soundproofing

You can do two main things to defeat sound in its tracks:

- **Create dead air.** Dead air traps sound and doesn't let it escape. You can trap air with a mattress, cushy furniture, or suspended (drop) ceilings.
- **Add mass and density.** A massive or dense object stops sound. For example, you can scream as loud as you want at a concrete wall, but you won't be heard on the other side. Because sound is produced by vibrating objects that push the air around them to create sound waves, a substance with little flex (like concrete) won't vibrate well. Less vibration equals less sound.

The best way to soundproof a home studio is to build a room within a room. After the normal drywall is hung, add sound batting, which is an absorbing material. Then hang another layer of drywall a few inches out from the original wall or ceiling. This creates a space between the walls to trap the sound, and it also adds to the mass and density of the wall. This is a common practice in professional studios, too. There are many books and resources available on soundproofing, so check the web, your local music store, and the public library near you.

FACT

A mattress makes a great baffle to use at home. Positioned a few feet in front of an amplifier or a drum set, the mattress will absorb and block some of the sounds from overpowering you. It's not a perfect solution since sound reflects to other places, but it can *really* help you out if you're in a pinch.

You can also isolate amplifiers by building an isolation box for them. By sealing each amplifier in a box, you create a mini–isolation room and prevent sound from escaping. You'll also need to insulate the inside of the box so the sound gets trapped there. Make sure the box is big enough to accommodate the microphone, and cut a small hole in the box to get the microphone cable out. Once you close up the box, you should be able to crank the amplifier and have little sound leakage. You'll never eliminate all extra sounds this way, but you can reduce the sound by almost 90 percent.

Acoustics

The science of acoustics is far too vast and complicated to get into in any depth here, but some basic understanding will help you in setting up an optimal space for your studio, wherever it might be.

Sound Absorption and Reflection

As sound travels through the air and interacts with surfaces, it's either absorbed into the material or reflected. Absorption is typically the least of your worries; most of the time it's a blessing in a home studio. Reflection, on the other hand, can be a problem. In a big space, reflections can have an ambient reverb, which is a good thing. Reflections are an essential part of a live concert hall, especially a classical hall, because they produce a natural reverb that is pleasing; reverb processors try to imitate the sound of a big room's natural reflections. But in a home studio that's set up in a small space, reflections can be as loud as the original signal, making it hard to mix and hear the real signal. If you have a space that is overly reflective, the easiest thing you can do is add some materials to absorb the sound and stop the reflections.

Foam for Your Walls

Foam is one of the greatest sound absorbers. Acoustical foam, special foam designed for studios and sound professionals, is a textured material with raised surfaces and depressions. It does a good job of cutting down the reflectivity of a room, and it's great when mixing with speakers. When you record, the sound of the room is recorded as well; this is called ambience.

Certain microphones pick up less ambience than others, but there's always something that gets picked up. If your room is overly reflective, you might get too much ambience in your signal. Acoustical foam can help tame those sources.

You can purchase foam from most major music stores or through online catalogs; it is sold by the sheet and can easily be mounted nondestructively to the wall. Acoustical foam does a bad job of soundproofing, so don't try to use it in this capacity.

The Direct Approach

If noise is a problem where you live, try as hard as you can to record direct sources. Electric guitar doesn't have to be miked; there are plenty of processors that do a great job of emulating that sound while the guitar is directly plugged in. The Line6 POD is a famous example of such a processor, and so is the Behringer V-AMP. With certain instruments, such as the drums, you have no choice but to use a microphone. The more direct sources you can use, the simpler your noise problem will be. It's possible to record all direct instruments (guitar, keyboard, bass, drum machine) and mix on headphones, thus creating zero audible sound.

Common Mistakes

It's a pretty safe bet that your first recordings will have some problems, so let's go over some very common ones and show you easy ways to fix them.

Recap of Signal Chains

Keep your signal chains simple. Don't use excessive wiring if it's not necessary—the simpler the chain, the better. This is especially important when dealing with gain stages; you have to be very careful about levels. Any device that can raise and lower your gain (any device with a volume control), such as a mixer, preamplifier, or input trim control, must be used carefully. It's easy to make mistakes like using two gain stages when only one will do, possibly adding noise or easily clipping the signal. Remember, once you clip a signal by overboosting it, your take is destroyed. You can't mix out clipping in a track. So be careful!

Ground Loops and Buzz

So you have some noise. Where is it coming from? There are a few very common buzzes, and most are easily remedied. Most buzz comes from bad grounding, which can create what is known as a ground loop. Modern houses typically utilize three-prong electrical outlets; the third plug is a ground, which draws excess electrical charges away from a power source. If an electrical outlet is not grounded properly, every device plugged into it might buzz. This can include your amplifiers or even your recording devices. Buzz is annoying and can ruin a recording. Fortunately, there are a few things you can do.

First, try the easiest fix: Plug the source into a different power outlet. Amazingly, some outlets buzz less than others. If that doesn't work, purchase a power conditioner, a device that regulates the type of power that comes out of an outlet, making sure the power is regular and clean. If that doesn't work and you have a really bad buzz problem, call an electrician to look at the wiring in your house. This can be costly, but it might be a viable option if the noise is rendering your expensive gear useless. Direct boxes are also susceptible to ground loop buzz. Thankfully, most direct boxes come with a ground lift switch that eliminates the buzz when activated. If you're planning to purchase a direct box, look for one that contains a ground lift.

Noises of All Kinds

Ground loop is not the only kind of noise. Electrical equipment, especially delicate equipment such as microphones and recording devices, is prone to interference. Interference from radio signals, televisions, and magnetic sources can create problems. It's not uncommon for a public address system to occasionally pick up a radio station or a cordless phone signal, and you might run into these problems in your home studio as well. The most common problem that home studio users face is from magnetic interference. If you've ever put a magnet near a TV, you've seen the color go haywire. Studio monitor speakers contain large magnets as part of the speaker. If you run a computer-based studio with a tube moni-tor, the speakers could interfere with the signal in the computer (not to mention that magnets should be kept away from hard drives). Look for monitors that are magnetically shielded. Many monitors are designed this way due to the popularity of computer recording, but you should double check to be safe.

CHAPTER 9

Microphones

There are so many brands, sizes, and shapes of microphones to choose from. This makes it hard for a novice to walk into a store and buy the right one. While there might be hundreds of microphones, there are actually just a few types to choose from. Once you get a handle on them, you can make informed decisions.

Polar Patterns

Directionality is an essential aspect of a microphone. To understand this, you must understand a little about polar patterns, because they are critical to picking the right microphone. Polar patterns are best understood by looking at one. Figure 9-1 shows the polar patterns you will encounter when microphone shopping.

Around the outside of the circle are degree markings. These degrees signify the origination of the sound in relation to where the microphone is pointed. Simply, the microphone is pointed at 0 degrees. The shaded areas in the circle show direction and scope of what the microphone can pick up and what it can't. In the case of the cardioid microphone, you can see that it's most sensitive to what's directly in front of it, at 0 degrees. If you were to stand behind a cardioid pattern microphone, at 180 degrees, the microphone would be basically deaf to anything you say. Out of the five polar patterns in this figure, there are only three main polar patterns (cardioid, omnidirectional, and figure-eight), and the remaining two (hypercardioid and supercardioid) are subpatterns.

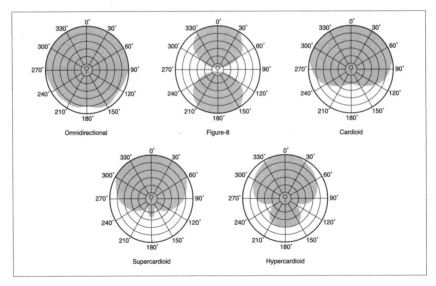

Figure 9-1: Microphone polar patterns

To repeat, a cardioid microphone is most sensitive to sounds in front of it. The subtypes, hypercardioid and supercardioid, simply change how much it can hear behind. You will see in Figure 9-1 that both hypercardioid and supercardioid have very little shaded areas behind them. This means that you can minimize microphone bleed by close-miking an instrument with a supercardioid microphone, since it rejects sounds from behind it so well. A supercardioid will only hear what's right in front of it. If you point this microphone right at your sound source, you won't experience much bleed from other instruments in other directions.

An omnidirectional microphone picks up everything from all sides. You can see in its polar pattern that the shading is all around the microphone. Omnidirectional microphones are great room microphones and work well with large groups.

A figure-eight microphone hears sounds only directly in front and directly in back of it, rejecting much of the sounds from the sides. Figure-eight microphones are best for recording two vocalists on one microphone, or for recording between two instruments, blocking out the sides.

Frequency Response

Frequency response is another factor to consider in selecting a microphone. Each microphone hears sound differently. Microphones will boost or cut certain frequencies across their range, which is what frequency response means. Many microphones aim for a flat response, which means there is little boosting or cutting of frequencies. With a flat response, you get as accurate a representation of the source sound as possible. There are limits to the minimum and maximum frequencies microphones can detect. The lowest frequency that most microphones

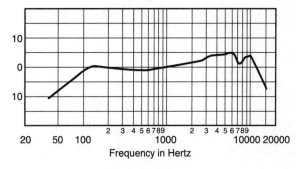

Typical Frequency Response

Figure 9-2: Microphone frequency response

can hear is 20Hz, and the highest frequency is 20kHz. You will see these numbers in product literature and advertisements (20Hz to 20kHz response). Figure 9-2 shows a frequency response chart for a dynamic microphone— a Shure SM57, a classic microphone that sounds great on guitar amps and snare drums.

However, not all microphones go down to 20Hz, and not all go up to 20kHz. So, why is this information important? Consider the boundaries of sound. The lowest note on a piano registers at 27.50Hz, which is about the lowest sound you can really imagine recording. The highest sound on a piano clocks in at around 4kHz. There are, of course, higher frequency sounds. We won't get into this here, but all sounds spread into many frequencies, and there are always higher overtones present. Microphones need to pick up these higher frequencies for our ears to accept the sound as "natural."

The loudness of any sound is measured by the level of sound pressure present, measured in decibels (dB). An airport runway is about 120dB and a normal conversation is about 60dB. Loud amplifiers, screaming singers, and certain drums can put out extremely high sound-pressure levels. If the microphone you choose can't handle the sound-pressure level, you can damage or distort the microphone over time, rendering the signal unusable.

Dynamic Microphones

Of the three main types of microphones available, let's start with the microphone most people are familiar with, the dynamic microphone. Dynamic microphones are the microphones you've most likely come into contact with if you've ever played on a stage, sung, or spoken into a microphone. Dynamic microphones are the ice cream cone–shaped microphones that we all know and love.

Construction

What makes this microphone "dynamic" is the way in which it picks up the sound and translates it into an electrical signal. It has a small diaphragm made of plastic, usually Mylar (a type of plastic), that is placed in front of a coil of wire, called the voice coil. The voice coil is suspended between two magnets. If you remember from high school physics, when you move wire between magnetic fields, you can induce current. As sound hits the diaphragm, the voice coil moves and induces current. The current is fed down the microphone cable into your mixer or recording device. Voilà, sound!

Using Dynamic Microphones

Dynamic microphones are great for vocals, miking amplifiers, and close-miking drums. Dynamic microphones are durable, well constructed, long-lasting, and—the best part—cheap. You can get a great microphone for under $100. A famous dynamic microphone, the Shure SM57, which is great on guitars and snare drums, can be found in just about every studio in the world. Shure also makes the SM58, which is used for speech and vocals in live settings, such as concerts.

FACT

> Another type of microphone is the ribbon condenser. Instead of using a traditional diaphragm as the dynamic and condenser microphones do, a ribbon condenser uses a very thin and flexible ribbon to pick up the sound. Ribbons are very fragile and can be damaged with mishandling. Recently, budget-priced ribbon condensers started to appear on the market.

Dynamic microphones hear sound in cardioid patterns, which means they hear sound only directly in front of them. This makes them great for close-up miking situations, such as vocals, amplifiers, and drums, situations calling for nothing but the sound coming from the source with little or no ambience. One of the most important points about the dynamic microphone is its ability to handle extremely high sound-pressure level (SPL). As a result, you can use them in loud situations. However, dynamic microphones don't have full frequency response, which is helpful in many situations, and all are a bit different in the frequency levels they respond to. For example, the AKG D112 Kick Drum microphone emphasizes the bass frequencies and falls off at the high range, where there is little signal from a bass drum.

Condenser Microphones

Condenser microphones are commonly found in recording studios but not often on stages because of the different way in which they pick up sound.

Condenser microphones use a diaphragm, just as the dynamic microphone does, but instead of sitting in front of a wrap of coil (the voice coil), the diaphragm sits in front of a stationary plate of metal called the back plate. The diaphragm in a condenser microphone is always made of thin metal or metal-coated plastic. Both the diaphragm and the back plate have polarized voltage applied to them. As the diaphragm moves back and forth in relation to the stationary back plate, a very small current is produced, which is the signal. Figure 9-3 shows a large diaphragm condenser microphone.

Figure 9-3: An M-Audio Luna II condenser microphone *Courtesy of Avid Technology, Inc.*

Condenser microphones are often classified by the diameter of their diaphragms. Obviously, large-diaphragm microphones are larger in size than small-diaphragm microphones. Large diaphragms are more sensitive to low-level sounds than small diaphragms. Small diaphragms can handle louder overall sounds, however. Condenser microphones can range from $100 to many thousands of dollars. The good news is that you don't have to spend a lot to get one that sounds good.

Condenser microphones are used for everything that dynamic microphones can't do. Condensers are more delicate and more expensive than dynamic microphones, but they are also more accurate. Condensers usually have a flat and wide frequency response, are sensitive to all frequencies, and tend not to boost or lower any particular frequency. This is why condensers are the microphones of choice for acoustic instruments such as piano, winds, strings (including guitar and bass), drum overheads, and vocals.

As for polar patterns, condensers are available in all polar patterns. This makes them ideal when you have to pick up a whole room with one microphone using an omnidirectional polar pattern. Couple this with the fact that some condenser microphones can switch polar patterns, and you've got one flexible microphone. Most condenser microphones can't handle superhigh sound-pressure level, however, so don't replace all your dynamic microphones with condensers. On certain condenser microphones, you might get a pad switch that lowers the microphone's output by 10dB or more in order to better handle louder sounds.

Microphone Extras

You mean there's more? Yes, you're not out of the woods just yet! The good news is that if you've hung on through all this, you really know something about microphones and what makes them tick. This will be invaluable to you as a home studio owner. So here's the rest.

Stands

A microphone doesn't just lie on the floor—you need to use a microphone stand to secure and position it. The following is a rundown of the basic kinds of stands you'll encounter:

- **Standard:** This is your garden-variety microphone stand. It has a wide base and allows for up-and-down positioning of the microphone only.
- **Low Profile**: This is just like the standard microphone, except it's very short. It's great for bass drums and amplifiers that sit on the floor. It provides up-and-down height adjustment only.
- **Low-Profile Boom:** This is a short stand coupled with a boom arm for much greater maneuverability in all directions, not just up and down.
- **Standard Boom:** This is a tall stand with a boom arm for maneuverability in many directions. It's great for vocals, drum overheads, and much more. This is a good all-purpose stand.

You can't go wrong with boom stands because they can work in practically any situation. If you microphone a lot of bass drums or amplifiers that sit on the floor, you'll need the low-profile stands to get down low, although you could also lean down a boom stand.

Shock Mounts

Many condenser microphones come with a strange-looking apparatus called a shock mount (Figure 9-4), which is a web of elastic string that encloses the microphone and is secured to the microphone stand.

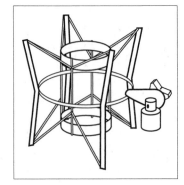

Figure 9-4: Microphone shock mount

The shock mount tries to isolate and cushion the microphone to prevent it from picking up sound traveling up the microphone stand. Keep in mind that sound can be transmitted through objects, and microphone stands are no exception. Condenser microphones are very sensitive and if you accidentally stomp a foot on the floor, or worse, hit the microphone stand while recording, the microphone will pick up the thump and ruin your recording. If you place your microphone stand on a bare floor, other frequencies in the room might cause the stand to vibrate. You don't have to use a shock mount, but if your microphone comes with one, you should use it.

Pop Filters

If you plan to record vocals or spoken word, you need a pop filter (Figure 9-5). Certain parts of speech called plosives make certain letters of the alphabet come out with much greater force than others. Words that start with the letters P, B, and T are the most common plosives. Recorded normally, the plosive sounds will "pop" and sometimes overload the microphone. A pop filter is simply a screen placed between the microphone and the singer's mouth to stop the plosive from popping the microphone.

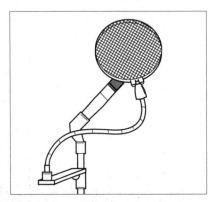

Figure 9-5: Pop filter

Pop filters are cheap, and you can even make one out of wire and nylon mesh or pantyhose. An added benefit is that pop filters stop spit from hitting your expensive microphones. Gross, but it happens!

Preamplifiers

As we have touched on in Chapter 4, a microphone puts out a very small signal through its cables. In order to use a microphone with a recording device, the signal has to be amplified to a level the recorder can detect. There's no way around this; every microphone needs some sort of preamplification.

QUESTION

Is a microphone preamplifier considered a gain stage?
Yes, a gain stage is any device that changes the volume of a device. A microphone preamplifier boosts the weak signal, so it is a great example of a gain stage. A gain stage could also be a mixer or the output knob on a guitar effects processor.

The good news is that most outboard mixers include a few microphone preamps, and so do studios-in-a-box and many computer interfaces. You can also purchase individual microphone preamplifiers. They are available in single- and multiple-channel versions.

Prices start around $40 and can go very high. Preamplifiers are an important part of recording, and the quality of preamplifiers varies from devices that simply make microphones louder, to those that truly improve the quality of audio that pass through them. You'll hear names like Neve, GML, and Great River in the upper echelons of mic preamplifiers. Like most higher priced units, if folks are buying them, there must be something to them.

Powered Microphones

Condenser microphones, except for ribbon condensers, need internal power to run, unlike dynamic microphones, which induce current on their own. Condenser microphones get power either from an internal battery or, more commonly, from an external source. The power derived from an external source is called phantom power. Phantom power is delivered to the microphone from the device it's normally hooked up to, which can be a mixer, microphone preamplifier, recording device, or computer interface.

The phantom power runs through the standard, ordinary microphone cable, so no extra supplies are needed. You need phantom power only when working with condenser microphones, and most recording devices automatically give you phantom power, but be sure to check with the manufacturers if you plan on using phantom-powered microphones, just to be safe. If you already own a recording device that doesn't contain phantom power capability, don't worry; there are plenty of condenser microphones that operate off battery power, so those might be a better choice for you.

So now you've learned the basics of microphones. If you feel unsure about anything, talk to engineers and other home studio owners to find out what they use and what they recommend. Happy hunting.

CHAPTER 10

Mixers

No piece of gear is more central to the studio experience than the mixing board, or console as it's referred to in larger studios. This is the place where the engineer sits and does all his most important work. For the home studio owner, the mixer has an uncertain future because many devices have integrated mixers, and software programs provide virtual mixers that can be accessed onscreen.

Mix It Up

In the twenty-first century, the outboard mixer is no longer a necessity, although many people will always use one. In professional recording studios, outboard mixers are an essential, irreplaceable part of the studio. Even as technology continues to change, the outboard mixer in some form or another refuses to go away.

The word "mix" is defined as combining or blending into one mass or mixture. In the case of recorded audio, a mixer serves as a control over many individual sounds, or channels (tracks). A mixer has two uses: The first is to manage many inputs of sound and help to route them into the recorder, including setting the appropriate recording input level and preamplifying microphones and instruments. The mixer can also be used after recording to provide balance and EQ, add additional signal effects, and provide a final master mix of your sound.

Do You Even Need a Mixer?

Twenty years ago, you had to have an outboard mixer, because there was no other way to control inputs to the recorder. These days, especially for home recording, you might not need one. For computer recording, every major brand of recording software provides a virtual mixer that allows you to change the balance of audio tracks and much more, all with your mouse. With a virtual mixer, you can even record the movement of the on-screen faders to be played back automatically during the final mix down (when everything is recorded to a single file) after you've finished mixing.

If you like the idea of moving volume sliders with your hands while using a computer, you can use "control surfaces" that move the onscreen faders. You can find more about control surfaces in Chapter 17.

Benefits of Using an Outboard Mixer

Even if you have the ability to mix built into your equipment, you might want a separate outboard mixer. Many computer-recording interfaces aren't exactly generous with the number of inputs and outputs they provide. Countless interfaces tout eight or more channels of simultaneous recording, yet they provide only two microphone inputs. So what do you do when you want to record more than two channels of microphones? In this situation, an outboard mixer is going to come in really handy.

ESSENTIAL

Whether you use an outboard mixer or a virtual mixer on your computer, you'll have access to the same features. The virtual computer emulations do just that—emulate the hardware version. Computer mixers are designed so that an engineer who knows hardware mixers will have no trouble transferring her skills over to a computer.

An outboard mixer will allow you to take eight microphones and mix them down to a stereo (two-track) mix that you can bring into the computer. That works great for the computer interfaces that have only two inputs. The only downside is that you lose the ability to change the volume of individual channels after you record. Some studio and live recordings are still done this way.

For recording devices that give you only two microphone channels and additional line inputs, you can take advantage of the microphone preamps that many, if not all, outboard mixers have built in. You can plug in additional microphones to the mixer, preamplify the microphones, and send their individual outputs from the mixer to the line inputs of the recording device. This is the easiest way to increase the number of microphone channels. Not only can buying an outboard mixer be cheaper than buying a new recording device or additional microphone preamplifiers, but having one comes in handy if you play live or have to mix sound. A few companies, such as Mackie, Behringer, Alesis, Nady, Carvin, and Soundcraft, make small outboard mixers appropriate for home studios. Some mixers even incorporate a FireWire or USB connector, allowing you to use your mixer as a two-channel interface.

Physical Layout of Mixers

One thing is for certain—mixers have lots of buttons and knobs. This can scare people at first, but like all things, it makes sense if you know what you're looking at. Figure 10-1 shows an outboard mixer and Figure 10-2 shows a screen from Pro Tools computer software. You can see that the two versions, hardware and software, look very similar in their overall layout. A mixer consists of three main elements: input/output, channel strips, and master sections.

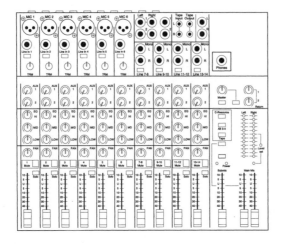

Figure 10-1: Mixing board hardware

Input/Output

The input/output section is the basic function of a mixer. This is where the physical connections are made on the unit. At minimum, a mixer will have a stereo "main" output, where all the individual channels are output. Some mixers give you alternate "bus" outputs that you can use (more on this later in this chapter). A bus is simply a path that audio can take. In the case of mixers, it's a path inside of the mixer. Better mixers give you individual outputs for each channel, but these mixers tend to be expensive.

Figure 10-2: Pro Tools 8 mixer

There will be one input for every channel that the mixer supports. Other inputs include channel inserts, which can be used to patch effects into individual channels, and auxiliary inputs, which allow effects to be assigned to any track in the mix. The better the mixer, the more aux effects you get. There is more about aux effects in our discussion of master sections later in this chapter.

Channel Strips

Figure 10-3 is a close-up of a channel strip from a mixer. These vertical strips are duplicated for every input channel your mixer has. If your mixer supports sixteen channels, your mixer will have sixteen identical channel strips, one after another from left to right. This takes up most of the space on a mixer.

They're also the reason that professional studio consoles are so massive—they contain many, many separate channels. From top to bottom you might find these common mixer elements, which are labeled in Figure 10-3.

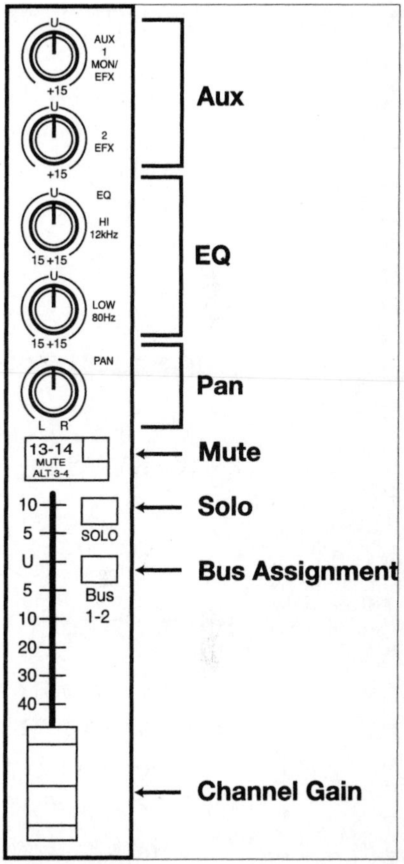

- **Aux Section:** This is where you mix in effects that are on the auxiliary channels.
- **EQ Section:** This is where you can adjust the equalization of the sound balance between high and low frequencies of a signal.
- **Pan:** This knob adjusts where the signal is placed from left to right of the stereo image.
- **Mute:** This mutes the channel from the main mix.
- **Solo:** This mutes every other track and solos the selected track or tracks; you can use this on multiple channels to isolate a few signals together.
- **Bus Assignment:** This sends the selected channel(s) to a bus output and bus fader.
- **Channel Gain:** This is where you set the volume of each track, using either a rotating knob or a vertical slider; channel gain is used for setting volume levels after you record, not during the recording.

Figure 10-3: Mixer channel strip

127

Master Section

So far you've learned to control individual channels, individual volume, and the like on the mixer. The master section (shown in Figure 10-4) is where you control the final output, after all the separate levels have been set. A simple master section contains one main volume control for the entire mix. You might get separate left and right channels, or the channels might be combined into one fader. A more advanced mixer goes beyond just master volume controls. If your mixer supports "buses," you will find those level controls here as well. Auxiliary effects and send and return levels can also be set here.

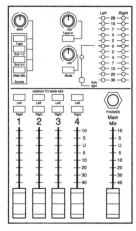

Figure 10-4: Master section

Insert Effects, Aux Inputs, and Buses

Mixers provide several different paths for the audio to take. To fully understand what a mixer is capable of, you'll want to know about insert effects, auxiliary inputs, and buses. Understating these concepts will make you comfortable on any mixing board, regardless of the brand.

Insert Effects

An insert effect is an effect that can be plugged into one, and only one, channel. You do this via the insert jack on your mixer, which sports a tip ring sleeve (TRS) connector made for insert effects. Insert effects are typically used only for compression and EQ because you cannot mix how much of the signal gets the effect—it's all or nothing. Because compression and EQ work fine in these cases, insert effects are perfect for this. Effects are covered in detail in Chapters 15 and 16.

Aux Inputs

Aux inputs are used for effects that require a blend of effected and noneffected signals. Effects like reverb, chorus, and delay sound terrible when you hear only 100 percent effects. Aux effects are also used when you wish to use the same effect on more than one channel. An aux input is plugged into the master section aux input/output, and each channel has a control for how much of the effected signal to blend in with the dry, unaffected signal. This is great when you have hardware effects processors and you have to make the most out of a few pieces of gear. On the computer side, aux effects do the same as their hardware counterparts. You can usually have as many aux effects as you want in software, because you can reuse the same plug-in on multiple tracks.

Buses

Buses act like a sub-master fader. That is, you can send a bunch of channels to a bus, and the bus fader will raise or lower as one, all of the signals fed into it. For example, let's say you're mixing a drum kit. You have four channels of drum sounds and you have the perfect mix between the individual drums. By itself, the drums sound great, but when you add in other instruments, you notice the drums' volumes are a little low. You could raise each drum track one by one, but that means that you lose that perfect balance you worked so hard to get.

If your outboard mixer or virtual mixer supports buses, you can assign all the drum tracks to bus one, which sends all four signals to one volume control (the bus). Then when you turn the bus up, all four signals fed into the bus get louder while retaining their individual balances. You can get multiple buses with the better outbound mixers. The more you spend, the more buses you get. All the major computer recording software supports buses. It's a great tool for recording, and it is commonly used to balance groups of instruments like drums and double-miked instruments.

Buses are also used when connecting to less capable audio interfaces. Many consumer audio interfaces allow only eight or fewer inputs total, so buses comes in handy if you need to consolidate four drum microphones to one or two channels, again regaining control of the final mix, not just the individual channels.

Getting Sound into a Mixer

Getting sound into a mixer properly is very important, and it's easy to make mistakes here. Start with the microphone channels. Attach your microphones to the microphone channels on the board. If your micro-phones are condenser microphones that require phantom power and your mixer supports it, flip the switch on the top or side of the unit that supplies phantom power. Now your microphones will be powered up and ready to go. Next, connect your line-level equipment, such as keyboards and line outputs from amplifiers and direct boxes.

Setting Recording-Friendly Levels

You need to set the level of each input you record through the mixer. Activate the solo button on the channel you are working on to isolate the sound. For microphones, set the input trim control so the microphone's loudest sounds do not clip the input. If your mixer has a meter that lights up (most do), make sure the loudest sound stays in the green lights and doesn't hit the red. Repeat this step for each microphone you have.

ALERT

When you set the microphone levels to record a drummer, make sure the drummer hits the drum really loud so you can get an idea of when clipping might occur. Set your gain so that even the loudest hit does not clip.

Line-level instruments connect to the line channels. You should adjust the gain on the keyboard or guitar amplifier, not on the recorder. The fader for those tracks should be set to "unity gain," which means nothing added, nothing subtracted. Unity gain is marked with a zero. This allows you room in either direction for volume changes later on. Also, check the level meter to make sure you aren't clipping. Taking time to check settings now will ensure that you don't clip and distort the inputs while you're recording.

Measuring Electrical Voltage

"Decibel" is a confusing term. Scientifically, the decibel is not a concrete measure of any one thing; it's a ratio of power or intensity to other factors. There are actually a bunch of different decibels that we deal with. The basic decibel measures sound pressure or the loudness of the sound pressure created. For instance, the sound of a subway car about 200 feet away is 95dB.

On a mixer, decibels are used in a much different way. The first way is as a measure of electrical voltage; the second way is as a level of sound output. When you look at a mixer's slider, you will see that it's marked up and down with decibel marks, ranging from negative decibels to positive decibels. See Figure 10-5.

Negative decibels? This seems to go against what we know of decibels. If you're comparing a volume slider to sound pressure, you will be confused. Think of the volume slider simply as a way of boosting or lowering the prerecorded signal. Negative dB values mean you are reducing the level that's been recorded, and positive dB values mean you are raising the recorded output.

So, as you mix, place all of your volume sliders at zero. At that setting the mixer is not artificially boosting or cutting anything. You hear the signal that you recorded from the instrument or microphone itself.

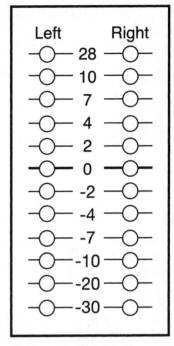

Figure 10-5: Mixer levels

Maximize Music, Minimize Noise

We've talked about setting levels high enough so that they are full and don't clip. This is because the louder the input signal, the less noise the signal will contain. Even if you are planning on using a soft track, record the input at a high level. Turning the track down later will help cover up any noise in the signal. Volume faders on mixers or computers can boost only a few decibels. They can, however, reduce signals to nothing. It's better to start with too much signal and reduce it later than to have too little signal and try to overboost.

FACT

Every signal, no matter how well recorded, will include some noise. This isn't usually a problem if you set the correct signal-to-noise ratio by recording tracks properly and setting the correct input levels. If the signal is loud enough, the noise won't be an issue if you've paid attention to your settings.

Output Scale

More decibel madness! When we discuss using faders to boost and cut input volume, we might naturally push the vocals +2dB to make them louder; increases in dB results in louder signal. Here's where the other side of the decibel confusion erupts, because when it comes to final output, decibels are measured using an entirely different system. We're now faced with a system called decibel full scale (dBFS). Decibel full scale simply considers 0dB as the absolute loudest signal you can have. Since decibels aren't a fixed ratio, dBFS calls 0 the loudest and works backward. When recording, mixing or mastering music, especially in the digital world, you can never exceed 0dBFS, ever. If you do, you will distort and clip the signal. Thankfully, you have meters that show you how loud you are. Meters even glow red when you've clipped.

Getting Sound out of a Mixer

How you get sound out of your mixer and connect it to your audio interface depends on how elaborate your mixer is.

Using a Basic Mixer

If you have a basic mixer that only features stereo outs, the mixer outputs to separate left and right channels. You will only be able to patch those two channels into your audio interface. Using the pan controls on the input channels, you can send certain sounds to the right channel and certain sounds to the left channel.

Using a mixer like this doesn't mean you lose total control of the sounds. By panning certain sounds all the way left or right, you force that signal into one of the two cables. Each of the output cables can go to a separate track on your recorder. Your mixer may have the ability to work as a USB or FireWire interface. With one of these mixers you will generally only be able to send the main stereo output channels from your mixer to your computer, and receive a stereo signal back to your mixer from your computer. The same panning ideas from above apply to these mixers.

More Sophisticated Mixers

If you have a mixer with multiple output buses, you can use those to connect your mixer to your audio interface. This gives you a greater degree of flexibility in how you can set up your recordings. For every bus you have, there will be another two outputs to your recorder. A decent-quality four-bus mixer will give you a total of four extra channels of output to your recorder. If you pan correctly and set the bus assignments well, you can route tons of signals flexibly to your recorder. If you use a lot of microphones and your recorder doesn't support many microphone inputs, this might be a cost-effective way to go—it's cheaper than buying all those microphone preamps separately.

Let's say you're recording drums, bass, guitar, keyboard, and vocal. Using a mixer that only offers you a stereo out, you must either record the instruments separately (or two at a time with the guitar and bass) or get the perfect balance of all the parts going into your computer. Now let's say you have a mixer with four stereo busses (or eight total outs) and an audio interface with eight inputs. With this setup you could devote three outs to the drums, one to the guitar, one to the bass, two to the keyboard, and one to the vocal.

CHAPTER 11

Recording Individual Instruments

No matter when you sit down to record, there will be different variables in the recording process. The type of song you are recording and the instrumentation will change from time to time; your approach will also change along with it. It's time to get your hands dirty with some specifics of instruments and how to record them.

Guitar and Bass

Guitar can be one of the easiest instruments to record—or at least it used to be. Back in the early days, musicians stuck a microphone in front of the amplifier and that was it. Now we are barraged with different amplifiers, effects processors, amplifier simulators, and realistic plug-ins in the computer-recording arena.

Direct Interfaces for Guitar and Bass

To record guitar and bass without the use of an amplifier, you will need a direct box (shown in Figure 11-1) in order to properly interface with the mixer or recording device. Some studios-in-a-box and computer interfaces feature a Hi-Z (high impedance) direct guitar/bass input. If you have this feature, you won't need a direct interface to record your instrument—you can plug right in with a guitar cable. These are becoming more and more common, especially with studio-in-a-box setups.

Direct instrument signals are usually high-impedance sources, so they can't be plugged into a mixer or recording device. In order to record them, you need to use a direct box to convert the high-impedance, unbalanced signal coming from the instrument

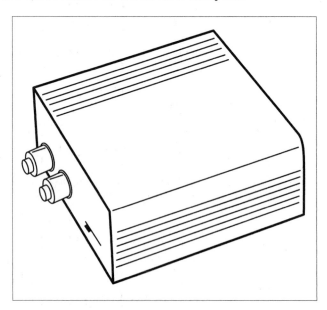

Figure 11-1: Direct box

to a low-impedance, balanced output. The output of the direct box will be a balanced cable, either XLR microphone or tip ring sleeve (TRS).

If your amplifier is equipped with a line out, you can run a cable directly from the back of your amplifier into your mixer or recording device's line input. The amplifier line out will have the correct output level and impedance. The amplifier's line-out jack is specifically designed for studio setups like this. You can also use this feature for live sound applications.

Unfortunately there's one catch to using an amplifier's line out—you might encounter a ground loop, which can cause some very unpleasant buzz in your signal. If this happens, plug your instrument into a direct box that has a ground lift switch. The direct box will take care of the buzz and you will have a good clean signal to work with.

Miking an Amplifier for Guitar and Bass

Miking a guitar or bass amplifier is pretty simple. Most engineers simply place a dynamic microphone a few inches from the center of the speaker. Placing a microphone close to a sound source is commonly called "close-miking." Close-miking is typically used with amplifiers, some acoustic instruments, and most drums.

The exact location of the microphone on the speaker will differ from amplifier to amplifier and microphone to microphone. It's common to place the microphone slightly off the center of the speaker. You can get different tones based on the location of the microphone. As you move the microphone farther to the outside of the speaker, the sound warms up. The closer you move to the center, the more grit and high end you can capture. Let your ear be the judge of what sounds best. Be prepared to spend a good amount of time moving the microphone around at first, until you learn what sounds best.

Recording engineers employ a few tricks in placing a microphone on an amp that might help you achieve some unique sounds. First,

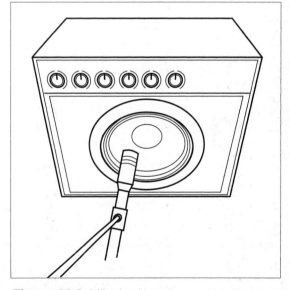

Figure 11-2: Miked guitar amp

you don't have to use a dynamic microphone. Many condenser microphones can handle high sound pressure level (although not the very highest), so if you're not cranking the amplifier to 11 (as in the movie *This Is Spinal Tap*), a condenser could be fine. You might get a richer sound by using the full range provided by a condenser.

Another trick is to use two microphones: a dynamic microphone to close-mike, and a condenser microphone farther back to catch ambience. By blending the two signals together, you can get a nice, rich sound. The farther away the condenser microphone is, the more ambience and natural reverb you'll get in the sound. Many engineers employ this technique to fatten up and widen the guitar and bass tracks.

Direct-Recording Preamplifiers

There's a wave of digital technology available to guitar and bass players found in the direct-recording preamplifier. Devices like the Line6 PODXT and the BOSS GT-10 emulate amplifiers and effects in one handy unit. What's even better is that they can output to line level, allowing you to plug them in directly, bypassing the need for an amplifier or direct box. These units are small and compact, and have become a staple for guitar players who record frequently. Many of the guitar sounds you hear on TV, radio, and studio recordings might very well have come from direct-recording preamplifiers or their computer plug-in brethren.

Wet or Dry Effects?

Effects such as reverb, delay, and chorus help give modern guitars and bass their unique tone. Most players come into the studio with a "sound" they always play with. Typically this sound is achieved with added reverb and other effects. The big question is whether or not to record the guitar with effects (wet) or without (dry). Some players consider the effects a signature part of their sound; it would be hard to duplicate those sounds later on when mixing. However, certain tones sound very good by themselves—but how they fit into a full mix is another story.

The biggest disadvantage to using wet effects is that you have no control over the effects after they're recorded. If you suddenly find out during mixing that there's too much reverb and the guitar sounds distant, there's little you can do to fix it. It's usually safer to leave reverb out of guitar and bass signals, because it's easy to add it during mixing. That way you have control over the final sound.

Computer Plug-Ins for Guitar and Bass

Computers have become a mainstay of recording studios. Both at home and in the professional world, plug-ins for DAW programs are being developed at a dramatic rate. Guitar and bass players have not been left out of this party. Companies such as Line6 and Fender feature digital modeling in their guitar amplifiers using DSP (digital signal processing). Computers use DSP to process recorded audio for effects. One of the coolest plug-ins available for guitar is Eleven by Digidesign. Another favorite is Native Instruments Guitar Rig 3, an impressive guitar amp and effects modeler plug-in with foot controller for live use.

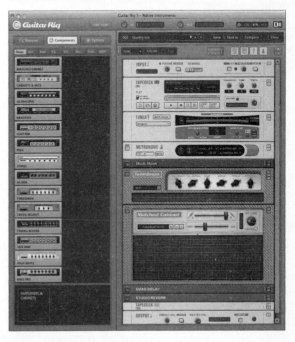

Figure 11-3: Guitar Rig 3

As you can see from the screenshot in Figure 11-3, the controls of Guitar Rig 3 mimic what you're used to seeing on amplifiers (they even resemble some of the classic gear). Not only are there a variety of modeled amplifiers, but the effects are built in, too! You simply plug your guitar directly into the computer and Guitar Rig 3 does the rest.

One of the ultimate features of a plug-in like this is its ability to change the sounds after you have recorded them. The audio track contains only the clean audio; it's the plug-in that does the rest of the work. That means you can change the sounds as you go along, without having to rerecord the part. That's something that wasn't possible before these programs were introduced.

Isolating Amplifiers

Many guitar amplifiers, especially tube amplifiers, sound best when turned up quite a bit—or even turned *all* the way up—because of how tube amplifiers saturate and create gain. To record with the amplifiers this loud, isolation of some kind is a must. Whether you banish the amplifier to a closet, another room, or a special isolation box, for the sake of your hearing, you need to do something. This is especially true when recording loud amplifiers with a band. Isolation can minimize the amount of bleed-through into the other instruments' microphones.

Vocals and the Spoken Word

These days, getting good vocals or spoken words recorded can be one of the greatest challenges of recording. The human voice is one of the hardest sounds to re-create because listeners are supercritical if it doesn't sound exactly as it should. We are, quite naturally, very used to hearing the human voice.

Choosing the Right Microphone for Voice

If you ever had the occasion to sing on stage, you probably sang into a dynamic cardioid microphone. Dynamic microphones are great because they handle loud sounds well, reject other noises from the sides, and are virtually indestructible. While dynamic microphones might be perfect for the stage, they aren't always perfect for the studio. Dynamic microphones don't re-create the full frequency spectrum very well, which can be a problem that sometimes shows itself in vocals that don't sound natural. However, a dynamic microphone is your best choice for live sound in most cases. For studio recording of any vocals, choose a large-diaphragm condenser microphone. Large-diaphragm condensers are those microphones with the large, fat heads. They allow you to pick up all of the frequencies present in a human voice.

Figure 11-4: Vocalist with condenser microphone and pop filter

Save your best condenser microphone for your vocal work because it will allow you to pick up the nuance and detail of the human voice. If you work with vocals a lot, investing in a good microphone will pay off time and time again.

Pop Filters

As discussed earlier, plosives can kill a recording by distorting or clipping the signal either to the microphone or input channel. Plus, they sound just plain awful. On digital recorders, anything that is clipped is instantly turned into garbage noise—a square wave, to be exact. Clipping ruins whatever you are recording. The simple solution—the pop filter—filters excess air through its mesh, and only the normal sound reaches the microphone. Pop filters are a must for vocal recording and can be obtained at a relatively low cost.

The Proximity Effect

Microphones exhibit a special phenomenon called the "proximity effect." Simply put, the closer you stand to a microphone, the more bass frequencies come through. As you step back, the bass diminishes. If you are close-miking a vocalist, this phenomenon creates a muddy sound. The easiest option is to have the singer step back a little, but then the track might sound distant. If so, you can do a few things to fix the problem. Many condenser microphones are equipped with a bass roll-off switch. The bass roll-off switch will usually cut the bass frequencies from around 100Hz and below (but it depends on the source),

Figure 11-5: Apple's Logic EQ plug-in

which is where most of the proximity effect occurs. If your microphone doesn't have such a switch, you can EQ either on your outboard or virtual mixer by cutting 100Hz and below.

Figure 11-5 shows what a 100Hz roll-off looks like in Apple's Logic EQ plug-in.

Voice Monitoring

The vocalist should monitor through closed-ear headphones. The level of the sound coming to the vocalist's ears is critical to getting the best performance. Hearing too much or too little of her own voice can cause major pitch problems. Adjust the mix until the singer feels comfortable and you notice that the pitch remains relatively constant. Typically, a singer doesn't enjoy hearing the dry sound of her voice through the headphone mix. Reverb is usually needed to sweeten up the sound and make the singer more comfortable. If you're recording in a DAW, adding reverb is easy enough: just insert a reverb plug-in and mix it to taste.

Isolating the Voice

Vocals are something you definitely want to isolate, because it's important to cut down a lot of the excess ambient noise in the room. Isolation will give the voice a relatively flat, neutral sound, which offers you the most control over the sound. Ambience can be added with reverb later.

Holding Pitch

For a singer, there are few things more important than holding good pitch. Not everyone is blessed with this ability, so you might have to rerecord until you get something you like. But that can lead to frustration on the part of the singer, which can make the situation worse.

Technology to the rescue! Melodyne (shown in Figure 11-6) analyzes the incoming pitches of any audio track and allows you to retune one or all of the pitches. Auto-Tune, a plug-in by Antares, first made pitch correction possible. Melodyne took it one step further and gave unprecedented control of not only the tuning of the notes,

Figure 11-6: Melodyne

but smaller nuances like formant and even the amount of vibrato. You can even change a note's pitch completely without hearing any ill effects.

If you work with singers, Melodyne is an amazing tool. A recent update to Melodyne has enabled pitch correction to work on polyphonic sources (like chords). In the past, you could only tune single-note lines. With the new Meoldyne DNA, you can tune or even change the pitch of a note inside of a guitar or piano chord! Amazing!

Electronic Keyboards

Good news! The keyboard is one of the simpler instruments to record. Any keyboard worth its salt is equipped with line outputs. The line outputs plug directly into your mixer or recording device. Better yet, you won't have to eat up one of your valuable microphone channels, because the output level is sufficient for recording (that's what line level means). You can set the level on the keyboard simply by adjusting the overall output level.

Recording in Stereo

Keyboards, especially modern synthesizers, utilize a stereo signal path internally. That means most of the patches are designed for listening in two-channel stereo—left and right signals. If you output only one of the signals to your recorder (perhaps to save inputs), you might not get a full sound. This is due to the way the keyboard pans the sound from side to side. To get the best sound, use two tracks for a keyboard. The exception is if you're trying to record an older analog-style keyboard that you know has a mono output; then you can get away with one track. By programming your synth's internal parameters, it's also possible to "sum" the output to just one channel, to combine the two signals into one. The term "sum" means to combine many signals. A mixer is a great example of a device that sums many signals into one stereo pair.

Monitoring Yourself

For monitoring, you have many options. If you're laying down solo keyboard tracks, you can just plug a headphone into the keyboard. If you play with an amplifier, you can plug into that as well. If you're working with pre-recorded tracks, you can monitor from the recorder with either headphones or monitor speakers.

MIDI or Audio?

Keyboards communicate with computers via MIDI. One of the benefits of using MIDI is that it's not audio, meaning you've got a lot more ability to edit the sound. With its simple code of commands to the keyboard, MIDI can be highly edited on a computer screen through all the major DAW programs. On the other had, if you record the keyboard signal as audio through an audio track, there's little you can do to change aspects of the performance. You would have to go back through the piece, decide what you want to change, and rerecord the audio. If you keep the performance as MIDI, you can tweak the part endlessly until you feel it is final.

ALERT

Many keyboards contain built-in sequencers, which are recorders for MIDI. While the built-in sequencers allow you to record and make music with the keyboard's built-in sounds, the screens are small and editing can be cumbersome. This is why computer-editing programs are so popular with keyboard players the world over—big screens and mice make for powerful editing.

At some point, however, you need to record the keyboard's actual physical sound. By itself, MIDI and MIDI sequencers don't capture any "audio" that you can print to a CD. So, you have to plug the audio outputs from the keyboard into a recorder. Recording the audio from the keyboard allows you to make the final mix and bounce a final product to an audio CD.

Drum Sets

How to best record a drum set is a slightly complicated subject. Most of the difficulty lies in the number of sounds you have to capture at once. A basic drum kit consists of:

- One snare drum
- Two toms (possibly three if there's a floor tom)
- One bass drum

- Two overhead cymbals
- One hi-hat cymbal

For those of you who weren't keeping score, that's up to eight different sounds to capture. And that's just for a basic kit; you might encounter far more complicated kits when you record.

How to Mike a Drum Set

There are a few different schools of thought on the right way to mike a drum set. The first school says "more is more." Place a microphone on as many separate parts of the drum set as you can so you can control the level and balance as you mix. Here is an example of a fairly extensive microphone setup for a basic drum set:

- One dynamic microphone for the snare drum
- Two dynamic microphones for the two toms
- One dynamic microphone for the bass drum
- Two overhead condenser microphones to pick up the two overhead cymbals and ambience of the drum set
- One dynamic microphone for the hi-hat cymbal

That's a total of seven microphones! That also means eating up seven microphone channels on your recorder. You could pare down (or sum) the inputs to fewer channels, but that would defeat the purpose of miking everything. If you have enough inputs and you can spare doing it this way, there's nothing wrong with it. You will have great control over the sounds when you mix. Most professional studios use multiple drum channels. However, this might not suit your needs when you consider everything else.

The other school of thought says "less is more." Use fewer microphones for a more ambient sound. The thought behind this is that a good drummer takes care of his own balance, so there should be little need for extensive tweaking. This is not always true; it really depends on the drummer. At a minimum, you can get away with two overhead condenser microphones to pick up the whole drum set. Although you can get a nice sound that way, it might not be flexible enough. Many engineers like to put effects on some parts of the drum set, and none on others. Snare usually gets some reverb, for instance. A simple overhead-miking setup won't give you the ability to add effects. For the most flexibility, the minimum you should use for a basic drum set is four microphones, as follows (shown in Figure 11-7):

- Two overhead condenser microphones
- One dynamic microphone on the bass drum
- One dynamic microphone on the snare drum

Using that setup will give you a more open sound that you won't have to spend days mixing together. Putting a separate microphone on the snare drum allows you to tweak its sound and add reverb if necessary. Putting the separate microphone on the bass drum allows you to set the EQ on that drum if it gets too much bass and sounds "muddy." You can get a great drum sound this way.

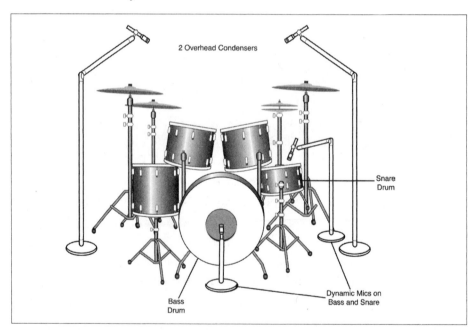

Figure 11-7: Drum-set microphone placement

Muffle

Bass drums, also commonly known as "kick" drums, are the lowest frequency in the drum set. Because the drum shell is so large, it's really easy to get an overly "thumpy" bass drum sound, no matter how hard you try to reposition the microphone to get rid of it. You can easily solve this by placing a muffle inside the bass drum to get rid of some the excess ring and thump. Towels, pillows and blankets work well in this regard. Experiment with the sound to see what you like. Some bass drums sound fine without any help, so you'll only hear what needs to be done when you test your microphones.

Tune Up!

Tune your drumheads. Better yet, replace them with new ones, and then tune them before a recording. New drum heads sound great and record well. There are many books available on this subject; just check out your local bookstore or music shop for information on proper drum tuning. Having a properly tuned drum set can make all the difference in the world.

Acoustic Instruments

Acoustic instruments can be more difficult to record well. You'll need to practice a few times until you get a sound you're happy with.

Winds and Brass

The wind instrument family can be difficult to record because of the way the instruments produce sound. With many wind instruments, the sound actually comes out of the whole instrument—finger holes leak sound and so on. So where do you put the microphone? This might seem simple, but certain instruments might fool you. Start by pointing the microphone where the sound comes out.

ESSENTIAL

Instruments may sound good by themselves, but when you add them to the rest of the mix, they may not fit as well. This is a common problem and can usually be fixed with some creative EQ and effects placements.

Trumpet and the other brass instruments have a bell where the sound shoots out. Simply place a condenser microphone slightly in front of the bell and you're good to go. For loud brass players, place the microphone back slightly to ease possible distortion. In saxophones, the bell delivers most of the sound, but there is also sound from the keys. Try to position the microphone in a way that allows you to hear both sounds clearly; then move the microphone around till you get a sound you like.

Piano

Acoustic piano is a difficult sound to get just right. If you are lucky enough to have a grand piano, open the lid to expose the strings. The best way to record piano is to use two condenser microphones, one devoted to the top strings and one devoted to the bottom strings. You can pan one microphone hard left and the other hard right to get a fairly wide-sounding stereo image (see Figure 11-8).

If you use just one microphone, choose an omnidirectional microphone for this job and place it dead center to get the best sound you can. For those who use upright pianos, which are far more common, take off the top of the piano's case to expose the strings. Follow the same technique noted earlier for either a single or double microphone setup.

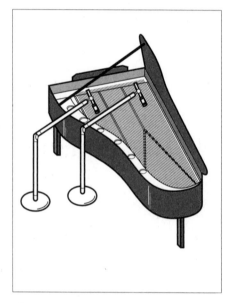

Figure 11-8: Miking a piano

Strings

For any single string instrument, whether it's a violin, cello, bass, mandolin, acoustic guitar, or anything else, place a condenser microphone close to the sound hole or *f* hole to get the most direct sound. You can place the microphone fairly close to get a good strong signal without much fear of distorting the microphone. Figure 11-9 shows an example of an acoustic guitar miked.

On bowed instruments, you might get excess bow noise if you are too close, so move the microphone around until you get a rich, pure sound.

For large groups of strings, like string quartets or groups of guitars, you can either close-mike each individual instrument, or use one or two condenser microphones set back to get the sound of the whole group. Stereo microphones work well for this sort of thing too.

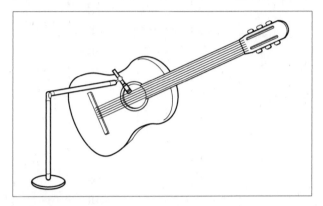

Figure 11-9: Acoustic guitar miked

Stereo Recording

When you record acoustic instruments or capture a stereo recording, you will utilize something called the "XY" technique.

The XY technique uses two microphones crossing at their heads, pointed in opposite directions, usually at a 90-degree angle from each other (see Figure 11-10). This works great on acoustic instruments and any time you want to record a simple stereo mix. There are other ways to record in stereo besides XY. Other popular techniques include mid-side, spaced pair, baffled omni, and the famous "Decca Tree" used by classical music engineers.

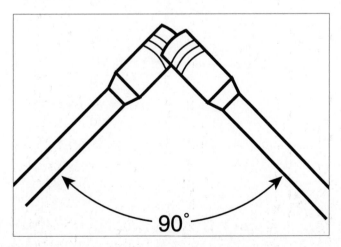

Figure 11-10: XY mike technique

CHAPTER 12

Digital Recording Software

If you're exploring digital home recording, chances are you'll work on a DAW software product. This book has talked about many important aspects of recording, each of which has to translate into software at some point. This chapter will take a broad look at DAW software and lay the groundwork for the rest of the book.

Introduction to the Visual Interface

The graphical user interface, or GUI, is your gateway to a software program. It's literally your key to using any software, so you'll want to understand how each software is laid out. Clearly, this book can't go into every possible type of software DAW; there are just too many titles to examine. This won't be a problem, however, as recording software is largely trying to digitally reproduce the analog recording tools that created the recording industry!

No matter how you slice it, a DAW needs to represent two main functions: a mixer and an arrange/edit page. Let's define these terms:

- **Mixer:** A software mixer is a virtual version of a hardware mixing board (see Chapter 10). Mixers control the volume of individual tracks, as well as side-to-side placement in the stereo field. Mixers are often used to interface with effects and to mute and solo tracks.
- **Arrange/Edit:** In the analog days, audio was recorded onto magnetic tape. Editing was done with a razor blade and tape. In the digital age, audio is recorded as data and can be manipulated. The digital tracks are broken into regions, and the arrange/edit window is the visual overview for all of your recorded regions. Many arrange windows also house the editing functions for looping, trimming, and manipulating your tracks. You'll also hear the arrange page talked about as a timeline, because tracks are laid out left to right, spread across time in a line!

Each and every software title encompasses some form of arrange/edit functionality and some form of mixing. Some, like Pro Tools, will do it in different windows for each function, while GarageBand will do it in a single window that contains both functions. Software programs are remarkably similar, even if their presentation is unique. Once you get the hang of what a DAW is trying to do, it's not hard to learn your way around.

Tracks

Tracks are at the heart of a DAW. Tracks are made up of regions, which can either be recorded digital audio or MIDI data. Tracks are shown in

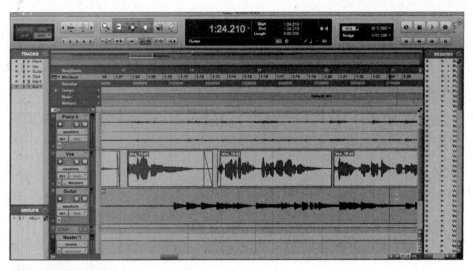

Figure 12-1: Multiple tracks in Pro Tools

your DAWs arrange view. It's easy to look at collection of tracks like the score for a piece of music. Each instrument takes a strip of horizontal space on the page. You stack multiple instruments on top of one another to create a score. In a DAW, each track takes up its own horizontal strip, with regions populating each track. You can stack multiple tracks and they play from left to right, moving past a point on the page, similar to a tape moving past a playhead on an analog tape machine. Figure 12-1 shows an arrange page with several tracks. Let's look more closely at the two types of tracks.

Audio Tracks

An audio track is probably the most common track in a DAW. Depending on your DAW, you can record mono tracks (from a single source) or stereo tracks for two sources (usually left and right). Some DAWs tag their audio tracks with a different color from other types of tracks to make it easy to see what's going on. You'll record regions on an audio track. How can you tell what's an audio region? Figure 12-2 shows a waveform, which is a graphical representation of an audio signal.

Figure 12-2: An audio waveform

The waveform in Figure 12-2 is unique in that it shows the overview of the digital audio. You can't see what pitch is being played in this view, but the vertical height (or amplitude) will tell you how loud the signal is at any given point. Audio regions, represented by waveforms, live on audio tracks—simple as that!

MIDI Tracks

MIDI tracks are used to record and edit MIDI data. MIDI regions look different than audio regions do. The distinctive waveform view is missing in a MIDI region as MIDI is simple data telling each note when you stop and start. If you've ever seen a player piano's roll, MIDI will make a lot of sense to you. Figure 12-3 shows a MIDI region.

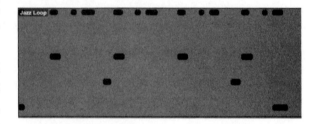

Figure 12-3: A MIDI region

The distinctive dots and small bars tell you it's a MIDI region, not an audio region. MIDI tracks can interface with hardware keyboards and samplers, triggering external instruments to make sound. MIDI regions can also trigger virtual instruments, something that you'll read more about in Chapter 13.

Typical Track Controls

There are some common controls that you'll find on many tracks. Some of these controls are duplicated on the mixer as well, but they're so commonly used that they're presented there as well. At the start of a track, it's not uncommon to find the following controls:

- **Record.** Typically seen either as an R or as a red dot. Toggling the R button will put the track into recording mode. (The color red is associated with recording in just about every DAW.)
- **Mute.** Typically seen as an M. Toggling the mute button will silence the selected track(s).
- **Solo.** Typically seen as an S. Toggling the solo button will silence all other tracks except the current track, soloing the selected track.

Figure 12-4 shows the track controls from Pro Tools. It's pretty easy to find your way around, even if you don't know Pro Tools; you just have to look for the Mute, Solo, and Record buttons. Every software program will look different, but you'll always find these common controls.

Figure 12-4: Pro Tools track controls

Virtual Mixers

Once you've recorded a bunch of tracks, you'll want to be able to mix and pan. In most programs, you'll access the mixing functions from a second window, although more and more DAWs give some ability to mix in their main arrange/edit window. A mixer is designed to look exactly like a hardware mixer, which you learned about in Chapter 10. Each track has its own corresponding mixer strip, a strip of vertical controls. The more tracks you have, the bigger your mixer will be. Figure 12-5 shows a single mixer strip.

This single strip contains a level meter so you can look at the track's audio level. Next to the level meter is a fader. The fader controls the volume of the track. As you pull the fader from bottom to top, the volume increases. The fader lets you place your audio in the stereo mix. In other DAWs, faders may be horizontal controls. Above the fader are the rotary panning controls.

You'll also notice the same record, solo, and mute controls from the track controls. They are duplicate controls. That's the basics of a mixer strip. You set the loudness with the fader and balance with the pan controls. Above the mixer strips are slots called inserts. This is where you insert effect plug-ins.

Figure 12-5: single mixer strip

FACT

One of the ways that GarageBand is able to simplify its user experience is by using a single window interface. The arrange page houses all the tracks, while the track controls alongside the tracks take care of mute, solo, record, and volume manipulation. It's a simple, uncluttered, and elegant way to present a DAW.

Inserting Plug-ins

Effect plug-ins are a great way to polish up your mix. Chapter 15 deals with the different types of effects and what they do, but we'll talk about how to utilize them here. In most every DAW, you insert plug-ins on the mixer strips. Typically, this is at the top of any single mixer strip. Figure 12-6 shows the insert section of a mixer strip in Pro Tools.

Figure 12-6: Pro Tools insert

DAWs let you insert more than one effect, so you'll see several slots. When you click on any single insert slot, you'll get a list of the available plug-ins you can insert. Once you've selected your plug-in(s), you can tweak them as you wish. Figure 12-7 shows how you select plug-ins.

Figure 12-7: Selecting a plug-in

Not all effects belong in insert slots. One of the most important things to remember about inserts is that they pass all of your audio through them. This is great for EQ, but not so great for reverb because you want to be able to mix the dry unaffected signal with your effected reverb sound. EQ doesn't require this. You can also place effects on buses and use sends (discussed in the next section) to route audio to those tracks.

Inputs and Outputs

Another important aspect of working with a DAW is controlling the physical input and output of your connected hardware. You'll typically find inputs and outputs controlled in the mixer window (although some have it elsewhere). With USB and FireWire interfaces sporting 8 or more channels, you'll want to make sure that each track points to the right input. Figure 12-8 shows the input selector in Pro Tools.

Each track will have a selectable input. When tracks are created, they default to an available input based on the number of input tracks you have. For example, if your interface has 8 possible inputs and you add 8 tracks, the inputs will auto assign to inputs 1-8. You can change this at any time through the input selector. Remember, if you're recording into a stereo track, you will need to configure both inputs!

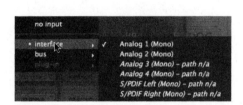

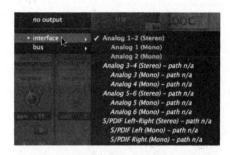

Figure 12-8: Input settings   **Figure 12-9:** Output settings

Outputs are typically much simpler. Most home recording and mixing is done with a pair of speakers plugged into outputs 1 and 2, so for the vast majority of users, as long as your speakers are plugged into the correct outputs, you're good to go since created tracks typically default to outputs 1 and 2. Figure 12-9 shows the output settings in Pro Tools.

Sends

Not all effects live happily as insert effects. Reverb is a great example of an effect that you typically don't put in a track insert. Instead, reverb is placed on a separate track, called an auxiliary track. To get your audio from your track onto the auxiliary, you have to send the audio to the auxiliary. Because you're sending a copy of the audio, you get a mix of dry uneffected audio and the reverberant sound.

To do this, you'll need to use a send on your track. Sends are typically under the insert effects. Most DAWs support sends as they're a basic way to route audio for mixing.

When you bring up a send, it won't show you effects. You have to think of a send as an invisible cable. If this were a real mixer, you'd have to connect the mixer to a piece of hardware with a patch cable. In a DAW, it's done invisibly, so it may be confusing if a DAW is your first mixer.

When you choose a send, you pick which path you're going to send the audio in. These are called buses. Buses let you move audio from place to place. In this case, you want to send your audio to the reverb auxiliary track. Pick an unused bus. On the auxiliary track, set that track's input to the same bus you just choose and insert the reverb effect. Now the two tracks are linked up. See Figure 12-10 for a shot of how this is done in Pro Tools.

Figure 12-10:
Routing to a send

Figure 12-11: Pro Tools send controls

On the audio track where you selected the send, you'll control how much audio you want to send to the reverb auxiliary. You'll need to determine how much level to send by listening to the source and the resulting reverb that comes out. Each signal is different. Let your ears guide you and dial this in for the proper mix (Figure 12-11).

Instruments Versus Audio Effects Plug-ins

There is more than one type of plug-in that you can use in a DAW. Plug-ins come in two main flavors: instruments and effects. An audio effect plug-in takes incoming digital audio and changes or manipulates the sound. Examples of effects are EQ, reverb, compression, and delay, just to name a few. An instrument plug-in takes MIDI input and pumps out digital audio. Instrument plug-ins can be pianos, synthesizers, and samplers, to name a few. These are also called *virtual instruments*.

Each DAW treats these plug-ins a bit differently. Generally, you can add an effect plug-in almost anywhere you want (except a MIDI only track).

Instrument plug-ins can usually be added only to a special instrument track, which is a track that records MIDI events and is made to host the instrument plug-in to realize the sound.

QUESTION

Why did I need to use a send for reverb?
Reverb is a synthetic recreation of a how sound reflects in a real room. When you use a send, you get a mix of direct and reverberated sound, which is as close to natural as possible.

You can add an audio effect to an instrument track. Once you've inserted the instrument plug-in, it's outputting digital audio. Effects plug-ins act on incoming digital audio, so once your instrument plug-in outputs audio, you can throw effects plug-ins to change the sound of your instrument plug-ins.

Editing Tools

Once you have all your tracks recorded and you have started to get a good sound with mixing and plug-ins, you'll want to take a look at one of the best reasons for using a computer-based DAW: the superior editing of MIDI and digital audio that DAWs offer.

Audio Editing

Audio editing is the process of trimming, cutting, and manipulating digital audio. The vast majority of audio editing takes place in the arrange/edit window of your DAW, although some will take you to a new window for more precise edits. No matter which DAW you choose, you'll be able to do the following things (although they may go by different names):

- **Cut.** You can edit sections of audio with precision. You can cut out large sections of audio to rerecord, or do microsurgery and remove single notes or errors in the audio.
- **Mask.** Just like masking tape, you can silence the start or end of an audio region. This is handy if there's a delay from the time you press

record to the start of your performance (the same holds true for the end).

- **Looping.** You can extend any region to loop over and over again with the loop tool.
- **Moving.** You can take any region and place it anywhere in the timeline you want. This is one of the key differentiators for digital audio versus tape. It's nonlinear, so you can place it anywhere you want.
- **Fades.** Manually or automatically fade in and out. An important technique when you're editing regions of audio together into a performance.

These basic tools are just the fundamental set of tools you'll see in a DAW. Modern DAWs also give you more advanced editing tools such as pitch correction and beat correction. Chapter 19 is an overview of some of these exciting new ways to edit audio!

Don't forget that when you edit audio in a DAW, you're editing it nondestructively. You can always change your mind because you're working on a copy of the original audio. This is true for all DAWs. Once you get used to nondestructive editing, you'll have a newfound respect for records that were cut and edited on magnetic tape!

MIDI Editing

Because MIDI predates digital audio by a number of years, MIDI editing has been around for a long time. There are some standard things you can do with MIDI in just about every DAW.

- **Quantize.** With MIDI, it's easy to correct rhythmic inaccuracies by quantizing. Quantizing places all MIDI notes and events on a rhythmic grid. You can quantize to different note values and even quantize to "groove" templates to inject a different feel.
- **Pitch**. With MIDI, changing pitch is very easy; just drag the MIDI note/event to a new note.
- **Velocity.** The volume of MIDI notes range from 0 to 128. You can edit the velocity of any individual note or group of notes.
- **Duration.** With MIDI it's easy to change the duration of any MIDI note/event.

- **Controller data.** MIDI allows you to control more than just the notes themselves. Continuous controllers allow you to manipulate parameters of your synth or plug-in. A good example of a continuous controller (CC) would be controlling the pitch bend with a wheel controller. You can edit this data, too.
- **Humanize.** A form of quantizing that has small errors in the timing. True quantizing is likely impossible for a human, so humanization helps you stay in time, without sounding like a computer.

QUESTION

Can I view my MIDI data as notation, rather than data?
Yes! More and more DAWs have score windows for viewing MIDI events as traditional notation. Pro Tools, Logic, GarageBand, Cubase, and Sonar all have score editors. Pro Tools can even send Sibelius files right to Sibelius, one of the most popular notation software programs in the world!

As you can see, MIDI is very malleable and powerful. With the wild popularity of virtual instrument plug-ins that respond to MIDI input, MIDI (now more than twenty-five years old) isn't going anywhere!

CHAPTER 13

Virtual Instruments

You've recorded your keyboards, guitars, bass, drums, and vocals, but there are still some sounds you need to add to your music. Maybe it's an ethnic instrument you've heard but never seen, or perhaps it's some strange synthetic texture that you hear in your mind's ear, but can't reproduce with the instruments you have. You don't want to compromise. You want to do it, and do it right. That's where virtual instruments come in.

What is a Virtual Instrument?

In the world of hardware synthesizers, there is a wide variety of synthesizers, and all of them have different goals—reproducing the sound of acoustic instruments, creating classic synthesizer and keyboard sounds, creating drum sounds, creating new and previously unheard sounds, and more. Computer–based recording gives you access to an incredibly vast array of instruments that can run on your computer.

At its essence, a virtual instrument (VI) is a synthesizer on your computer. The variety of virtual instruments available and the power of these instruments is unequalled in hardware. While many VIs are meant to emulate or replace actual instruments, there are many brilliant developers creating instruments with capabilities that have never been seen before. From incredibly detailed pianos that require large, fast hard drives to run to collections of instruments from all corners of the globe, from hybrid instruments that allow you to mangle sounds until they're unrecognizable to synthesizers you can "build" to suit your needs, VIs can play a major role in your music.

Figure 13-1: A Logic virtual instrument: ES1

Included Versus Third Party

At this point, most DAWs come with at least a few included virtual instruments. Some have enough VIs to supplement your songs; others have enough for making complete productions using nothing but VIs. Regardless, you can always add more VIs to your palette. Cakewalk, MOTU, Digidesign, Ableton, and Steinberg all offer VIs that you can buy and add to their products. Apple's Logic Studio ships with more than a dozen VIs and more than forty gigabytes of loops, samples, and other content, making it a truly complete VI production package. Having plenty of things to choose from is beneficial. That's where third party virtual instruments come in.

Included Virtual Instruments

The VIs that come with your DAW offer certain advantages. The most obvious is that you have already paid for them. From a practicality standpoint, you can be reasonably certain that the developers have made sure that their VIs will be stable in their DAW. All of their included VIs will be useful at the very least, and some will be as good and as powerful as any similar VI on the market. Some may even be unique instruments with no real competition.

Some included Vis may have disadvantages, minor though they may be. For one, you might not like the way some of them sound. Perhaps you just don't find them particularly inspiring. It's likely that you just can't find an included VI to do what you want to accomplish. Some DAW manufacturers offer additional VIs that only work in their products, but they come with an added cost.

Third-Party Virtual Instruments

There are many developers that offer VIs you can add to your DAW. In fact, Steinberg, MOTU, and Cakewalk are among the developers who sell VIs that can be used in other DAWs. You can find third party VIs whose price tags range from free to over $1,000. Most retail VIs run from $50 to $500. You can find some for sale in retail stores and online, while others are available exclusively online.

ESSENTIAL

There are many online communities that are devoted to different virtual instruments. Some manufacturers host forums for their products, and some enthusiasts host communities for particular products. One community that is devoted to a broad range of third-party developers is *www.kvraudio.com*. Here you can find news, product announcements, forums, and a large, searchable database—it's a one-stop destination for researching third-party VIs.

There are advantages to using third-party VIs. First, you can easily find VIs that are different from those in your DAW. There are many unique and powerful VIs available from third-party developers. You can often find extra content or presets for a third-party's VIs on the Internet. Since many VIs come from small developers, you can frequently get excellent support from the developer. Some third-party VIs can even be run in standalone mode, meaning you can run them as their own application without using them in a DAW.

There can be disadvantages too. Not all developers are as talented or as thorough as others. Sometimes, this means a VI can cause instability in your DAW. Not all VIs are available for both Mac OS and Windows, or even for all available plug-in formats on either system. Sometimes third-party VIs reach a point where they are no longer supported, or the developer goes out of business. Still, the advantages usually outweigh the disadvantages, and a little bit of research before you buy can go a long way toward protecting your third-party VI investment.

Controlling Virtual Instruments

You have your VIs and you want to make some noise with them. Since many VIs are keyboard oriented, or at least are related to traditional keyboard instruments, a MIDI keyboard controller is an obvious choice to manage your VIs. If you're not a keyboardist or are looking for alternative ways to control VIs, don't despair! VIs can respond to a variety of different kinds of input. How you control your VIs can be as personal as your music! You can use hardware controllers you actively play, controllers that have nothing but knobs and sliders on them, or simply your computer keyboard and mouse.

Playing Virtual Instruments

VIs can be played by any kind of MIDI input. You can use your mouse to create and edit MIDI information in your DAW's MIDI editors. You can even use your computer keyboard to play notes into your DAW. Those aren't the only alternatives to MIDI keyboards, though. If you play guitar, you can use a MIDI guitar to control VIs. There are MIDI drum kits, MIDI wind controllers, and MIDI pad controllers that can give any musician easy and familiar access to VIs. Just like MIDI keyboard controllers, all you need to use these

MIDI controllers with your VIs is a MIDI interface. Many of these nonkeyboard MIDI controllers even come with USB capabilities.

Programming Virtual Instruments

Perhaps you've found a VI with a sound that is almost perfect for your song, but you want to tweak it just a little. As you saw in Figure 13-1, there are plenty of on-screen controls that you can manipulate with your mouse, but there are other ways to program your VIs. Many MIDI controllers offer knobs and sliders. These can be assigned to control different parameters in your VIs. This can make programming your VIs much easier because it feels more like using a "real" instrument. Some VI developers even offer hardware units that can be used for programming their VIs, and other third party VIs.

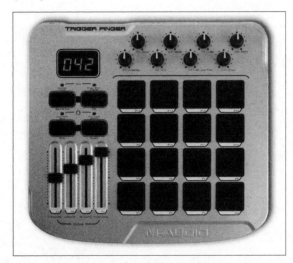

Figure 13-2: A MIDI pad controller: The M-Audio Trigger Finger *Courtesy of Avid Technology, Inc.*

Overview of Popular Virtual Instruments

Let's be honest—there are a ton of VIs on the market. To give you an idea of what's out there, and to give you an introduction to some of the industry standard VIs, it's time to introduce you to some specific products.

Native Instruments Komplete

Native Instruments is one of the oldest and most respected names in the VI market. It offers a wide range of VI products, from real instrument emulations to powerful, groundbreaking synthesizers. While all of its products are available individually, it offers an all-inclusive package called Komplete.

Komplete is a suite of ten VIs plus Guitar Rig, a guitar amplifier, and effects pedal emulator. The VIs in Komplete include Kontakt, Massive, Reaktor, Absynth, Battery, Akoustik Piano, Elektrik Piano, B4, FM8, and Pro-53. Kontakt is an industry-leading sampler, which ships with an extensive library of sounds.

Reaktor, Massive and Absynth are three of the most popular and powerful synthesizers on the market. FM8 and Pro-53 are excellent emulations of a couple of classic synthesizers. Akoustik Piano, Elektrik Piano, and B4 emulate acoustic pianos, electric pianos, and Hammond organs respectively. Battery is a top-flight drum sampler. Together they form a fairly complete—Komplete, if you will—VI solution.

Figure 13-3: A few Native Instruments Komplete plug-ins

Native Instruments also offers hardware controllers that are perfect for controlling its VIs and other VIs. Native Instruments Kore 2 is a hardware controller designed not only as a front end for Komplete, but as a VI host on its own, effectively turning your computer into a workstation that competes favorably with expensive keyboard workstations. It can also be used to control VST and Audio Units plug-ins, and to control your DAW. Maschine is a hardware pad controller combined with a software interface for creating and manipulating samples and beats. Of course, it can be used as a MIDI controller too. For Guitar Rig enthusiasts, Native Instruments offers a hardware controller that allows you to use Guitar Rig like a multieffects pedal.

Synthogy Ivory

Ivory is a highly detailed acoustic piano virtual instrument. It requires 11GB of hard drive space to install, and it was the first of a growing list of extremely large piano libraries. If Ivory's 11GB of piano samples aren't enough for you, there are add-ons that give you access to new pianos such as an Italian grand piano and a number of upright pianos.

Spectrasonics Omnisphere

Spectrasonics makes some of the most highly regarded VIs on the market, and their most recent offering, Omnisphere, continues that tradition. One of the most important hardware synthesizer sound designers and sample library developers of the last twenty-five years started Spectrasonics, so their pedigree is unrivaled. Spectrasonics Omnisphere is a powerful synthesizer capable of traditional synthesizer sounds and radical new textures. It is easy to use for beginners, but it has a programming depth and flexibility that will make even the most experienced synthesists happy.

u-he Zebra 2

Among the many small, independent developers, u-he is one of the most impressive. With a unique slant on user control and a sound that rivals any synthesizer on the market, u-he's Zebra 2 is a prime example of the capabilities of independent developers. Zebra 2 is a synthesizer that gives you as much or as little control as you need; you can build synthesizers with unique routings, or simply tweak presets.

Managing Resources

As computing power grows, developers continue to push this power to the limits. While there are plenty of VIs that run very efficiently, others can bring your computer to its knees. They can tax the computer's processor, RAM, and hard drive. Even if you're running efficient VIs, using a lot of them at the same time can affect your computer's performance. However, this shouldn't scare you off from using VIs. Fortunately there are a few things you can do that can help you use some of the most advanced VIs in your music.

System requirements are one of the most important things to consider when buying a VI. Just like your DAW, most VIs have minimum system requirements, and they often have recommended system requirements too. Some may need a modest processor or virtually no hard drive space, but some programs require extremely fast processors, lots of RAM, and large, fast hard drives. Some VIs are very processor intensive but use little hard disk space. Others don't require a lot of processor, but they do utilize huge libraries of samples that need their own hard drive to run efficiently. Knowing what kind of computer performance your VIs need is important to incorporating them in your songs effectively.

Using Processor Intensive Virtual Instruments

You're working on your next big hit and you have a sound in one of your VIs that you want to use, but you know it's going to eat a lot of your computer's processing power. You want to have as much of that power available later for working on other parts of the song. Are you going to have to forget about using that sound? No way. There are a couple of different tactics to deal with this situation.

If you are done recording your VI part and are happy with how you played it, you could simply bounce the track down as an audio file and add it back into your song. You can then apply any effects that you want to the audio file. Using effects is discussed in Chapters 15 and 16, and bouncing audio is discussed in Chapter 17. Another way to deal with this situation is to freeze the VI track. Many DAWs offer this ability. Basically, this is similar to bouncing the track down, but instead of adding the new audio file to an audio track in your DAW, the DAW automatically plays the frozen track on its original track. Freezing tracks does have one disadvantage, though—you generally can't make any changes to the original track or add any effects to it unless you unfreeze the track and then refreeze.

Using Disk Intensive Virtual Instruments

Because computers are so powerful these days, and because memory and storage are so cheap, it has become possible for developers to create VIs that access huge libraries of samples. A sample is a recording of a sound that a sampler plays back. To create incredibly detailed samples, some developers will sample an individual note on an instrument sixteen or more times, each sample at different volumes, each lasting as long as the note can ring. Then they may even add in other samples of that same note, including any noises the instrument might make mechanically while playing that note. Then they repeat the process for every individual note on the instrument.

ESSENTIAL

To help you realize how much space these samples take up, think of a piano. Eighty-eight keys times sixteen velocity layers is 1,408 samples, all of which last until each note decays completely. Then, add in all sorts of other noise samples the hammers might make, plus resonance sounds the piano makes from using the pedal!

Fortunately, extra hard drives are cheap. Maxing out your RAM is also pretty cheap. To maximize the performance of VIs that use large sample libraries, you'll want to get all the RAM you can put in your machine, plus an additional, fast hard drive. The hard drive can be internal if your computer allows it, or external. Regardless, dedicating a separate drive to samples will improve the performance of your entire system if you are using large sample libraries.

Plug-In Formats

One last consideration when buying VIs is checking to make sure the VI is compatible with your DAW. Many VIs are available in multiple plug-in formats, but not all of them are. Some may even be available in only one plug-in format. As you can imagine, since some VIs are not available in all plug-in formats, there are also a lot of VIs that are only available on Mac OS or Windows. Again, remember to check the VI's minimum system requirements! It can save you a lot of money by helping you avoid buying a plug-in that won't work on your system.

CHAPTER 14

Editing

Word processors redefined the publishing industry with three simple words—cut, copy, and paste—and a new form of editing was born. Musicians got their first taste of the power of a similar kind of editing with MIDI in the 1980s. Digital audio editing on the computer brings this power into the home studio.

Making Changes

Editing is the art of altering a performance. While it might seem counterintuitive and nonmusical to go back and change things, the reality is that no one is perfect every time. The outtakes from movies come to mind. Veteran actors are sometimes unable to keep a straight face or deliver the correct line. It's also very common for a motion picture to be shot out of sequence and reordered later. What you see at the end looks cohesive, but it might not have been shot that way. Music is no different. It's possible to record separate instruments, heavily edit the performance, move sections around, and have it sound perfect—like one straight take.

Some styles of music rely on edits less than others. Classical music is almost never edited. Jazz music is often not edited either, although many artists edit some parts—just not the solos, which are typically left intact. Rock and pop music might be highly edited; in fact, that's usually the case. Oftentimes, parts for rock and pop music are composed on the fly, in studio. If your band or project can get it right the first time, more power to you. For everyone else, welcome to editing!

What Editing Used to Be

Back in the good old days of analog recording, editing involved physically cutting and splicing a new section of tape. Edits were done on a special piece of metal called a splicing block and the cuts were performed with a razor blade . . . ouch! Editing like that was difficult, to say the least. Finding the exact spot to make the edit and getting the new material to line up perfectly was no small feat.

With multitrack tape, everything got more complicated. Each track occupied a small section of the tape. Making an edit to just one track meant cutting a small window in the tape and pasting in a new one. Edits were used to fix only blaring mistakes and other tragedies. Many engineers would push for a better take rather than perform miracle surgery. Editing was seen as a last resort.

What It Is Now

Editing sure has changed! Digital audio has changed the way we all work, and it's one of the main reasons the home studio is so powerful—we get to edit just like the big boys! Digital audio recording is based on the principal of nonlinear editing. Tracks don't have to be in line together as they are on a tape. A digital audio mix is simply several audio files read at the same time off the disk; they can reside anywhere on the hard disk. This is because the files don't need to be read by the recording machine or computer as if they were sentences. Because of this, they can be edited with great ease.

ALERT

There are plenty of situations where a simple stereo (left and right) recording will more than suffice. Multitrack recording can put artificial control over a group's sound, balance, and vibe. Before you dive with both feet into the multitrack arena, try a simple stereo microphone setup and see what you think. You might save a lot of time and trouble in the editing department.

For example, suppose you're recording your latest hit. You are laying down the guitar track, and you mess up the melody in the second half of the song. Coincidentally, you played the same melody earlier in the track and you played it perfectly. Do you have to scrap the whole track? Maybe years ago you would have, but not now. Just copy the correct performance from the beginning of the song and move it to the end. Intrigued? Read on.

Just Because You Can . . .

Just because you have the tools to edit with an amazing degree of accuracy in the digital world does not mean you should. Let's use Band X for an example. You buy Band X's album and you think it sounds great. The CD is well produced, all the instruments sound great, the performance is top-notch—in short, this band is kicking. You purchase concert tickets eagerly anticipating seeing Band X live. The day comes and you head out to the concert. The lights, the stage . . . Band X takes the stage and sounds horrid. The signer can't sing on pitch, and the band is falling apart. You leave the concert very upset. What happened? Did Band X have a bad night? Maybe so, but it's more likely they might have fallen into the trap of overproduction. That is, the band might have recorded their music one track at a time and perfected each track before releasing their CD.

Editing can be a bit of a trap, especially the high-precision computer editing where you can change a single note of a solo you thought was "off." The result might be a standard that can never be replicated live. You want your work to be perfect, and you should try to make it as good as possible, but it's easy to get carried away. Just because you have these tools doesn't mean you should overuse them. Fact is, a great album isn't a perfect album.

Computer-Based Editing

Since computers use nonlinear editing technology, DAW programs give you a great deal of freedom in moving around information. Your masterpiece of music is nothing more than chunks of data to a computer. It doesn't care what order they're played back. By default, the computer plays back your music just as you recorded it. What's different is that you can drag pieces of your music to and fro at will. Let's take a look at a sample Pro Tools session for some visual aids.

Figure 14-1: Pro Tools session

As you can see from the simple four-track mix in Figure 14-1, each track occupies its own lane. The different tracks are shown by visualizations of what the audio looks like. Suppose you wanted to add space at the beginning for an intro that you were going to write and record later. At the same time, you want to double the length of each track by copying them end-to-end. Take a look at the finished product, shown in Figure 14-2.

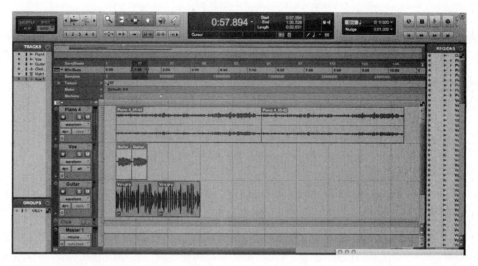

Figure 14-2: Edited Pro Tools session

You'll see that the window is a bit smaller to accommodate the length—that's purely so you can see it all in one window. All we did was drag all the files to the right by thirty seconds to make room for the intro. After that we made a copy of each track and put it end-to-end with the original, which allowed us to repeat a part of this song to double its length. Simply done. All it took was some dragging with the mouse.

As you can see, it's very simple to build up arrangements and change large sections or small pieces of your song. And this is just the tip of a very large iceberg, because this is only the beginning of what you can do.

Digital Micro-Editing

Editing is regularly used to fix mistakes and redo parts that weren't quite up to par. But editing can also take you in unimagined creative directions. Sometimes creating arrangements from disparate sections can yield some really exciting results.

All vocalists have sung a few "special" notes in their day, notes that just stand out and say: "I'm out of tune!" With micro-editing it's possible to change just one note in a phrase. It's hard to do because two things have to be going your way for this to work. First, you have to be able to isolate that one note, which might be a chore in itself. Second, the new edit that you add in has to sound natural, not as if it was added in later.

Now in order to micro-edit, whether you're taking out one note or an entire solo, we need to talk about a few things. The first is zero crossing.

Zero Crossing

Simply put, sound is a combination of frequency (the pitch of a sound) and amplitude (loudness). To edit correctly, you need to find what are known as zero crossings. A zero crossing is a part of the audio where the amplitude or volume is zero, which happens quite often. To find this, you need to zoom in on the waveform on the computer or use the "find zero crossing" function. Why do you need to find the zero crossing? If you don't edit at a point where there is no volume, you will get an audible pop or click between the new files. Zoom in on your computer screen to see this better.

Figure 14-3: Zero crossing

Figure 14-3 shows a magnification of a screen showing a zero crossing. See where the wave hits the middle line in the center of the picture? That's a zero crossing that Pro Tools found automatically. Cutting your audio files at this point ensures that your edits remain seamless and undetectable.

Punching In

Do you really think you're going to hit the record button at exactly the right point and hit stop at the end . . . exactly in time? Survey says, no, probably not. Have no fear; punching in is here to save you. Punching in is simply a way to automate pressing the record button. Every DAW has a function for automating the record process of punching in. You simply tell it where to start and stop recording and it takes care of the rest for you. Look at your manuals for your system to find out specifically how to do this in your DAW. Automated punching in is a key feature on digital systems. If you work alone, automating the recording process is essential to working efficiently. It helps separate the engineer from the musician.

Cross Fades

If you are planning on doing a lot of punch editing in your music, you will love cross fades. As you might have already noticed, even if you find the correct place to edit, chop your file up nicely, and add in the part, getting the volume levels perfect between the old and the new can be difficult. Sometimes this can cause the new part to stick out a bit. What you need is a cross fade. Take a look at an edit with cross fades in Figure 14-4.

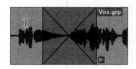

Figure 14-4: Cross fades

A cross fade is an automatic volume change. The very last few milliseconds of the first file gets its volume dropped down while the beginning of the next file starts low in volume and comes up to normal. This volume exchange between the edit points makes a world of difference. It prevents any abrupt shifts in volume from being noticeable. Cross fades are an indispensable part of editing. Learn to use them effectively.

Combining Performances

Since we're big on examples here, let's give another one in the category of "combining performances." Let's say that you recorded a band recently. You used multiple-miking technique with great isolation, making edits possible. The band recorded three straight takes of the same song. Unfortunately each time, a different person made mistakes along the way. On the first take, the guitar solo was a piece of art. On the second take, the vocalist nailed his part, perfectly in tune (a rare occurrence). On the third take, the drums were better than on the rest of the takes. So what do you do? Go for a fourth one? Nah! Edit!

QUESTION

What do I do if I can't find a good point to cut my file?
You might not find a natural place to punch in. Certain performances are very hard to edit this way. When in doubt, try recording the whole section again.

Certain things have to be in place to make this kind of edit, which, by the way, is done all the time in professional studios. First, you need to have very good isolation when you record, otherwise when you piece the parts together you might get leftover bleed in certain tracks that you can't get rid of. Second, the band needs to play to a click track, which is a steady metronome-like pulse that keeps the band from speeding up or slowing down; it ensures a consistent tempo. If each take was performed at a different tempo, you'll have a hard time fusing them into a super-take. If all of this works, it's pretty easy to cut out sections and glue them together. This can be done easily in a DAW. Try it one day; it just might come in handy.

Loop Editing

In Chapter 7 we talked about using loops and loop-based software. Loops are great if they are a certain length, matching exactly with the beat, but what it you have an extended phrase that you want to turn into a loop? What if you have some dead space in your audio file either before or after the section you want to loop? No worries! You just use some of the tools you've just learned about to edit your loop to perfection.

First, you want to figure out exactly what section of your audio you want to loop. This should be easy enough; just listen to the track. Maybe make a note of the time you want to start and end the loop to make it easier to find the section you want to use when looking at the wave-form. Note how many bars the loop contains. Now you can edit your loop by deleting any other unwanted audio or dead space from around your loop.

With loops, particularly drum or rhythmic loops, you want to be very mindful of searching for zero crossings that occur as close as possible to the absolute beginning of the first beat and absolute end of the last beat. Imagine finding the perfect loop and not finding the zero crossings. Hearing the same pop or click at the beginning or end of the loop would get annoying very quickly. Once you edit your audio to the perfect loop length, you can convert your newly created loop into whatever loop format you use.

MIDI Editing

MIDI has had powerful editing from its beginning. Audio has played catch-up to MIDI for years, so it's really unfair to compare the two. Audio is a complex waveform that is hard to replicate digitally. MIDI is made up of simple text commands. We touched on these techniques in Chapter 12, but let's get deeper into what you can do with MIDI editing.

Quantize

Since every MIDI note is a separate event, taking control of single notes and moving them around is quite easy. One of the things you can do with MIDI is quantizing. Quantization sets up a rhythmic grid for all of your notes to follow. For example, a MIDI drum part that needs to be right in time can be hard to record correctly, but the quantize feature can help. Quantization pulls notes that are slightly ahead or behind right onto the beat you tell it to. It makes parts rhythmically very exact.

FACT

Like to swing? Many quantize functions allow you to align notes to a swing grid. A swing grid is another type of quantization that allows for a jazz or swing feel, which is different from a straight rock groove. Swing quantize is great for jazz drum parts that need to swing!

The only information you need to quantize is the speed of your fastest note division. It uses the standard musical note durations of whole, half, quarter, eighth, sixteenth, and so on. You select the quantize value (your fastest note), and it will make a virtual grid for all of the notes to cling to. It will make the part play exactly in time. Quantizing can really steady up recorded performances.

Humanize

One of the unfortunate side effects of quantizing is a "stiff" rhythmic feel. Let's be honest, no one plays every single note right on the beat, no matter how good they are. Quantized tracks can sound too perfect sometimes.

To combat this, many sequencers have added a humanizer preset, which randomly moves selected notes off the grid, ever so slightly, to simulate the imperfect performance. It does so subtly; it doesn't sound wrong. The slight imperfections in timing that it produces can take the mechanical feel out of quantizing. Some programs call the humanize command the randomize command.

Groove Templates

A groove template is another kind of quantization. Instead of drawing your notes to a mathematically placed grid like quantization normally does, groove quantization has a preset grid that creates a nice "groove feeling." Your notes are drawn to a preset grid that is slightly out of time at certain points. Unlike humanizing, groove quantizing is preset, while humanizing is random. Again, this can add some life to otherwise mechanical sounding performances.

Looping MIDI

Do you have the same one-bar drum pattern repeating throughout most of the song? Don't play it fifty times in a row; play it once and loop it in the sequencer. This will save you a lot of time and energy. Looping MIDI is like cutting, copying, and pasting in your word processor.

Transposing

Feel like changing the key of your song after the fact? Or maybe the singer you brought in has a lower range than you thought. Your work is not lost. MIDI is very easily transposed into different keys. On your sequencer, highlight the section you want transposed and tell the sequencer how many semitones (half steps) up or down to move it. Instant transposing.

Tempo Changes

MIDI adheres to tempo maps, and every sequencer has tempo indications. It's very easy to speed up or slow down a performance you've already recorded by just changing the song's tempo. You can do this globally for the whole track, or you can create tempo changes for only certain parts. You can even change the tempo while the sequence is playing back. Since each program is a little different in how it treats tempo and tempo changes, refer to your documentation for more specific instructions. Most programs have the tempo indicator right next to the play, pause, and rewind button, which is called the "transport." The transport is where you control pause, fast forward, rewind, and record functions. Usually, tempo is coupled next to the standard transport controls. You can even set up different meters such as 3/4 time for the first ten bars, and 4/4 time for the rest. With MIDI, anything is possible!

CHAPTER 15

Tweaking Your Sound

Once you've laid down your recorded tracks, it's time to start mixing and adding effects to achieve a final, polished sound. Proper mixing can make even the simplest recording sound great. Effects add a layer of magic dust and final smoothness to recordings. Without proper mixing and effect placement, you won't get the sound you're used to on professional recordings. This is one of the most important parts of the recording process!

Essentials of Sound

As a recording engineer in training, you'll have to know a little bit about sound waves and electricity, because they are pivotal to understanding recording. In this chapter, you'll see why music can't be separated from science—the terminology is everywhere, impossible to escape. Have no fear!

Sound Waves

Sound is emitted by a source and travels in waves that vibrate back and forth, pushing air molecules around them. The sound waves create sound pressure (volume) as they push through the air molecules, which make our eardrums vibrate and pick up sound. Without a medium for sound waves to travel through, there is no sound.

FACT

Sound needs a medium to carry its waves: air, water, and the earth itself can all transmit sound. Certain media carry sound better than others; you might notice that it's more difficult to hear under water than it is on dry land. In space there is no sound, because in a vacuum, there is nothing to transmit sound.

The speed that a sound source (a monitor speaker, for example) vibrates tells you the frequency of the sound that comes out. If a speaker is playing a perfect A (440Hz) tuning note, such as one found on metronomes and tuners, it is vibrating back and forth 440 times a second. The faster the source vibrates, the higher the sound; the slower it vibrates, the lower the sound, or pitch, you hear. Sounds are rarely made up of just one frequency; actually there are many frequencies present in any one sound. The science behind it is beyond the scope of this book, but just understand that when you play or sing one note, there's more than just one frequency present.

You might be saying to yourself, why do I have to know this? That's a legitimate question, and here's the short answer: Understanding frequency and how sound works is essential to mixing and almost all effects. We don't just talk about "low sounds;" you'll see on your EQ knob that "low" might have "80Hz" next to it. Your microphone might have a "100Hz roll off" on it.

You might read an article about boosting the 10kHz band to improve presence and clarity. Wouldn't you like to know what that all means? Simply put, the audio community, of which you are now a full-fledged member, deals with terms like hertz and kilohertz, so you should learn what they mean to avoid confusion!

Ranges of Sound

Let's talk a bit about the ranges of sound you may be used to. Your stereo might have a bass and treble knob. These knobs are used to boost or cut a certain range of frequencies. The specific range of frequencies involved will differ from system to system, but the process is generally known as equalization (EQ). Equalization is simply the boosting or cutting of certain frequencies of a sound. The most basic EQ you will encounter is a three-band EQ on a mixer (either outboard or virtual).

Figure 15-1: Mixer EQ Controls

As you can see in Figure 15-1, there are values in Hz next to the knobs. The values show what ranges of sounds are affected by turning those knobs. If you really want to learn about EQ, twist knobs and listen. Like any other skill, you need to practice. Don't be afraid to turn knobs and listen to what happens.

Effect Types

Studios use a few different types of effects. The first, EQ, isn't really an effect per se, but for our purposes, we'll lump it in with the rest. There are many flavors of EQ, from a simple three-band EQ found on many four-tracks and mixers to elaborate parametric equalizers that give a great deal of control over individual frequencies. Dynamic processing involves effects that control the volume or dynamics of sounds. Effects like compression, limiting, gating, and expanders all control the volume of tracks.

Special effects usually encompass delay and its many incarnations, such as tape delay and multitap delay. Modulation effects like chorus and phasers and flangers change the sound by utilizing a delayed signal mixed in with the original signal, which either delays that signal or changes how the delayed signal sounds.

Reverb is the most important effect to learn how to utilize well. Every sound we hear has some reverb. Reverb, which is short for reverberation, is a natural occurrence when sound waves reflect and bounce off surfaces. The larger the room, the longer it takes the sound to come back to your ears—giving you the feeling of space and distance. Reverb is such an important part of acoustic sounds that when we record without it, it sounds quite strange.

Hardware Versus Software

Years ago, effects were done exclusively by rack-mounted outboard effects units. Certain effects processors were multifunction units and could produce reverb, delay, and other effects all within one unit. Other gear, like a compressor, performed one specialized job. The great part about outboard gear is that it sounds really good.

ESSENTIAL

Even with the innovations of software plug-ins, many professional engineers opt for tried-and-true hardware devices over plug-ins. Some of this is habit, and some of it is because hardware just sounds better. When you walk into a professional studio, notice the many racks of hardware devices still in use today.

Early outboard gear used analog technology to produce effects. As technology improved, manufacturers turned to digital signal processing (DSP) chips to improve the quality of the sound. The digital-effects processor was born. It was only a matter of time before a computer was able to do the job of DSP. Indeed, that day has come. Now, instead of needing floor-to-ceiling racks of gear, you can re-create all the effects you want through software. This is where the home studio became powerful. No longer do musicians need all the space and expensive gear they used to! Through software, a computer can do it all.

Equalization

Equalization is the process of boosting or lowering certain frequencies, or groups of frequencies in a sound. Equalization can have a dramatic effect. However, EQ can only boost or lower what's already there; it can't add frequencies that aren't there. In a recording, EQ helps balance the sounds between groups of instruments and alters the color of individual tracks so that they either stand out or fall back in the mix. Equalization can also fix problems such as proximity effect and noise in recordings.

There are several different types of EQ that you can use to help equalize the sounds in your music. Here are the terms you might run into:

- **High pass:** Lets the high frequencies through and blocks the low frequencies.
- **Low pass:** Lets the low frequencies through and defeats the highs.
- **High shelf:** Controls a specific frequency and all frequencies above it (similar to your stereo's bass and treble knob).
- **Low shelf:** Affects a certain frequency and all the others below it.
- **Parametric:** Lets you boost or cut a specific frequency (to boost just one little part of a sound). This is also called a peak filter.
- **Notch:** The opposite of a peak filter: this lets you remove a specific frequency.

Figure 15-2 shows each kind of EQ running in Apple Logic Pro 9.

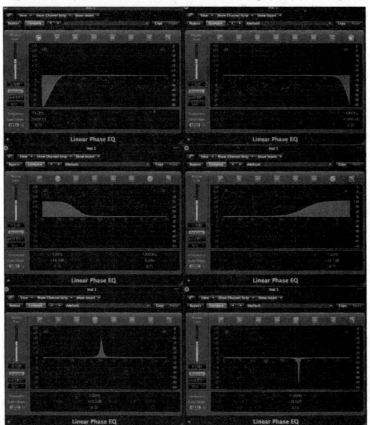

Figure 15-2: Types of EQ. Top row, left to right: high pass filter, low pass filter; middle row, left to right: high shelf, low shelf; bottom row: parametric EQ, notch EQ

The Parameters of EQ

Thankfully, EQs don't have a ton of parameters to set, so let's go through them one by one. Figure 15-3 shows a plug-in window from Digidesign Pro Tools 8.

As you can see in this figure, there are only a few things you can set:

- **Input:** This is where you can set the level of incoming signal. You wouldn't usually change this, because you don't want to overload the plug-in.
- **Type:** This is where you choose from the six types of EQ we listed earlier. From left to right, the symbols are high pass, low shelf, peak (parametric), notch, high shelf, and low pass. These same symbols are used in most EQ software or units.

Figure 15-3: Pro Tools EQ plug-in

- **Gain:** This is where you select whether you are boosting or cutting frequencies. 0dB is no change, –dB cuts, and +dB boosts.
- **Frequency:** For each type of EQ, this setting has a different meaning. On a low pass, the frequency you set here determines where the cutoff starts. In the parametric or peak EQ, the frequency identifies the specific frequency that will be boosted or cut.
- **Q:** The Q value widens or narrows the frequency range that's affected.

 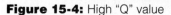

Figure 15-4: High "Q" value   **Figure 15-5:** Low "Q" value

Take a look at a graphical representation of both a high Q and a low Q, shown in Figures 15-4 and 15-5.

The graphical display on the plug-in gives you a visual approximation of what your EQ curve will look like. It's easy to visualize low frequencies on the left side of the display and higher frequencies on the right side.

Knowing When to Use EQ

There are many uses for EQ. You can use it to enhance the bass in dance and electronic music. You can use it to add sheen to vocals by boosting some high range. You can take the thump out of bass drums by lowering the low end. You can help an instrument come out of the mix more by enhancing certain frequencies. You can eliminate proximity effect by using a high pass to remove the bass rumble associated with it. The list goes on and on.

But EQ is not a magic cure-all for sound problems. Actually, most of the time you shouldn't need to EQ much at all, because much of your EQ comes from microphone placement. It won't fix harsh-sounding instruments or poor microphones. It can certainly help things, but over-EQing will sound unnatural.

Graphic EQs show a visual depiction of sound frequencies. Red lights pop up and down along with the frequencies present in the recording. This makes a great demonstration of how different instruments sound and what frequencies give those sounds. Being able to see with your eyes will help you make a connection to your ears. Listen to your own recordings as well as to professional CDs to learn what a good, smooth mix sounds like.

Reverb

No effect is as organic as reverb. Every sound reflects off surfaces and comes back to the listener. The time it takes to do this creates a feeling of aural space. A great concert hall is made specifically to control the reflections and provide a rich, warm reverberation. Electronic devices, hardware, and software try to emulate this sound. In recording, it's one of the most commonly used effects, and it's almost universally necessary for some instruments, especially voice. When mixing, reverb has the effect of bringing certain sounds to the foreground or pushing them to the background of the mix, in addition to creating a natural ambience.

The Basics of Reverb

Reverb is a very fast echo. However, there are many different types of reverb today. They fall into two categories: room emulations and "old school," such as plate and spring reverb. Room emulations try to re-create how the sound reverberates in rooms of different sizes. The larger the room, the larger the natural reverb you'll get. You typically see "small room," "medium room," and "hall" as popular reverb choices. In the early days of recording, reverb was simulated by sending the audio either through a spring or on a large plate of metal to simulate the sound of reverb. Spring and plate reverb have their own distinctive sounds and are now emulated by modern reverb processors and plug-ins.

Reverb and New Technology

One of the really amazing new technologies in reverb is called convolution. Convolution takes an audio snapshot of a real room (typically recording the sound of a starter's pistol) and mathematically re-creates that room in software. This is called an impulse response. When you get a convolution reverb, you can download different rooms as impulse response files. These rooms range from famous recording studios to historic spaces like Carnegie Hall. You won't believe your ears—it sounds like your music is inside these real rooms. One of the best convolution reverb plug-ins is Altiverb, although many DAWs like Logic Studio are shipping with included convolution reverbs.

The Parameters of Reverb

Unlike EQ, reverb has many parameters to deal with. Let's look at the D-Verb plug-in by Digidesign (see Figure 15-6) to see what kinds of control it gives you. Its parameters include:

- **Input:** This is where you set how much input signal volume comes into the reverb plug-in.
- **Mix:** Specifies how much of the effected signal is mixed in with the original. One hundred percent wet and effected signal will sound very odd, as though you're in another room very far away, while lower values will incur less reverb. Play with the mix until it sounds natural and good to you.
- **Algorithm:** The algorithm is the computer's model for different rooms and means of reverbs. Each algorithm will sound different and has unique characteristics. You'll find a few you like.

- **Size:** Based on the algorithm you choose, you can set how large the emulated room is. The bigger the room, the more echo and reverb you get.
- **Diffusion:** Diffusion simulates a room's reflectivity. The higher the diffusion setting, the more "live" the room will sound.
- **Decay:** How long will the reverb hang around? If you set it long, the sound will bleed around and get very "mushy." You can get some cool effects by playing with the decay. For a natural sound, don't set it too high. A decay time less than one second will do nicely in most cases.
- **Predelay:** Since reverb takes a short time to appear in a natural environment, the predelay is useful in making your sound feel real and natural. Experiment with the predelay time to find out what suits you best. For most situations, fifteen to forty milliseconds will sound the most natural.
- **HF cut and LP filter:** High frequency cut and low pass filter are holdovers from our EQ discussion. In a reverberated room, high and low frequencies react and decay at different rates. Every room will yield different results. Usually adding some of these parameters will help your reverb sound more natural.

Effects built into studio-in-a-box and hardware will have similar, if not identical, parameters.

Every reverb processor includes presets—explore these to get an idea of what you like and how they work. Pay attention to how the different algorithms, room sizes, and decay rates influence the overall sound. Tweak to your heart's content—you might be able to improve the presets and make them your own.

Figure 15-6: D-Verb reverb plug-in

Knowing When to Use Reverb

Reverb, in some subtle way, is used on almost every part of a recording. This is not to say that you're going to apply gobs of reverb everywhere. Reverb is one of those things that is hard to detect when it's applied well. And that's usually the point: Emulating a natural sound shouldn't draw attention to itself. Unless you're going for a special effect, hearing the reverb is a bad thing. It's a mistake many musicians make because reverb tends to make things sound really good. It's a bit of a drug and it's hard to stop, but go easy.

Certain instruments need reverb more than others. Bass typically has little reverb applied to it. Guitar—especially acoustic guitar—will need some reverb. Vocals will almost always get reverb; vocals without reverb will sound dry and unnatural. Drum sets tend not to get reverb applied to the whole set. However, snare drums typically benefit from some subtle reverb. Because of how cymbals ring, it's not wise to put reverb on; the same goes for bass drums. Acoustic pianos should not need much reverb, but a subtle amount might warm things up. As for other instruments and other situations, trust your ears.

ALERT

Reverb is a great effect, but it's easy to get carried away. Here is a very easy way to set reverb properly. Start by applying a reverb on an auxiliary channel. Start mixing in the reverb until you can hear that it's there. Then back down slightly. It seems easy, but if you can hear an effect, you are probably overusing it. Dial it in and then back off a touch.

While you could make an entire album with just EQ and reverb, there are other essential effects that engineers use to craft recorded tones. The next chapter will detail everything else you need to know about effects, including how to get them into your recordings.

CHAPTER 16

Using Other Effects

Beyond the basics of EQ and reverb lives a whole other world of effects. Chorus, delay, distortion, and various other effects help shape your sound in unique ways. The little things will put your recording over the top! This chapter also covers what you need to know about the techniques engineers use to apply effects to music.

Chorus

Chorus is a commonly used effect. The term "chorus" comes from the idea that two performers playing the exact same part wouldn't be exactly in tune and exactly in time with each other. The delay might be only several milliseconds, but that's enough to create an effect of multiple players. Applied to one part, chorus makes it sound as if more than one person is playing; the end result is that they sound richer. Chorus achieves this by copying the signal, delaying it a bit, and detuning it through a modulation effect. Modulations are changes to the pitch that rise and fall in a steady pattern. The change in pitch gives chorus its distinctive sound.

Parameters

The amount of control you get from chorus varies depending on your equipment. A traditional chorus effect will give you the control of these elements:

- **Delay:** Controls how long it takes for the second, copied signal to appear. The amount of time is generally kept fairly low—usually between fifteen and thirty milliseconds.
- **Depth:** Controls the amount of change in modulation or pitch of the sound. The higher the number, the weirder it's going to sound!
- **Rate:** Controls how fast the pitch will rise and fall.

Some choruses really go to town. Take a look at how much control Pro Tools gives you (see Figure 16-1). The extra control can yield some incredible sounds.

You have to tinker with the parameters for chorus. It's impossible to give you standard chorus presets because everyone will use them differently. Play around and have a good time. Check the included presets, too.

Figure 16-1: Digidesign's AIR Chorus

Uses for Chorus

Chorus is used on many different sounds. Guitar players love it for creating clean sounds. Keyboard and synth players commonly use it to thicken up their sound. For vocals, chorus can help cover up subtle pitch problems. Chorus can also add the illusion of width to a sound, making it appear fuller and wider. Wherever you use chorus, go easy and don't go overboard.

Compression

Dynamic effects change and control the aspects of volume in a recording. While not as dramatic as reverb and chorus, dynamic effects are some of the most important tools in recording—and the ones that are easily forgotten or misused in home recording. Dynamic effects come in a few flavors: compressing, limiting, and gating.

ALERT

Dynamic effects are subtle and don't alter the character and tone of a sound; they affect only volume, and only in a subtle way. If you slap on a reverb, you can instantly tell what's going on. Something changes right away. Grab an EQ knob and you impart some change immediately. But with dynamic effects, you get a less obvious change.

A compressor is an effect that automatically stops volume from rising too high. When instruments spike their volume wildly, as drums and bass do, for example, the sound can be unpolished and hard to listen to. A compressor, when set correctly, keeps sudden volume changes from occurring. It compresses the loud signals, makes them less noticeable, and smoothes out the overall volume level of a track.

Compression has many uses in the studio. It controls instrument levels when you're tracking. It helps bring tracks to a smoother volume level when you're mixing. It also compresses the entire song to smooth out the volume when you're mastering.

Let's take a drum track, for instance. Drums produce a wide range of sounds, from very soft to quite harsh. In other words, their dynamic range is pretty wide. In order to set the volume level correctly, you need to account for the loudest hits and make sure they don't clip the channel. This can be a challenge and usually means turning down the track, which can make the softer parts harder to hear. Applying a compressor limits the loudest hits from getting too loud and lets you raise the overall level of the track without fear of clipping. This helps make the drums fit into the mix better and also serves to smooth out the sound. This is one of the most common uses of compression.

Parameters

A typical compressor has a few controls that set its action:

- **Input:** Sets the input volume of the plug-in. On the 1176, a popular compressor, you can raise the input to make the compressor act faster and compress more quickly.
- **Output:** When using a compressor, it's typical to boost the gain because you will have more volume range to work with at the top.
- **Attack:** Controls the length of time (measured in milliseconds) the compressor takes to actually start to change the sound level after the volume reaches the threshold.
- **Release:** Controls the length of time (in milliseconds) the sound is held by the compressor after the volume level falls below the threshold.

Figure 16-2: Digidesign's Bomb Factory BF76

- **Ratio:** Here is the most important parameter! The ratio is the difference between incoming and outgoing signal. A 4:1 ratio says that when 4dB of sound come past the threshold, an increase of only 1dB comes out the other side. Higher ratios will sound more squashed and compressed. On the 1176, try pressing all four buttons at once for a unique effect!

Figure 16-2 shows the Digidesign Bomb Factory BF76 Compressor (a digital update of the popular 1176 compressor) plug-in.

How to Use a Compressor

Setting up a compressor isn't hard; you just need to be aware of a few parameters that help it sound natural. The threshold should not be set so low that the compressor is always working. You really want to compress only the upper end of the dynamic range. The ratio depends on how much fluctuation the source has. If it's a snare drum, you might want a 4:1 ratio or even higher. If you're trying to lightly compress a guitar track, choose a lower ratio.

ESSENTIAL

Try bypassing your effects often so you are able to hear them before and after the effects are applied. This way you can judge how you're doing. Bypassing effects is commonly referred to as A/B testing. ("A" is with the effect on, and "B" is without any effect.)

Attack and release are where compression is won and lost. Attack is not as critical as release. If the release is long, then the instrument will sound unnatural. You have to listen for the instrument's natural volume decay and try to match that with release time. As mentioned before, compression is not a dramatic effect, and it might take you quite a while to hear if it's even there.

Limiting

A limiter ensures that no signal gets too loud. It sets a "do not pass this" level, and anything that gets near that level gets squashed. A limiter is actually a super compressor with a ratio of 10:1 or more, and many limiters use a ratio as high as 100:1! Limiters are good for turning up an entire track via the gain parameter with absolutely no fear of clipping.

The controls of a limiter mimic the controls of a compressor because that's what limiters are—compressors. However, the ratio of a limiter is higher than that of a normal compressor, or it may be preset. Because of the dramatic squashing effect that limiters incur, you should use them carefully and only on sources that really need it. Compressing is usually used more often than limiting. Limiting is used often in mastering to get a full, loud signal.

Gating

A gate, or a noise gate, is basically a backward compressor. While a compressor limits the high end of the dynamic range, a gate quiets the low end. For example, when an instrument is not playing, there is a break in the sound. If the drummer doesn't play for the first chorus of the song, the microphones might be picking up other instruments or noise. Instead of tuning the volume down manually and raising it up again, a gate can be set to close the channel until a certain volume level is achieved. This can cut down on noise and bleed from other sources. Figure 16-3 shows a gate plug-in from Logic Pro 8. You'll notice that the parameters are very similar to those of a compressor:

Figure 16-3: Logic Noise gate

- **Threshold:** Sets the volume level at which the gate opens and closes. The gate will open when a real signal is present at that level and close when the signal falls below that level.
- **Attack:** Sets how fast the gate acts after the volume reaches either the open or close threshold.
- **Hold:** Sets how long the gate stays open after it falls below the set threshold.
- **Release:** After the hold releases the signal, release sets how long until the gate fully closes.
- **Lookahead:** This lets the plug-in act sooner by looking at the audio before it comes into the plug-in. This is very helpful when using sidechain inputs, for example.

Experiment with gate settings to get rid of noise and other low-level volume problems in your tracks. You can even use the gate for some creative effects—your creativity is unlimited and you can tinker as much as you want!

All-in-One Tools

On a large mixing console, it's not uncommon to find EQ, a noise gate, and a compressor on each channel. Because these are the most commonly used effects, it's useful to have them hard-wired. Plug-ins can also combine EQ, compression, and gating into one plug-in. These plug-ins are so useful, you might even use them on every track in your mix. Figure 16-4 shows a shot of ChannelStrip by Metric Halo.

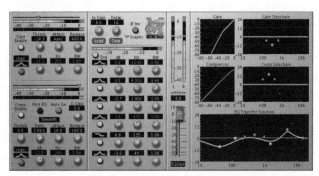

Figure 16-4: Metric Halo's ChannelStrip

There are plenty of other examples of "all in one" processing solutions, and you may have one included in your DAW of choice. They are a great place to start when processing your tracks.

Guitar Simulators

Guitar effects processors have been a popular choice for guitarists for many years. Traditionally, these processors exist in hardware versions. With the flexibility and power of computer plug-ins roaring at us, it's no surprise that plug-ins focused on guitar are becoming very popular. One such plug-in is Guitar Rig 3 by Native Instruments. This plug-in for Windows and Mac allows you to mix and match your favorite guitar amps, cabinets, microphones, pedal effects, delays, reverbs, and even toys like a "Loop Machine" for real-time phrase sampling. You also get a hardware pedal for stomping effects on and off just like you're used to with real pedals.

One of the best reasons to use guitar plug-ins is that you always record your audio without effects. That's right—you plug your guitar straight into the computer and it records clean, boring, direct guitar. The plug-in itself does all the work in real time. The largest win for you is that you can change your mind about your tone without needing to rerecord. You can start with a great Fender emulation and then decide to go for a Marshall amp. The sky is the limit! There are other plug-ins to choose from—Amplitube by IK Multimedia, 11 by Digidesign, and Revalver by Peavey remain popular choices.

Other Effects

There are even more effects you can use! The most common basic effects are covered here, but feel free to experiment with other effects now that you have a good idea of what the parameters do.

Distortion

Remember how we said that overloading a circuit is bad? Well, most of the time it is, but ask any guitar player and he will tell you that distortion is good. Distortion amplifies the incoming signal wildly, letting it distort, but this doesn't incur "bad" clipping like overloading a recording channel does. When you overload a recording channel, you ruin the recording; distortion gives the effect of overloading a circuit on a guitar amp. It can make for an interesting effect when used. It's a great way to add "dirt" to a sound.

Delay

Delay is a simple effect that copies your signal and re-creates it, only it does so at a specified interval after you play. This can range from short delays of milliseconds to long delays of many seconds. A short delay will thicken up a track much as a chorus will. A long delay can have many musical possibilities. If you set the delay right, it will follow you around, playing back what you played. Delay has long been a favorite of guitar and keyboard players. Try it on your tracks to see how it sounds.

Noise Reduction

Noise reduction is one of those amazing effects that you can't live without once you've used it. Unlike a gate that limits noise when you're not playing, a noise reducer listens to the signal and gets rid of all unwanted noise. Hums and hisses? Gone. Crackles and pops? Gone. Simply talking about iZotope's RX plug-in can't possibly convey how amazing it is. These tools are able to not only take out noises, but also repair audio. If you find yourself recording in less than ideal situations, you'll want to check out RX.

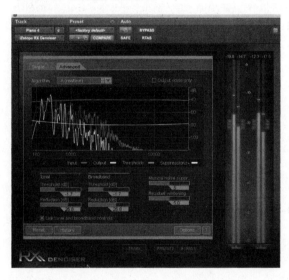

Figure 16-5: iZotope's RX noise reduction plug-in

Using Hardware Effects in a Digital Studio

What if you own some great hardware and you'd like to use it with your computer-based DAW? It's not uncommon to have some great hardware reverbs and EQs, especially with the current vintage craze in audio effects. Working with hardware inside of a DAW is pretty simple. Here's what you have to do:

1. Send the output of the track your want to process out of your DAW on a specific hardware output on your interface—let's say you'll use output 3.
2. Connect a cable from output 3 to the input of your hardware effect.

3. Connect a cable from the output on your hardware effect to an unused input on your audio interface—maybe you'll use input 5.
4. Create a new track in your DAW and set its input to the same channel you plugged into in step 3.
5. Record enable the track you've just created and initiate recording.

Your DAW will start playing, sending the track out of your interface, into the hardware effect you want to use, and back to an empty track. The new track will be printed onto the track you've just created.

The last step is to mute the old unprocessed track in your DAW so you hear only the effected track. Be aware that latency comes into play here. Every track you send from your DAW, out and back in again, will incur some latency because it takes time for that audio to convert from digital to analog and back again. Some systems provide plug-ins that compensate for this delay automatically, but you may simply have to adjust the track by hand. Thankfully, you have the original track (the unprocessed one) to use as a guide. If your DAW tells you, you can determine the exact round trip latency in milliseconds and simply move that track back by that number. Apple's Logic Pro comes with a plug-in called "I/O helper" that makes this routing an absolute snap! Other DAWs are starting to follow suit, adding plug-ins to help with external processing.

ESSENTIAL

Don't worry if this process sounds intimidating; most new DAW users feel the same way. Patching in and out of mixers, into hardware, and back into tape machines used to be simply part of the job description of recording audio. In today's DAW, all of that routing and patching is done for you.

Now that you know what the effects do, let's actually get to the nitty-gritty of how and when to use them. Effects can be added to your system in various ways. The common ways to add effects are through inserts, auxiliary channels, and patch-throughs.

Insert Effects

An insert sends your entire signal to the processor and mixes all of the signal back. Insert effects work well with dynamic effects (compressing, limiting, and gating), which take your entire signal and affect the total volume of that signal. With dynamic effects, there is no need for mixing how much effect you use, so inserts work perfectly with these effects. But because you have no control over mixing when you use inserts, they aren't appropriate for all effects. Effects like reverb and chorus, for example, would be overpowering because you couldn't control how much of the reverb or chorus is mixed with your signal.

On a mixing board, EQ is a good example of a "hard-wired" insert effect. All of your signal passes through the EQ and then gets mixed out to the stereo pair.

In software programs, insert effects are usually listed above the virtual mixer's fader for each individual channel. This varies from program to program, so check your manual to be sure.

Auxiliary Effects

Use auxiliary effects when you want to use a mixture of processed and unprocessed signal. This makes auxiliary channels perfect for reverb and other processors that you want to assign to more than one track. On most DAW systems, you use bus or auxiliary tracks to send signal from one track to another track, which holds the auxiliary effect. The send acts as a virtual patch cable, connecting the two tracks together. Sends allow you to control how much of the signal to send to the auxiliary effect, usually through a volume knob. The track that holds the auxiliary effect has its volume control for setting how loud the effect should be mixed into the track. This is the standard way to use reverb, for example. You should use one reverb plug-in on an auxiliary track and send your individual tracks to it through sends (which are sometimes called buses). Do this rather than placing individual reverbs on each individual channel.

Patch-Through Effects

Usually, you want to record instruments without any effects on them. This allows you much greater control later on when you mix. If you record with effects, the effects are "printed" to the track; you can't get rid of them. But there are some circumstances when this is okay. Guitar players, for instance, tend to use reverbs, delays, and choruses to make up their signature tone. It would be hard to replicate their exact sound later, so it might be best to allow them to record with their normal effected sounds. Keyboard players also do this on their synthesizers—adding effects into their patches. In these cases, it's okay to let the players "patch-through" their effects.

The Pros and Cons of Software Plug-Ins

It's no secret by now that the computer and plug-ins are becoming the cornerstones of the home-recording market. Computer effect plug-ins have specific advantages over hardware. Here are some of the pros:

- You can use them as many times as your computer's processor can handle. For example, you can have five different versions of the same reverb on five different tracks, or aux tracks—all with different settings on each plug-in.
- You gain the ability to use one plug-in as an insert effect or an auxiliary effect at the same time.
- You can conceivably have a compressor on each track, all for the price of one.
- You can save and recall patches from song to song automatically.
- You won't need cables, patch bays, and rack mounts—there's no space required, except virtual space.
- You might get to upgrade your plug-in version for free if the maker updates it to improve the sound.
- You can automate the settings of any plug-in within a song.

There's always a downside:

- Just because you bought a plug-in doesn't mean you'll be able to run it.
- The more plug-ins you use, the slower your CPU becomes, and the fewer tracks you can use.

- Many professional engineers believe the sound of software plug-ins isn't as good as hardware versions.
- You can't use plug-ins anywhere but in a computer, which makes hardware versions handier for live sound or instruments.

As you can see, there are ups and downs to plug-ins, but most people will agree that the flexibility and cost-benefit ratio make computer systems and plug-ins very attractive.

CHAPTER 17

Mixing and Mastering

Mixing and mastering are two of the hardest subjects to describe in writing. By its very nature, audio is an art of the ears—not the eyes. If you spend enough time in studios, talk to enough engineers, and read through the important work on the subject, you'll see some similarities in how engineers work and how they mix. But there will never be a substitute for getting your hands dirty and mixing yourself.

What Is Mixing?

Mixing is the second stage in the recording process, which comes after the tracking has been completed. In a basic sense, mixing isn't that hard to understand. Mixing involves blending all of your separate tracks into one stereo pair suitable for listening to on any radio, iPod, or car stereo. Mixing also involves adding effects to polish up the sound.

While the idea may be simple, the art of blending disparate sounds is very difficult. When you hear an acoustic band, the blend is taken care of for you; the reverberation is natural from the room. As soon as you start close-miking instruments, reproducing the sound in a realistic fashion becomes a challenge. While you might not know how to make a good mix yet, you certainly know a bad one when you hear it.

Mixing is all about perception. Can you perceive that this group of instruments really sounded this way? The best mixes sound natural, and they try to replicate how those instruments should blend together. If the mixing engineer has done his job, nothing out of the ordinary should be noticeable. That is, nothing catches your ear as unnatural or out of place. As you know, it's easy to spot a bad mix; there's just something that's not right.

Many engineers talk about hearing in multiple dimensions. Understanding those dimensions can help you figure out what's going on in a good mix. Here are the basic dimensions you'll encounter in mixing and what it means to work with them:

- **Foreground/background:** Bringing sound forward and backward in a track using volume
- **Depth:** Using effects like reverb to create the feeling of closeness or distance
- **Up and down:** Using EQ to help tracks sit in their own distinct part of the frequency spectrum
- **Side to side:** Placing sounds from left to right using the pan controls

Without oversimplifying the process too much, these four dimensions give you an idea of what goes into a mix. Now let's look at what goes into working with these dimensions so that you can start mixing like a pro.

Foreground/Background

The basic element of mixing is the loudness of each track. This is the first place you should start as a budding engineer. No matter what system you own, from the four-track on your iPhone to Pro Tools, volume manipulation is the first part of a mix. In visual artwork, such as paintings and photographs, there is the background and foreground; the more important visual elements usually come to the front of the work. It's the same with audio—the important parts need to be brought to the foreground to be heard.

ESSENTIAL

The mute and solo buttons are the two most important buttons to use in mixing. Get to know and love those buttons. When you mix, you'll never be able to work on a full mix all at once—it's just too much sound. Isolating sounds or groups of sounds played together is the best way to go, especially when working with EQ problems. Focus on small parts and build your mix around them.

The volume control on a mixing board or your software recording device is called a "fader" because it allows you to fade the sound in or out at will. The first thing you should do is set your faders for each track to create a basic feeling of foreground and background. In most music that includes vocals, the vocal track is usually the point of interest and should be the loudest element. But how loud? How much louder than the accompanying guitar? You have to trust your ears on this. At a basic stage like this, do your best to get it to sound as balanced as possible. Volume of the tracks is only one very basic element of a mix. But it's a great place to start!

Depth

The element of depth is taken care of by effects. Depth shouldn't be confused with volume. Depth is the feeling of how far a sound is from your ears and has little to do with volume. Just imagine that you're listening to a symphony orchestra. No matter how loud or soft the violins are, they will always sound closer to you than the brass section that sits in the back of the orchestra.

The way to demonstrate depth is to use reverb, which re-creates the natural reverberation and ambience of a space. Something can be quite loud in the mix, but if it's drenched in reverb, it can sound far away. And using less reverb can make the sound sit right up front, as if the player were right in front of you. Other popular depth effects are chorus and delay, which are all very closely related to reverb.

FACT

If you have a track that seems to get lost no matter how you mix, try using a chorus effect to thicken up the track. Chorus adds a second copy of the original signal and slightly delays it to give the illusion of more than one person playing. It's a great way to add depth to the track and help it stand out a bit more.

All of these effects help to widen the perceived music. Remember that mixing is perception, and using effects correctly can let you manipulate your mix in some very neat ways.

Up and Down: EQ

So you've spent hours manipulating the volume and depth of your track, and yet, everything sounds bad. No matter what you do, it just seems sonically cluttered, so to speak. EQ may be the answer, but in a different way than you might think. Until now, we have discussed EQ as a way to shape the sound of individual tracks. When you mix, EQ takes a slightly different role.

EQ and Mixing

Remember the idea that any single sound is made up of many frequencies? Think of sounds as analogous to building blocks; each sound is a differently shaped building block. Not all sounds will just fit together without some light sanding. For example, the bass guitar and the bass drum sit in the same frequency range—the low frequencies. Depending on how the instruments were recorded, when you play them back together, you'll most likely hear a bit of sonic mud because of so much sound coming in from the lower frequencies. What's happening is that both the bass drum's and the bass guitar's low frequencies are covering each other up, making your mix very bass heavy. You'll notice that it's also hard to hear both the instruments clearly.

Welcome to EQ Carving!

When you mix, sounds should not compete with each other. If you load up a mix with a bunch of instruments in the same frequencies, you'll get mud. Start to separate the sounds so that each sound can occupy its own layer. Try cutting the bottom of the bass guitar so the bass drum has some room. Or try the reverse and cut the bottom of the bass drum. By doing this, you open up a space for the other instrument to fit in. You make a mix much the same way you make a building—one layer on top of another. EQ helps the pieces fit together.

You probably consider a bass drum's sound to be fairly low in frequency. However, whether you realize it or not, the bass's sound also consists of high frequencies, albeit very quiet ones. You can barely hear them, but they're there! If you have a low-frequency sound, cutting high frequencies won't have much effect. The same is true with high-frequency sounds—you won't affect them if you cut the low frequencies. If you properly trim sound frequencies, the tracks have a better chance of sitting one on top of another without clashing too much.

Trimming with EQ is also called carving EQ. Just think about each sound and how it sits in relation to the other tracks. If you have sounds that compete, try cutting from one sound so that the other has room. Mixing is like building a layer cake: each track gets its own space and EQ is a great way to keep tracks in their own spot.

Side to Side

Panning is the control of sound placement. In stereo recording, music is panned between the left and right speakers. Until music is heard in surround or 5.1-channel surround sound, left and right is all we have. Just as EQ carving determines how frequencies sit on top of each other, panning controls how the sounds sit from right to left in the stereo field.

For a basic test, don't pan anything; set the pan controls exactly at 0, which means equal distribution to both the left and right speakers; this is also called center pan. Now that you've set all the sounds to the center, you have created a narrow and crowded mix. The sound is most likely muddy and indistinct. It's easy to understand that no matter how well you EQ, if all the sounds sit in the same pan position, you're going to get even more fighting over sound! Now, start moving instruments around. Put the guitar to the right, the bass to the left. That simple move opens up the mix a lot.

ESSENTIAL

If you're having a hard time getting the bass and bass drum to sound good together, make sure to pan them away from each other. No matter how well you EQ the sounds, if they're sitting in the same pan spot, they will interfere with each other. Moving them around can alleviate many EQ and balance issues.

To really pan well, try to imagine a stage. Think of where the sound comes from: guitar on one side of the stage, vocals in the middle, bass on the other side. Drums are often in the center but reach right and left because they physically take up a lot of space on stage. Now try to pan your mix that way. Push the guitar and bass to opposite sides of the mix and keep the vocals in the center. Let the drum mix mirror how the drums are set up—snare and kick basically in the center, a tom to the right, a tom to the left, hi-hat cymbal on the right, and ride cymbal on the left. The amount of left and right pan that you use is up to you and your ears. Each song might have very different pan ideas that suit the song, and no two mixes will be the same.

Audio in Motion

Here's something vital: Music breathes, and so should your mix. This doesn't mean just turning up the volume of an instrument for its solo! Your audio should always be in motion; even the slightest movement of volume levels makes the mix feel alive. Minute changes during the playback of the songs will do wonders, making your music feel more alive. It's a trick that so many engineers use. Keep those faders in motion, even just slightly. It will make everything sound better.

Automation

If you own a studio-in-a-box or computer recording system that supports mixing automation, you'll enjoy this section. Mixes aren't static. You can't just "set it and forget it" as the TV infomercials often say. A song and its resulting mix is a living, breathing thing that changes. Guitars get louder for solos, drums duck under vocals during verses; things change. If you're working on a system that you can't automate, such as a tape-based studio, or if you're using a mixing console, you'll have to know exactly what's going to change throughout the songs and adjust the levels and other parameters live upon playback. In the old days, this was called "playing the console" and was an art all to itself.

Digital technology allows you to plan all the movements of faders, effects, and pan settings in a process called automation. You go through the tracks as you mix, and you record the motion of the faders into a special track called an automation track. Once you've recorded all the movements, the automation track plays back and takes care of all of the changes in faders and so on. It's a great thing to have if you work alone. Most studios-in-a-box support some level of automation, and computer systems give you an incredible amount of control.

Fades

How will a song end? Take a good listen to the end of some of your favorite albums, and you'll realize that none of them just stop; they all have some kind of smooth fade. How do you achieve a smooth fade? If you use a digital system, you can use the fade-out option in the editing menu. If you have automation capabilities, just automate the master fader at the end of the tune. For those of you who have to move the fader by yourself, just evenly yank the master fader to zero at the final mix down to achieve a smooth fade.

"Flying fader" is the name given to a mixing board with motors that move the faders automatically. After you've recorded automation for your songs, the fader "flies" by itself along with the volume changes you've recorded via automation. Flying faders were once found only on the most expensive mixing consoles, but now more and more manufacturers are putting motorized faders in home studio products.

Control Surfaces

In the digital home recording studio, a control surface is an amazing tool. Back in the day, you had consoles with lots and lots of knobs and faders to manipulate in real time. In the first edition of this book, studios-in-a-box were still popular and came complete with control surfaces that you could use to manipulate the volume, pan, and other effects on your computer.

Today, computer DAW systems are becoming the standard way for users to record, so many users miss out on the experience of having tactile control. Another important reason to think about a control surface is that manipulating onscreen controls with a mouse can feel a bit unnatural, especially if you're used to real knobs and faders. Thankfully, you can buy control surfaces that allow you to get "hands on" control of your mixing.

Figure 17-1: Control surface with integrated interface *Courtesy of* Avid Technology, Inc.

Control surfaces exist in two flavors: dedicated control surfaces and interfaces that combine physical inputs and outputs with control surfaces. Figure 17-1 shows an integrated control surface, which combines a control surface and an audio interface.

One of the big wins with a control surface is that you can record your physical actions into controller automation—your DAW will record and play-back your movements automatically. Another big win is that the faders on many control surfaces are motorized, so they recall back to their correct positions when you come back to a mix or move your song position. Once you invest in a control surface, you may wonder how you ever survived without one!

Buses

We've talked about using bus and auxiliary inputs for certain effects like reverb, but you can use buses for other things as well. A bus is simply a path that sound can take. For example, let's say you have four drum tracks that you've mixed together. The balance between the drums is perfect, but they need to be a little louder in the mix. You could try to raise all four faders equally, although you might find that difficult to do.

A better option is to send each of the drum tracks the same bus, which would act as a volume control for all the signals it's fed. When you take a bunch of signals and mix them down to a single track, this is commonly called stems. Buses are a great way to prepare stems. They're also a standard way to get many tracks to a single reverb or other audio effect.

The End Result

Okay. You've slaved over your work. You've mixed and remixed everything and now it's time to finish up. There are a few things to do before you're done. The first is format—what are you mixing down to? These days, you either burn to a CD or bounce into a digital file, either a compressed MP3 or an uncompressed WAV or AIFF file. Either way you cut it, the end result is about taking many tracks and bouncing them out to a stereo pair.

Final Mix Down

The final mix down entails sending all of your work to a simple stereo pair of left and right signals. All the levels and effects need to be taken care of in advance. Whatever you commit to, the final file is it! If you're working with automation, get that in order too. At this point, you should feel comfortable that you have a good product. Remember the fade-out at the end if you want that effect.

QUESTION

Where do I start if I have sixteen or more tracks to mix?
The drums are usually mixed first, starting with the kick drum. Bass is added next. Vocals are usually last. Compression is added on a track-per-track basis on the instruments that need it, and effects are added to auxiliary channels. Once the engineer has a rough mix, she starts tweaking EQ, setting all the effects levels perfectly and starting to craft the mix.

Bounce to Disk

On digital systems, most notably computer systems, the process of a final mix down is achieved by "bouncing" to the disk. All the audio is bounced together onto the hard drive into a file (usually a stereo file) that can be burned. Bounce to disk is the same as mixing down to a tape or any other format. On many computer systems, bounce to disk is not something you control. This means that you can't play with levels and ride faders while it's bouncing. Many programs just do it quickly while you wait. The reason they do this is that all of the software available lets you automate movements of faders and other parameters. If you can automate, then you should. Once you have the final file, you can burn it to a CD using your favorite CD burning software, like iTunes.

Dither

The standard for encoding digital information onto a CD is 16bit/44.1kHz audio. Every CD available today plays back that way. The newer computer audio systems advertise better-than-CD quality, and if you're getting into computer recording you might be able to record at that quality. Nowadays, most computer audio systems record at 24bit/96kHz or higher.

Without getting too technical, the higher the numbers, the better quality you get. The problem is that if you record at 24bit/96kHz, you can't just burn that to a CD, because it's not compatible with current CD quality, which is called red book standard. You have to do something called "down sampling," which means mixing down to 16bit/44.1kHz. In your software program, this is easy to do. In the bounce-to-disk window, you'll always be asked what rate to mix down to. If you are making a CD, you always need to mix to 16bit/44.1kHz.

QUESTION

How long does it take to mix a song?
Well, how long do you have? Mixing takes a very long time; you will most likely listen to the entire song twenty to fifty times before you get close to finishing. Now you know why bands take so long to release albums.

Okay, so now to dither. When you "down sample," you lose some of the audio quality because the computer goes from a higher sample rate to a lower one. Dithering was invented to make up for the loss in quality. If you're recording at better-than-CD quality, you need to dither your music down. On many systems, dithering is a plug-in you put on the master fader. On some systems, it's a box you can check in the bounce-to-disk window. Either way, if you record at anything above 16bit/44.1kHz, you must dither it. If you don't, you can hear the difference. Your recording will sound better with dithering.

Compare

Now that you have your mix in your hands, you need to start playing it on as many systems as possible. Play it in your car, on your stereo, on your mom's stereo . . . you get the picture. Play it everywhere you can. The goal here is to make sure that it sounds the way you want it to sound on every system. Certain mixes sound great at home and quite bad in the car. Most professional recordings sound good on almost every system they're played on. If you find some problems, you can always go back and remix. It's also good to play the song for as many different people as you can, especially musicians. Opinions at this stage in your development are very worthwhile.

Mastering

Mastering is a term that's thrown around a lot but rarely understood. It's also the hardest to pull off at home. Mastering is the last stage in the recording process. Mastering takes all the separate songs for an album and puts them together so they sound good together. If mixed well, each song will sound good by itself, but that doesn't necessarily mean all the songs you put back to back on a CD will work together. Subtle differences in loudness and EQ from track to track can really hurt the sonic impact of a record. Mastering balances the sound from song to song so that the album sounds cohesive.

It's All about Balance

Mastering balances the levels of a group of songs, making sure that each song is as loud as it needs to be. It also makes sure that the tracks are relatively equal in volume and tone. Mastering might also apply some compression to smooth out the dynamics of the entire song. In many cases, some subtle EQ is applied to help polish up the tracks. Mastering deals only with the final stereo mix down, and it's not considered mixing anymore.

Mastering is tricky because the folks that do mastering professionally invest a small fortune on the acoustic perfection of their mastering studios. To truly listen to music in detail, your room must be tuned properly. Irregularities in the room can make certain frequencies sound more pronounced than they really are. Mastering speakers are on the whole very neutral sounding and mastering engineers invest heavily in their quality. Many mastering engineers also rely on outboard effects instead of plug-in effects. As a point of fact, mastering is a different art than recording and mixing. Most engineers specialize in one or the other, rarely both.

ALERT

Limiting is something that you can abuse, and too much will absolutely destroy the sonic quality of a track. Louder is not better. Just do a quick Google search about the Metallica album *Death Magnetic* to hear exactly what happens when limiting goes bad.

Mastering Tools

Compression and limiting are the most common processes applied during mastering. In order for a track to be heard as it was meant to be, it has to be loud enough. Even if you did a great job of setting levels in your recording, mastering sets the final loudness. Some compression might be applied to reduce the dynamic range of the audio. The negative effect of this compression is that you lose some of the volume of the track because the compression squeezes the sound together. Limiting then takes the compressed signal and boosts it to make tracks as loud as possible without clipping or going over the threshold you set. Once the track is compressed and boosted, it will start to "sit" better on the album. When this is repeated from track to track, you start getting something that sounds more like an album, rather than eight tracks thrown together on a CD.

Tone and Sequencing

When you put several songs together on an album, especially ones that were recorded over a long period of time, you might notice that the songs sound quite different from each other in regard to EQ and overall loudness. When you master, you can apply EQ to help the tonal balance of the songs fit together better. This typically means going though each song and listening for its EQ or looking at a graphic representation of the frequencies in your mastering program. Once all the tracks sound cohesive, the next step is deciding the sequence they should appear on the record. Unless you're recording a suite of songs that has a predetermined order, mastering is the stage when the order of songs occurs—this is called sequencing. Sometimes you can't help that certain songs sound different from one another, so in those cases careful sequencing can help them fit together on the album.

It's entirely possible for you to master at home, and you might even get good results. However, mastering might be the one part of recording you won't want to do at home. Mastering and a good mastering engineer are worth their weight in gold. Mastering really is an art—not to mention that mastering studios have hundreds of thousands of dollars of mastering equipment that can make your CD sound incredible.

If you've worked very hard at home and you want to get the CD you've created put on the market, get it mastered by a professional. You'll be amazed at what a professional can do to a final mix.

Mastering Software

If you're going to take on the job of mastering, you'll likely want to look at some mastering software. What's mastering software? Well, in truth, you can master audio in just about every DAW you own, but there are plenty of reasons to look at software titles designed specifically for mastering.

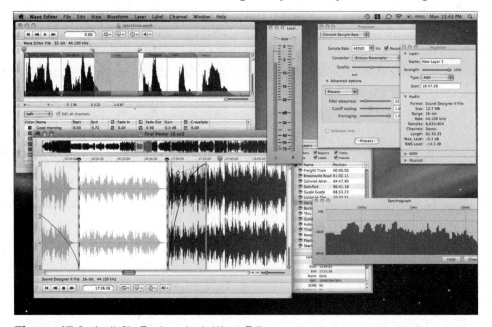

Figure 17-2: Audiofile Engineering's Wave Editor

Since mastering typically deals with stereo files, and not multitrack audio, all of the bells and whistles of your full-blown DAW just aren't needed to work on the final details in a mastering situation. You can find software that excels at working with stereo tracks, making it a science to add the EQ, compression, and other effects you may need to finalize your mix. Mastering software enables you to burn a CD, but it will also deliver your tracks in a specialized format called DDP, which is what CD replication companies will need to mass-produce your CD. You can add in other information, such as CD-TEXT and ISRC codes that are used in commercial CDs. Some notable names in mastering software include Steinberg WaveLab, Audiofile Engineering Wave Editor, Sonic Studio soundBlade, and BIAS Peak. Figure 17-2 shows a shot of Wave Editor in action.

These applications are great for audio editing, in general. No serious audio engineer should be without one!

CHAPTER 18

Advanced Recording Tips and Techniques

At this point in your journey, you've gained a lot of general experience and have a good foundation to build upon. Your music sounds good. Your recordings are clean; there are no problems—yet they don't sound quite as amazing as you had hoped. What's missing? Every experienced engineer employs some tricks of the trade now and again. Here's a collection of those tips and tricks.

Multiple Microphones

Deciding on what microphone to use can be a difficult task. If your studio is large enough to hire a helper, it's not a problem to check microphone after microphone while you sit in the control room and listen. But let's get back to reality! You don't have a big studio, and chances are it's just you working there. While you could set up a microphone, do a short recording, and repeat this several times with other microphones, that's inefficient and makes it hard for you to compare each microphone to each other. But how can you get around it?

If you have a few microphone inputs available, set up as many microphones as you feel like (or have available) in front of your sound source. Let's use a guitar amplifier as an example. Set up four microphones on the speaker, each at varying distances and locations around the speaker and record them all at the same time. When you play back the tracks, use the solo feature to listen to them one at a time and see what you like best. If you find a microphone that stands out as the winner, delete the other tracks and you're done. You might also find that blending several microphones at once gives you the sound you're looking for. In any case, keep track of which microphone goes to which input!

Surgical EQ

The art of EQ is a subtle one. An experienced engineer can listen to a sound with such acute listening skills that she knows just what knob to turn to get the sound perfect. Some of us aren't quite that skilled. Here's a great trick to find the frequencies that need help. (This trick works well on snare drums to find the frequency on the annoying ring that most snare drums exhibit.)

FACT

On a three-band EQ, you typically have no control over which frequency is boosted or attenuated. The three bands are set by the manufacturer and sweep through a general range of frequencies. This doesn't mean you can't necessarily use a three-band EQ effectively; if the frequency you need is built into one of the bands, then you're set.

On a parametric or graphic (not a three-band) EQ, set the Q—the width of the EQ—as high as possible. This lets you pinpoint a very small range of frequencies, allowing a precise cut. Now set the level control as high as it will go, giving a maximum boost. Slowly change the frequency control, sweeping from the low to the high frequency. When you find the frequency that is responsible for the ring or any other sound problem, you'll hear it easily. Because your EQ is boosted as high as it will go, that sound will jump right out of the speaker.

Once you find the culprit, reduce the gain until the offending sound goes away. Repeat this as many times as you need to achieve the sound you desire. This is an absolutely essential trick as you learn about proper ways to EQ.

Thicken Up Vocals

If your vocals seem to lack body and fullness, you might like this next tip. Duplicate the track so you have a second copy of the original. On the copy, add a slight chorus effect and set the mix control to 100 percent full wet mix, so you hear only the effected sound. On that same copy, reduce the overall level of the track and pan it in the opposite direction of the original track. Placing the second copy in the other speaker will make the overall sound large and wide. You can substitute a short delay for a chorus effect for similar results. This technique of duplicating vocal tracks was used on many Beatles recordings.

Side Chains

Many effects utilize something called side chains, which are extra inputs. These are either physical inputs for hardware effects or virtual inputs for plug-ins. A side chain listens for the audio present in the side chain input and uses that information to trigger some part of the effect. The best example of this, called a ducker, is used in radio broadcasting: A compressor is applied on the music source's output. The side chain inputs are from the announcer's vocals. When the announcer starts to talk, the compressor kicks in, lowering the signal of the music and letting the voice come through clearly. The music "ducks" under the voice.

ALERT

On a piece of hardware, side chaining involves patching with audio cables. With a plug-in, side chaining is done virtually by the computer. You set the inputs and outputs and the computer routes the audio for you.

Side chains like this are great for controlling guitar and vocal interaction. In most pop music, guitar is the focus when there isn't a vocal present. Using a compression side chain on a guitar track can help the guitar get out of the way when the vocal is present. Simply route the vocal track into the side chain inputs of the guitar's compressor. When the vocal is present, the guitar lowers slightly and then rises back up after the vocal drops down. This can save you from having to manually "ride" the volume of the guitar track.

Abusing Compression

Compression just might be the most important effect to master, but it's also easily abused. Compression reduces the dynamic range of audio. Dynamic range is a natural part of sound. When you manipulate it, you are changing a big part of the sound. If it's done wrong, it can sound unnatural and harsh.

Breathing and Pumping

These are two common compression no-no's, and both are the results of overcompression. Let's talk about how you can avoid them. Pumping typically occurs with bass drums, which have sudden loud bursts and can get too loud. Compression can help tame this, but if the kick drum is only one of many sounds fed into a compressor, you might have a problem. The bass drum will kick the volume up, and the compressor will respond by turning everything down with it, suddenly. Since the kick drum is rhythmic, the effect is noticeable because the volume pumps up and down in rhythm. The easiest way around this is to put the kick drum on its own separate compressor, or lengthen the attack time on the compressor.

Breathing is a side effect that occurs when vocals are overcompressed. If the compression is set too high, there is little difference in volume between the loudest sung phrases and the quietest inhale. Breathing occurs when inhales and exhales of air are as loud as the rest of the sung parts. Not the nicest sound. You can get around this by setting the ratio lower and adjusting the threshold so that the quiet parts stay quieter and the loud parts get squeezed slightly.

Overcompression: Hitting the Wall

Compression is the limiting of dynamic range. Dynamics are also referred to as nuance. If you overcompress a final mix, you'll make the whole song very loud and won't allow it to vary and have nuance. Your music will suffer. NO ONE LIKES TO READ SENTENCES WITH ALL CAPS. IT'S ACTUALLY ANNOYING. That is a dramatic example, but that's what a listener hears when your mix is overcompressed with no dynamic range. This is also very prevalent in dance/house/club–style music. Don't let your music fall victim to the current trend of louder is better—it's not always so. Subtle compression will help a mix sit and sound nice, but overcompression will kill it.

On any compressor, the ratio control sets the amount of compression. The ratio of 10:1 is considered a very high ratio. It might work for some instruments, but anything over 6:1 is considered heavy compression. If you are experiencing breathing or pumping, look at your ratio first.

CHAPTER 19

Amazing Technology in Your Home

As if all of the digital recording technology you've seen in this book isn't remarkable enough, there are some tools that truly push the limits of technology and define the cutting edge. This chapter will detail some of the amazing trends in the audio and technology markets.

Pitch Correction

In the past, the pitch you recorded was the pitch on the final track. But today, you can play around with the pitch on your recordings to perfect it or experiment with different effects.

Auto-Tune

In the mid-1990s, a company called Antares changed the world for recording professionals. Auto-Tune was the product that heralded one of the greatest shifts in recording production since the invention of multitrack recording: perfectly in tune vocals.

The premise was simple: Auto-Tune would analyze the incoming audio, figure out what pitches were being sung and correct them on the way out. The premise is simple enough, but it's a difficult technical challenge to pull off. Auto-Tune started out as a hardware processor but quickly moved to an effects plug-in. When used properly, a marginally talented singer is polished to absolute perfection. When used incorrectly, Auto-Tune had some interesting side effects, most notably on Cher's "Believe" where the pitch correction was intentionally overused to make her sound robotic.

When used correctly, you're not aware of it. Auto-Tune was used on almost every recording of the past few years. Auto-Tune is not the only solution for pitch correction. More and more DAWs include pitch correction integrated into their software. Sonar and Digital Performer have excellent integrated pitch correction.

Melodyne

One amazing new technology is Celemony's Melodyne, which started out as an easier-to-use alternative to Auto-Tune. Melodyne offered the same end result as Auto-Tune, but accomplished it much more easily. In Melodyne, you see all of the pitches in a MIDI-style piano-roll editor. You can adjust individual pitches by hand or quantize them to the grid. You can even edit the formant and vibrato to shape the performance. Melodyne upped the ante on Auto-Tune because you could edit the timing of the notes as well. Melodyne allowed monophonic audio editing as flexibly as MIDI editing.

For both Auto-Tune and Melodyne (and the included correction in DAWs) pitch correction only worked on single line, or monophonic sources. This was well suited for vocals, but there were other instruments that could benefit from pitch correction. In 2009, Celemony broke through the technical barrier with Melodyne Direct Note Access (DNA). This program includes polyphonic pitch detection, allowing users to select and edit the pitches of multiple tones at once. That means that if you feed the program a piano or guitar chord, you can edit one of the notes of that chord separately from the rest. This was a feat few thought would ever be possible.

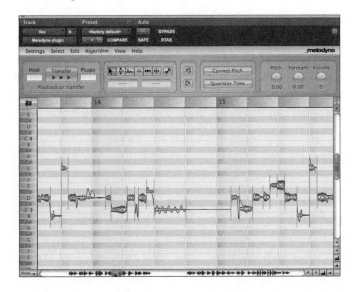

Figure 19-1: Melodyne's pitch correction in action

Melodyne still remains one of the most impressive technical breakthroughs for digital recording in memory. The jury is still out on the simple question of whether or not pitch correction is killing the public's perception of art and musicianship. No matter what side of the debate you sit on, if you want perfectly in tune vocals, it's just a plug-in away.

Figure 19-1 shows Melodyne in action.

Pitch to MIDI

One of the most vexing problems in recording has always been the exclusivity of MIDI controllers. Historically, if you wanted to input MIDI, you used a keyboard or drum pad. With virtual instruments changing the way that musicians make sound, MIDI is as important as ever.

Guitarists have always wanted to get into MIDI, but the complexities of the instrument made this a challenge. A MIDI controller is a simple mechanical switch, which is why we've seen keyboard controllers drop in price in recent years. For a guitar to transmit MIDI, a complex process called pitch-to-MIDI is required. A computer listens to each pitch on the guitar, calculates the pitch, converts it to MIDI, and sends it out a MIDI jack. If this sounds complex, you're right! It is.

MIDI guitar has been around since the late 1970s when manufacturers started trying to get guitarists into the largely keyboard-only world. Early attempts at pitch-to-MIDI conversion were slow and plagued with high latency and errors. If you're a guitarist who tried MIDI guitar, you probably weren't impressed. Like all technology, advances yield better results. In the past few years, MIDI guitar has improved dramatically.

QUESTION

Can any guitar be a MIDI guitar?
MIDI guitar only requires a special pickup, which can be attached to almost any guitar. There are even guitars from Godin that ship with the pickup already installed. Gibson's new Dark Fire guitar also offers an interface to MIDI through the standard Roland 13-pin interface that both Roland and AXON use.

There are two main companies in the MIDI guitar game: Roland and AXON. Roland has been involved with MIDI guitar since the beginning and has kept the format alive throughout the years. Roland makes the GI-20 and the VG-99, both of which offer MIDI guitar conversion (the VG-99 does a whole lot more than just MIDI and is worth a look), while AXON has the AX 50 and AX 100. Both Roland and AXON do an amazing job of converting a guitar output to MIDI.

If you're a guitarist, you owe it to yourself to check out MIDI guitar. MIDI guitar will unlock the world of MIDI, synthesis, virtual instruments, and notation to any guitarist. It's amazingly cool! Famous guitarists like Pat Metheny and John McLaughlin have used MIDI guitar for years.

Elastic Time

In Pro Tools 7.4, Digidesign introduced a new technology called Elastic Time that changed the way to you could work with audio in Pro Tools. Elastic Time didn't take place in a separate window; you did it right in the main edit window, in line with all of your other MIDI and audio tracks. Elastic Time made editing the timing of audio as flexible as MIDI. In a MIDI sequence, you can easily shift notes in time. With audio, this was nearly impossible. You could edit, slicing up audio regions and reorganizing them, but it was very difficult and never sounded right.

Elastic Time allowed you to take an audio region and change the timing of each individual note. For example, you can start with a drum loop and move a snare drum hit earlier or later in the same drum loop without any change in the quality of the audio.

You can quantize all of the audio events to a grid just like you do with MIDI. You can even conform Elastic Time events to a groove template, so all of your tracks can have the same rhythmic feel. Elastic Time works on monophonic audio, polyphonic audio, and rhythmic/loop-based music. It even has a setting for varispeed, which is the old style tape speedup and slowdown effects. Figure 19-2 shows an audio region with Elastic Time switched on.

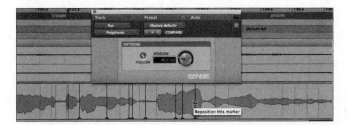

Figure 19-2: Pro Tool's Elastic Time

In Figure 19-2 the vertical white lines are called warp markers. You can drag these freely to change the exact placement of any audio event and you can even add your own warp markers. Elastic Time is a boon for rhythmic editing and is one of the coolest things to come to the DAW market in a long time. Other manufacturers have time stretching, but what makes Elastic Time so special is the quality of the algorithm. Time stretching has historically degraded the audio when used in anything other than small doses. Elastic Time allowed a greater range of time stretching with minimal degradation of audio quality. The ability to move an individual rhythmic event and audio quantization is nothing short of revolutionary for Pro Tools users.

Audio Analysis

Have you ever wanted to see exactly what was going on in your mixes? It's easy enough to understand EQ, but it's sometimes hard to know which knob to turn and why. Wouldn't it be great if you could see what was going on, frequency by frequency, so you knew what to tweak? Better yet, you could use your favorite commercial mixes as a point of comparison and learn from the masters. You can! The digital age has brought some great advances in audio analysis.

One of the first programs to do this in real time is Metric Halo's Spectra-Foo, which started life as a Pro Tools TDM plug-in and now runs as a stand-alone application on Mac OS X. There are other audio analysis programs, but many professionals still consider SpectraFoo the best of the bunch.

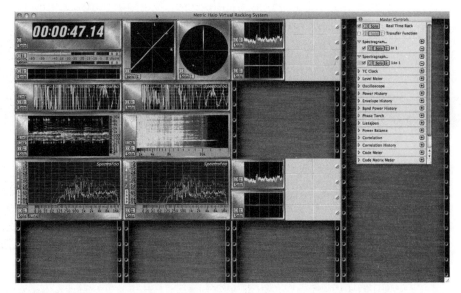

Figure 19-3: Top to bottom: Spectragram and Spectragraph in Metric Halo's SpectraFoo

SpectraFoo offers a bevy of tools. You can see your mix in a spectragram, which shows frequencies on the Y axis. A frequency's strength is shown by the color it registers, much like thermal imaging for audio. You can easily see what frequencies are present and how strong they are. You can look at a spectragraph, which shows frequencies along the X axis, while the strength of that frequency is on the Y axis. This simple graph shows you, in real time, what's in your mix and what's not. Audio analysis tools show you more than just frequency; they can help maintain phase coherency, correlation, and level metering with different ballistics. Figure 19-3 shows SpectraFoo in action

Logic has frequency analysis built into their Channel EQ plug-ins. You can get audio analysis plug-ins and add them into your favorite DAW. Check out companies like Audiofile Engineering, Blue Cat Audio, and RNDigital Labs for audio analysis tools that you can integrate into your DAWs.

Audio Restoration

Have you ever had a really great recording that was plagued by a few pesky problems? Did a cell phone ring during recording? Do you pick up hum from a single-coil equipped guitar? There are myriad problems you can have when working with audio. New computer tools can do some amazing

things to repair audio. Boston-based iZotope has released RX, a full suite of audio restoration tools. It's great for all forms of audio restoration and for taking out hum, broadband noises, and clicks and pops, which makes it great for digitizing vinyl. Figure 19-4 shows RX in action.

RX works as a standalone application and as a plug-in in every major DAW. RX is simply amazing. You can even remove

Figure 19-4: iZotope's RX

chair squeaks and cell phone rings from live performances with RX. Buzzing guitars and bad electricity are easy to fix with RX. Even wind noise from an outdoor performance was no match for RX. RX isn't the only restoration tool; you can find noise reduction built into some DAWs and available as plug-ins from several manufacturers.

CHAPTER 20

Share Your Music

You've written your music, gotten your equipment, gotten your software, learned to use everything, and have finally finished mixing and mastering your hit record. You're ready to take the world by storm. People are knocking down your door trying to . . . wait a minute . . . people! You haven't gotten your music out there for people to hear. Sure, your family and friends have heard it, but what about the public at large? There's a whole world of potential listeners out there that you need to reach.

Getting Your Mixes Out

For years, the only way to get your music to the masses was through radio, TV, and record stores. Agents, lawyers, and contracts were all a part of what made the music industry go. You needed to have someone believe in you before you could reach ears around the world. Sure, people produced recordings locally and had albums, cassettes, or CDs manufactured to sell at shows. Some even had local airplay, but getting beyond the local market was extremely difficult on a good day. The chances of having someone on the other side of the world hear your music were almost nonexistent. That's all changed.

Creating Tracks

The first things you need to do to get your music out are to mix and master your songs. To mix your songs, you need to set the levels and panorama of your tracks so that they sound as you want them to sound when others will play back the final mix on their computer, MP3 player, or stereo. You can add effects to individual channels and on the master channel to achieve the sound you desire. Make sure none of your tracks are clipping, and then you're ready to bounce the track down to a single stereo audio file. Every DAW has a bounce function for this reason. Once you have bounced down all of your songs, you should master them. This involves creating a consistent sound and volume level from one track to the next, so that they sound like they all belong together.

One way to help ensure that your tracks stand out is to normalize them. During this process, the application you are using analyzes an entire audio file, finds the highest peak, and raises the level of that peak to the maximum volume possible before clipping. It then raises the volume of the entire audio file relative to that peak. Check out Chapter 17 for more in-depth mixing and mastering techniques. Once you have done all of this, you're ready to get your music out!

Distributing Your Tracks

The world is getting smaller. The Internet age has completely changed how we communicate.

For example, a small news item can be sent from one person to another almost instantly, and it can gain a life of its own, becoming a huge story within a few hours. Music benefits from this kind of worldwide access too. Someone can browse the Internet from their home in Anytown, USA and discover brilliant artists from parts of the world they've never even heard of. People all over the world find new music online everyday. Your music belongs out there too!

Formatting Your Music

On the Internet, most music is distributed in MP3 or AAC formats. MP3 is the standard format that most people use on their websites and on social networking sites, while AAC is the format that is used in the iTunes music store. Both are compressed audio formats. This means they don't require as much storage space on your hard drive as WAV files do. When you convert an audio file to a compressed format, the application uses complex algorithms to shrink the file size by removing some of the information, mostly sub- and ultrasonic information, to reduce it to about 10 percent of its original size. This makes the file easier to distribute on the Internet because it takes much less time to upload and download.

You can use the iTunes application to convert your songs to MP3 or AAC. First you need to decide which format you want to use.

MP3 is best for most Internet uses. You can select MP3 by opening iTunes preferences and clicking on the Import Settings button. In the Import Using menu, select MP3 Encoder. Now when you add music to your iTunes Library, it will automatically convert it to MP3.

Once you have added a track, right-click on it and select Get Info. This opens up a window that gives you the ability to enter information about the song—its title, artist, genre, and so on. When you are done adding the information you want to add, click OK. All the information you added in that window is embedded in the MP3 file, so other people will be able to see it when they download your song.

MySpace Music

Now that you have converted your songs to MP3s, it's time to get your music on the net! One of the largest and most important sites on the Internet for artists who are trying to get their music out is MySpace. MySpace is a social networking site where everyday people can join, find their own friends, and find other people with similar interests. For musicians, it's a great place to share their music and promote their songs.

There are a few different kinds of MySpace accounts. To create a musician account, go to *www.myspace.com* and click the Sign Up button near the upper right corner of the page. This takes you to a page with a form you can fill out to join. Guess what? This isn't the form you need to fill out, and this is what confuses many musicians.

If you look to the right side of the form, you will see that there are three kinds of accounts you can sign up for—musician, comedian, and film-maker. In the box for musicians, click the Sign Up Here link and fill out the form on the page that link opens. It asks for your e-mail address and for a password of your choosing. Next you need to put the name you are using to promote your music. Are you going to use your own name, a pseudonym, or a band name? This is where you enter that information. Under that box, you select the genre that best describes your music. This makes it easier for fans of a particular style of music to find you!

Figure 20-1: A MySpace music page

You can now edit your profile to add information about you or your band, upload photos, tell people where your upcoming gigs are, and—most importantly—add your music. Click the Edit Profile link to access all of these features. Once you have reached the Edit Profile page, select Manage Featured Songs to upload your MP3s to MySpace.

You can decide whether you want other users to have your songs play in their profiles, whether your songs will automatically play when someone comes to your MySpace page, and whether the songs will be randomized when people come to your page. Then click the Add Songs to Your Profile link in the Current Songs box at the upper right corner of the page. The page that opens asks you to enter the song title and other information like the album name, the year it was released, and the lyrics if you so desire. There is also a box you can check to let other users download your song. Once you click the Update button, you are directed to a page that asks you to upload your MP3 to MySpace. Click Choose File, find the MP3 on your hard drive, click Choose, and then click Upload. Your song is now on MySpace, ready to be heard by the masses!

Selling on iTunes

Now that you're on MySpace, you're getting some positive attention from people on the Internet, and you want to try making a little money from your music. It's time to try to find a record company, right? There's no other way to sell your music on the Internet, right? Wrong. Anyone can have their music placed on iTunes. How, you ask? TuneCore.

TuneCore (*www.tunecore.com*) is a service that charges you a series of small fees to place your music on iTunes, Napster, Amazon MP3, Rhapsody, and eMusic, among others. It's pretty simple. As of this printing, TuneCore charges you 99¢ for each track you want to sell, and 99¢ per store you want to put your songs on. They also charge $19.98 per album to maintain the album on their servers for one year. So, if you were to make a ten-song album that you wanted to place on ten of the stores that TuneCore has access to, it would cost you $9.90 to upload your ten tracks to TuneCore. Then it would cost an additional $9.90 to put the album on the ten stores you selected. Finally, add in the yearly $19.98 maintenance fee. That comes to a grand total of $37.98 for distribution of your album! All royalties go to you. If you want to have your album up for another year, it just costs another $19.98 for maintenance.

One thing to be aware of: you must upload your music to TuneCore in WAV format. If you recorded your music to AIFF, you can convert your music to WAV using iTunes. Just change the Import Setting to WAV and add you your AIFF files into your iTunes Library.

CD Baby

Maybe you've decided you want to make CDs of your music, but you don't know how you're going to sell them online. Never fear. CD Baby (*www .cdbaby.com*) is another Internet site for distributing your music. Originally designed as a site for musicians to sell their CDs, CD Baby also sells downloadable MP3s. CD Baby handles things a little differently than TuneCore. They handle most of the work, and as a result they charge a little more. You send them five CDs, and they open one, rip and upload the music, scan the artwork, and create a webpage for your album. This costs you a one-time $35 fee as of this writing. They also take 9 percent of every MP3 sale and $4 of every CD sale, but you are allowed to price your music as you see fit.

Other Marketing Channels

Remember, the Internet is a vast, open market with new distribution methods appearing frequently. Keep your ear to the ground to find out what "the next big thing" in networking and marketing will be. Whether it's music technology or marketing strategy, you always want to stay ahead of the curve!

Facebook

Facebook (*www.facebook.com*), the immensely popular site for social networking, is a great place to explore music connections. You can find and add musicians to your list of friends and use the Facebook events system to advertise your next gig or CD release. You can also use the fan pages to promote your music and gigs. Facebook and other social networking sites are great in that your network grows with each and every new connection you make.

Twitter

Twitter (*www.twitter.com*) has exploded in popularity recently. If you haven't checked out Twitter, it's a new micro-blogging service that's becoming an important tool in social media. With Twitter, you post small microblogs that are limited to 140 characters. Since the character limit is small, it's perfect for posting from cell phones and smart phones. People can follow you on Twitter and learn about what you're up to. Musicians are using Twitter to expand their audience and keep in touch with their fans. You can announce gigs, new tunes, or new albums on iTunes. You can learn a great deal about new trends in technology just from following the right people on Twitter, and it's a really interesting way to get information out.

Wordpress

The other promotional avenue to explore is full-on blogging. When blogging first started, it was fairly bland, only giving you access to text-based posts. Nowadays, blogging has turned into a rich web experience. Wordpress (*www.wordpress.com*) is the open-source blogging platform that makes it possible for anyone to blog in style. Because it's open-source, it's not only free, it's in active development. A Wordpress blog can look like anything you want, thanks to the thousands of pre-made templates and add-ons available. A nicely made Wordpress site looks like a website, not a blog. You can add pictures, music, and video. Wordpress could be a perfect landing spot for your band to showcase their music and recordings.

CHAPTER 21

Tips for Recording a Demo and Getting Some Work

Recording a demo is one of the major reasons to invest in a home studio. Many of you probably got into home recording specifically for this reason. So, as a culmination of all of your experience and knowledge, it's time to get to work on a demo recording. After your demo is complete, we'll put it to work for you—gigs and recording contracts await!

So You Want to Make a Record?

It's time to stop fooling around—you need a demo recording in order to further your career, get gigs, and spread your music to a wider audience. At some point it became clear to you that you can do this yourself, at home. For the cost of one professional-level demo, you can start building the studio of your dreams and record as many demos as you want. Now that you've learned some techniques for recording and honed your skills, it's time to work on the details of the process.

Getting Organized

Organizational skills are critical to getting anything done—and not just on a demo. Too many groups decide to start a demo without thinking it out, and eight months later they still aren't done. You should have a clear plan of what you're going to do and how you're going to do it. Here is a list of things to consider:

- What material will you include?
- What purpose will the demo fulfill?
- Are you well enough equipped to handle the project?
- Are you well enough rehearsed?

These are just some of the things to think over. Consider this: If you were going into a pro studio at an hourly rate, you'd go in prepared and well rehearsed so you wouldn't waste your money. Don't treat yourself and your home studio any differently; strive to be as productive as you can be.

ESSENTIAL

Being serious and productive in your home studio does not mean that you shouldn't have any fun. The pressure-free environment of recording at home is a major plus. Plus, you'll have some solid material for a bonus release of outtakes and b-sides!

Setting Up a Session

Plan your dates and session times in advance. Treat this just like anything else—have a goal for when you'd like to finish. A lot of this process depends on the size of your group, the complexity of your music, and what kind of studio you own. Bottom line: Approach the sessions just as you would in a pay studio. Too many times bands encounter the "we can do it next week" thinking and things keep getting put off later and later. Just because you aren't paying someone else per hour, don't let that change the efficiency and drive behind your own work.

Picking a Convenient Spot

Where will you record the demo? You might own the equipment, but your living conditions might not be suitable for live drums or loud guitars. Maybe you know someone who has a large basement you could use. Finding an adequate spot is key; the fewer compromises the better. If you're really in a pinch for space, you might be able to rent rehearsal spaces that are well soundproofed and that fit the bill. Sometimes opting to pay for a larger room in order to record the full band all at once may be a better option than playing one track at a time in your basement. Your demo will be your personal calling card and the key that will open many doors for you. Opt for the scenario that makes you sound better, even at a cost.

Rehearse, Rehearse, Rehearse!

Entering the studio, no matter what level studio, should be the last step in a long process of preparation and rehearsals. There is nothing worse than wasting time because you have a loose idea of what you're doing. The studio is usually a place to capture a final product. The only exception to this is when you go into your home studio specifically to write music together and record it. Many bands work this way—most with the luxury of booking eight months in a studio and having the recording company foot the bill. The other exception is to try recording your rehearsals. You might get a good enough take during a rehearsal to make into a demo.

The Fine Details

Depending on your situation, the details of recording a demo will be different from case to case. Variables such as the number of players, space limitations, and equipment all play a role in deciding how you'll go about accomplishing your task. Here are some common scenarios and ways to work with them to the fullest.

Solo Demos

If you're working by yourself, it's a little easier to get organized because there are no other schedules to organize and generally you work when you want to. As most recording sessions do, you should probably start with a drum track. If your music doesn't need drums, find the track that has the strongest rhythmic elements, such as a strummed acoustic guitar, for example. Recording those elements first will give you a strong rhythmic base to lay the other tracks on top of. Once your rhythm tracks are down, there's no set order to how you should record the remaining tracks, although many people like to record the vocals last. If you use the studio as a compositional tool and write as you go, you might go about this process differently, and that's just fine—whatever works for you.

FACT

There's no set way to make a record. Everyone works differently. Find out what works best for you and work it to your advantage. If you're a night owl, make sure to invest in some soundproofing so you can work at night with disturbing your neighbors and family.

Group Demos

Group demos require a little more planning because you'll likely have more technical hurdles and variables to deal with. One such hurdle is equipment. Suppose you picked up a home studio for yourself and joined a band later. Your current gear might not be the best for group work. The big question is, will you want the band to play together, or do you want to do it track by track, one player at a time? A few things influence this decision.

Do you have the space for a live demo? For many, fitting four or more players plus live drums into a recording space isn't a possibility. Even if you do have the space, can you capture instruments well enough to minimize bleed-through from microphone to microphone? And does your recording equipment/interface allow enough simultaneous inputs? Once you start recording a full band, you enter the "big leagues" of home recording, and the equipment that accommodates this can be expensive. You might be forced to record one or a few instruments at a time, building up a multitrack arrangement if your gear is limited in this fashion. Don't worry; many big-name albums are produced this way by choice, not by limitation.

Multitracking One Player at a Time

If you need to record one player at a time, there are a few things you can do to help you start smoothly. First, record the drums. You will thank yourself for having a rhythm track down first. Bass guitar usually comes next. Then you can record the guitar and keys, finally adding in the vocals. The hardest thing about recording a group track by track is a certain feeling of disconnection when you split a group up like this. After all, you don't rehearse this way! Some of the magic and interaction between players can be lost. It's hard to get a vibe and a feel going when you break up the instruments, but the feeling of disconnection can be overcome. On the bright side, one player performing at a time means the overdubs and mistakes can be fixed with much less hassle.

ESSENTIAL

When recording any direct instrument—one that doesn't use a microphone—nothing says you can't have the rest of the band playing along. Since there are no microphones involved, you won't hear the other instruments on the recording. Having the other players there might help the feel tremendously.

Using a Click Track

Do yourself a favor and record with a click track, especially if you multitrack your demos. Live bands can usually regulate a good tempo together, especially one that breathes naturally, but when you take that element away, you might need a click to hold things together. In addition, it will help lock everything together anyway!

If you have drums, use the click track when recording the drums. Once that track is done, the click is no longer necessary because the drums act as a click from that point on.

Being Productive

Making the most of what you have, especially your time, is crucial. Here are a few pointers to get you going along the way. First of all, have a plan. Know exactly what you're going to record, when you're going to do it, and in what order things need to be accomplished. The more complex your band and recording situation, the more work you need to put into these preliminary steps. It might seem like overkill, but constructing a solid battle plan will make things go much more smoothly for all involved. You'll most likely have more fun and have a better final product, too!

Sticking to a Schedule

Try your best to set a realistic schedule for how long you think it will take to record each element of your demo. Just because multitrack audio allows you to go back as many times as you want doesn't necessarily mean that you should. Set time limits for various parts of your sessions to help the recording move forward. For example, set aside an afternoon for the guitar solos and promise yourself that whatever sounds the best that day is what gets to be on the demo. Period. Remember, it's a demo.

Budgeting

What will this cost you? Maybe nothing. If you have a home studio capable of doing what you want and you have the space and time, this might be a no-brainer. But for many people, extra costs might be involved—additional microphones, renting out ample space for recording, and so on. Budgeting is a responsibility that everyone in the project should share equally. You might have invested in the recording machine alone, but everyone involved can help split some of the additional costs such as studio time, additional microphones, and any other accessories that are needed.

Studio Log Sheets

Keep a log of each session you do and document details such as what microphones were used on what instruments, approximate microphone placements, microphone preamp settings, effect settings, and any other pertinent information you might need later. If you need to go back to fix or change something, you can get the sound the same by using the exact same variables for each instrument listed on your log. Log sheets like this are standard in pro studios. It's just a good idea to keep track of what's going on from song to song.

Keep Everything

There's no such thing as a bad take. A mistake here and there is no reason to delete anything. Hard drive space is dirt cheap and getting cheaper by the minute. Almost every DAW system is nondestructive when it comes to recording audio, so you will keep all the old takes unless you specifically choose to delete them. It's a good idea to save everything you record because you never know what you're going to need later on. Especially in the case of multitrack recording, you might be able to assemble a "super" take, combining performances into one perfect take from past performances. If you ever make it big, you'll have your first "bonus" materials on your first greatest hits album: alternate takes!

Finalizing

At this point, you've completed the tracking stages and are ready to finalize the project through mixing and mastering at home or in a professional mastering house. It's time to turn your demo into a reality.

If you're working alone, mix to your heart's content. However, it's always a good idea to get some fresh ears on your work every once in a while. Opinions do count here. If you're working in a band situation, don't mix alone, even if you have the equipment. It's a band project and everyone's opinions count. Listening to others ensures that you get everyone's input and help. The more ears on a mix, the better it will most likely come out. Once you've decided on a final mix candidate, burn out a few copies and listen to the work on as many different systems as possible. Try cars, home stereos, computers, iPods—you name it. If it sounds good and clean, you might be able to put it out for the world to hear. If it doesn't, go back to the studio to even out the rough parts.

ESSENTIAL

When mixing for extended periods of time, it's important to pace yourself and take breaks. Ear fatigue can make mixing very difficult. For every hour you mix, take a fifteen-minute break. Get up, walk around, grab a bite to eat, and let your mind wander.

In recording, mastering is the last stage in album production. For a demo, however, you might not need it. Mastering generally deals with loudness, balance, and song sequence. If you've done a good job with levels during your recording, you might not need any loudness maximizing to make your signal strong enough. Depending on the purpose of the demo, mastering might not be worth the extra money. If the demo is not destined for release and is solely for solicitation of work and record contracts, mastering might not be necessary. If you feel that you need it, try mastering at home. There are many mastering plug-ins available for the computer-recording world.

Optimal Sound Quality

How does it sound? Good? Really good? What, exactly, sounds good? Is it just that you captured a good performance, or did you create a sound that stands on its own? If this demo is going to serve you well, it should sound as great as it can. You saved a ton of money recording it at home, and you also kept all of your creative control. Now's the time to ask the hard questions. Did you mix it as well as someone else could? Does it need to be mastered? Did this demo turn out to be album quality after all? If you answer yes to any of these questions, you should investigate some options.

If you intend to distribute your recordings, gain radio airplay, or establish music industry ties, your recording needs to sound professional. Professional sound doesn't mean just mixing, noise, balance, and effects, but more important, loudness. Loudness is one of the most critical parts of the mastering process, and it's one that should not be overlooked. We've all been frustrated by commercials that play too loudly on TV, forcing you to lower the volume—and then, *bam!* The next show comes on normal volume and you can't hear a thing. That rogue commercial wasn't properly mastered.

Imagine that your demo gets into the hands of a club owner who takes the time to listen to your work. If she can't hear it properly due to mixing and mastering issues, then you might have closed that door. It might make sense to take your work to a professional mixing and mastering studio to help you put the finishing touches on your work. If something doesn't sound right and you're not quite sure how to fix it, investigate some professional options. You'll also learn a lot.

ALERT

Like diamonds, recordings are forever! That quick two-song demo you gave out at your first gig might appear on the Internet after you have hit it big. It would be a shame to have a poor performance follow you around. You'd be amazed at how file sharing, legal or not, has made it easy to spread music around the globe. Anything is fair game.

Don't let obvious mistakes remain part of your recording. No matter what your original intent was, this demo has taken on a deeper purpose if you've decided to go public. Even if you started out wanting to simply utilize your new gear and you got a better result than you expected, polish it as best you can. Fix the mistakes your public will hear. If you intend to sell this recording, your demo is your personal calling card. Obvious mistakes in your recording ring out as clearly as spelling errors in a typed resume. You never know who's going to listen to it.

Define Your Purpose

When you're working on recorded music, it's really important to understand that there are different standards for different purposes. What's this for? Is it just to get a few local gigs? To get a record deal? If you're looking for a local gig, you might be able to get away with slight imperfections and rough edges in the recordings. But if you're looking for a record deal, then the stakes change and the rules are different.

Getting Gigs

If you're looking to score some gigs, you need to do your homework. When looking into clubs, find out what kinds of crowds and what sorts of people frequent the establishments. You need to ask yourself, "What will this owner or booking agent want to hear?" While it would be wonderful to believe the owner is into music for music's sake, you're not being realistic. Live music plays one role—to make the establishment money.

ALERT

When handing out a CD for a prospective gig, make sure to place your contact info and phone number as many places as possible. Make sure to mark the CD itself, because CD cases often get separated from their contents. Don't assume the proprietor is going to do to your website to listen to music. Always give a hard-copy CD in addition to any online formats you may choose to use.

In turn, you are compensated based on several factors. You may get a cut of the door, meaning that you get paid a percentage of the admission fees. If no one shows up, you don't get paid. You may also get a cut of the bar tab, but this is becoming increasingly rare these days. Bottom line, proprietors want to hear music that fits into their normal mold, and they rarely take chances on new formats and risky groups.

With that in mind, you need to customize your demo to address the most important need for each potential client. What that means is putting what you consider your best and strongest material for a particular client on the first track of the tape or CD. Chances are, the client won't even listen to the second track. It's very common to put together multiple demos with different track orders and song content for different purposes. One size might not fit all in this case.

On the first track, which might get only one minute of play time, the club owner simply wants to hear that you aren't a joke. He most likely won't listen very carefully to your content. The club owner wants to make sure you fit into the mold so that regular customers are happy with your sound and new customers are drawn in by it.

Getting a Record Deal

If you're an ambitious sort, you might want to seek a record deal. After all, your home studio has allowed you to produce quality content just for this purpose. While sound quality is always important, it really comes into play if you want to get a record deal. Chances are, the person hearing your music is involved with music production and listens to music all day long from bands that either go the home studio route or pay top dollar for professional demos. If your recording sticks out because of poor quality, soft levels, and other anomalies, you might be dismissed right off the bat. That's why getting it right the first time is ideal—you might never get a second chance.

Do You Need a Record Deal?

This is an interesting question, one that's changed dramatically over the last few years. With the success of the iTunes Music Store, independent bands can get into the same distribution channels as the big record labels. It used to be that getting a CD into a record store was a big deal and required a substantial investment on the record company's part. Nowadays, anyone can get into the iTunes store. But that brings about new challenges for musicians. Since the iTunes store is so crowded, how do you stand out? You'll need to promote your music in as many places as you can. Give out links to your website, give out free sample CDs, and get your music into as many places in the virtual world as humanly possible. The beauty is that with iTunes, you can sell just as well as any band. The only deciding factor is the quality of your music. Welcome to the new world!

Making Good Connections

Making blind submissions (sending your recording to a club or company you've never contacted or made a connection with) is as good as sending your demo to the trash. Most record companies on principal throw out all blind submissions due to the large number of submissions they receive—you aren't the only one who wants a record deal, you know! Club owners often act the same way. They open the envelope, see a CD they don't recognize, and toss it into the trash. You have to make some connections beforehand.

Talk to the Right People

In the case of clubs and other performance venues, a simple phone call beforehand will usually suffice. let them know who you are and ask if they are accepting submissions. They might respond with questions about your music and the audience you typically play for—this is usual. After you make the initial contact, send your demo by mail or preferably show up in person and place your demo right in their hands. After that, back off. Give them time to listen and then follow up a few days later.

QUESTION

How can I get in touch with agents and managers in my area?
Ask other artists and bands who they've worked with and had good experiences with. For every good agent, there are ten agents who won't help your chances of success. Start with someone you know has been successful. It's all about who you know and their connections.

Making recording industry contacts is much more difficult. The sheer number of people who try to initiate contact with artist relations persons makes this part difficult. You might be very hard-pressed to get anyone on the phone at all. Most companies will tell you they don't accept unsolicited submissions, which is a nice way of saying: Don't call us; we'll call you. How can you overcome these difficulties? Many times agents and managers can make these connections for you. If you're serious about getting into the industry, seeking the help of an agent or manager could open doors. Really good agents and managers already have connections and close ties with record companies, and their submissions often have a chance of getting noticed.

Fill a Need

The other aspect of doing your homework is understanding what "they" want. "They" can be record companies, clubs, venues, and concert promoters . . . you name it. The name of the game is filling a need. If you don't read this part correctly, then your demo will end up in the trash again. When looking into prospective avenues to distribute your demo, make sure you're close to what "they" are looking for. For example, you're wasting your time and money sending a heavy metal demo to a jazz club. The same goes for record companies—make sure you've got a similar style to other artists on the company's current roster. Otherwise, the company won't take your demo seriously and you'll end up simply wasting your money.

Be Professional

The presentation of your demo makes a big difference, so package your demo in a great-looking press kit. A basic, professional-looking press kit includes these elements:

- **A CD:** Always give a physical CD, even if your music is online. Just about everyone's car has a CD player. Not everyone has Internet access all the time.
- **A label with contact information and track listing:** Make sure you place a nice label on your CD—don't just write on it with a black marker!

Label it using a very inexpensive adhesive CD labeling kit on your home computer. Include contact names, phone numbers, and track listings.

- **A group biography:** Include a well-written, typed bio of your group. The more information you provide the better. You might want to list places you've played, awards you've won, and so on.
- **A picture (optional):** A picture helps to humanize the group and elevate a boring press kit and make it a human reality.

All of these elements should be packed in a nice folder or bound together in some way so they don't get lost or separated.

No matter how good this demo of yours is, if you don't act professionally, you're not going to get very far. Anyone who's been involved in the recording industry will tell you that product is not always as important as personality. Getting your demo to work for you will invariably involve phone calls and mailings, and it's to your advantage to speak and write as professionally as you can. That means being polite and considerate during your phone calls, especially when talking to the people who book gigs for concerts and clubs. These people are often overwhelmed with other responsibilities, so they might appear to blow you off. It's so important to keep your perspective here and exercise an extra bit of patience. Remember, you need them; they don't need you. There are other demos they can likely choose from, so make a good impression by being nice.

When writing and e-mailing, make sure to use good English and practice your written communication skills. Just because it's becoming normal not to capitalize words in e-mail and text messages doesn't mean it's correct. Don't take that habit with you when you correspond with prospective clients. And please, please spell-check your work!

The more pleasant, easy, and fair you are to work with, the better. This will pay off in your search for contacts, in winning repeat gigs, and in finding success in putting your demo to work.

Copyright Protection

One thing we've left out of this discussion until now is how legally to protect your songs. If you're writing your own material, you own the intellectual property fully. But if you don't take the proper steps to protect yourself, you might get yourself in trouble, or worse yet, give away your music. Here's the lowdown on the copyright process and how to secure your rights.

From the minute you record music, you own it. The law protects you as the creator of the work. However, if things get messy later on, you might regret not having filed a formal copyright application with the U.S. government. It's easy and inexpensive. All you have to do is fill out a few forms and send a check for each work, which typically totals $30 for a full album. If someone tries to use your music in the future without your permission, you will have a much better footing in court if you choose to litigate for copyright infringement of intellectual property. It's so simple to do; you really should take a few minutes and do it.

FACT

For more information on how to obtain copyrights, go to *www.copyright. gov*, the website of the U.S. Copyright Office. Websites and resources for other topics of interest to the home studio owner are listed in Appendix B in the back of this book.

The American Society of Composers, Authors, and Publishers (ASCAP) and Broadcast Music, Inc. (BMI) are two organizations that serve to protect copyrighted music and its writers and publishers. Typically, you will need to join both ASCAP and BMI after you sign a record contract; most likely someone at the recording company will take care of setting all this up for you. If your song gets played on the radio, the organization—ASCAP or BMI—would make sure you get paid the proper royalty. It's very rare to have music on the radio without a label behind you—not impossible, but not common.

Selling It

If you plan on selling your music yourself, you will enjoy a few benefits and face a few hurdles, too! The first benefit is that you keep all the money after you subtract the cost of making the product. Nowadays, you'll make more money per CD or download if you sell the music yourself than if a record company sells it for you and gives you a cut. The only difference is the volume of sales you can achieve with a company backing versus selling it yourself. In either case, before you sell your music, you have to get it ready for duplication if you want to make physical CD copies.

CD Duplication

The simplest way to duplicate your music is to burn it at home on a CD burner. The CD burner can be either a standalone system or part of your computer. Blank CDs continue to plummet in price, so the cost of making CDs at home is an attractive option. You can even produce professional-looking computer-printed labels for the front of the CD and the insert materials for the jewel case. Considering the price of good-quality printers these days, you can yield some impressive results at home with a relatively small investment.

FACT

If you're opting to use iTunes to sell all of your music, do consider having some CDs available, even if you burn them yourself. The Internet is great, but there is an immediacy to physical CDs. Plus, a CD is a tangible item that you can hold in your hand. Even if your fans never put the CD in a player, they will have your band's name attached to a physical product. They can look you up online and get your music digitally if it's easier for them.

For those who want to leave the duplication to the professionals, you'll find many options. Usually, these duplication companies deal in large runs, say of 500 or more CDs at a time. While you can order fewer, the difference in price between 100 and 500 is small enough that most people opt for more. You submit either a burned CD or individual stereo audio files and the company takes care of the rest. You can supply the art or pay to have it designed for you. Professionally made CDs look better than homemade ones because the duplication company uses better printers and it inks the CD labels onto the case rather than applying inexpensive adhesive labels. It also shrink-wraps the CDs in plastic. There are literally hundreds of places that duplicate and package CDs. You can find them by searching the Internet and local music magazines and papers.

Selling at Gigs

Now that you have a CD ready to sell, either from home or a duplication house, the most logical place to start selling it is at your gigs. You can generate a lot of sales and buzz at live shows. Having CDs for sale, especially if you tour around, is essential for promoting yourself, not to mention for making extra money. Most bands that sell CDs at gigs don't charge record-store prices, and this can make the CD attractive to an audience member. If you come across people who don't want to buy your CD, consider having some postcards printed with the same cover art with a link to the iTunes store or another digital distribution site you're using.

ESSENTIAL

The website *www.cdbaby.com* is hooked up with the Apple iTunes Music Store, so any music you sell through CDBaby will also be available for sale through Apple's legal download service. This is a great way to spread your music.

Barcodes

If you plan to sell your CD online or through stores you'll need a barcode. CD manufacturing houses typically provide barcodes, but you can also get them yourself by registering for one through a CD duplication facility. Whenever your CD is purchased, the barcode is read by Sound-Scan, a service that tracks record sales. If you're interested in having real sales data to show a record company, get all of your CDs equipped with barcodes.

Promotion

Promotion and the art of self-promotion are key. Here are some tips on how to get your music heard outside of your immediate area:

- Give away your CD to clubs and restaurants—or any other place that plays music. It's a great way to get heard. With luck, it just might get played, and someone is bound to ask, "What was that?"
- Get your local record stores to stock your CD. It's great exposure.
- Start with your own website. What, you don't have one? Get one! It's now expected that you will have one. Get your CD and sound samples on there too.
- Post a page with a site that hosts songs for free. Sites like *www.mp3.com* are haunted regularly by many adventurous Internet music seekers looking for up-and-coming music. You can create a WordPress blog for free and host your music, or make a MySpace Music page, also for free. You get a simple page with your music, links to your site, and places to buy your CD. Many bands have gotten their start this way and you can too. Harness the power of the Internet.

Promotion is all about creating excitement and buzz about a product. The more work you do to create excitement for your project the better you will do. Use the examples provided or try your own. In the end, success is the end result of a great deal of legwork and hard work. Promotion takes patience and diligence. You can do it!

APPENDIX A

Recording Equipment Manufacturers and Suppliers

Recording Equipment and Software

ABLETON
www.ableton.com
Live recording software

ALESIS
www.alesis.com
Keyboards, effects, and recording devices

ANTARES AUDIO TECHNOLOGIES
www.antarestech.com
Auto-Tune and other plug-ins and hardware

APPLE
www.apple.com
Logic Studio and Apple Macintosh computers

BEHRINGER
www.behringer.com
Full range of entry-level recording equipment

CAKEWALK
www.cakewalk.com
Sonar recording software

CELEMONY
www.celemony.com
Melodyne software

DIGIDESIGN
www.digidesign.com
Pro Tools software and hardware

IK MULTIMEDIA
www.ikmultimedia.com
Computer plug-ins (AmpliTube, SampleTank, T-Racks)

LEXICON
www.lexicon.com
Really nice hardware and software effects

M-AUDIO

www.m-audio.com

Manufactures and distributes everything from audio interfaces to software to MIDI keyboard controllers

MACKIE

www.mackie.com

Mixers, speakers, and control surfaces

MARK OF THE UNICORN

www.motu.com

Digital Performer, MIDI, and audio interfaces

METRIC HALO

www.mhlabs.com

FireWire audio interfaces, plug-ins, and measurement software

NATIVE INSTRUMENTS

www.nativeinstruments.com

Virtual instruments and samplers

PRESONUS

www.presonus.com

Audio equipment for studio recording

ROLAND

www.rolandus.com

Makers of just about everything from keyboards to recording equipment

SIBELIUS

www.sibelius.com

Professional sheet music software

SPECTRASONICS

www.spectrasonics.net

Amazing virtual instruments

STEINBERG

www.steinberg.net

Cubase, Nuendo, Wavelab, and other software

UNIVERSAL AUDIO
www.uaudio.com
High-end recording equipment and the UAD system

WAVES
www.waves.com
Really nice computer-recording plug-ins

YAMAHA
www.yamaha.com
Recording equipment and software

Microphones

AKG MICROPHONES
www.akg.com

ELECTRO-VOICE MICROPHONES
www.electrovoice.com

NEUMANN
www.neumannusa.com

RODE MICROPHONES
www.rode.com.au

SENNHEISER MICROPHONES
www.sennheiser.com

SHURE MICROPHONES
www.shure.com

STUDIO PROJECTS MICROPHONES
www.studioprojects.com

EARTHWORKS
www.earthworksaudio.com

Internet Sites to Shop

www.audiomidi.com
www.musiciansfriend.com
www.samash.com
www.sweetwater.com
www.zzsounds.com

APPENDIX B

Additional Resources

Magazines

COMPUTER MUSIC
www.computermusic.co.uk

ELECTRONIC MUSICIAN
www.emusician.com

EQ
www.eqmag.com

MIX
www.mixonline.com

RECORDING
www.recordingmag.com

SOUND ON SOUND
www.soundonsound.com

TAPE OP
www.tapeop.com

Websites

www.ascap.com
Music licensing

www.bmi.com
Music licensing

www.cdbaby.com
Sell your CD online.

www.groups.yahoo.com
Discussion groups for everything you can imagine, audio too!

www.harmonycentral.com
Music industry news

www.homerecording.com
An informative site

www.loc.gov/copyright
U.S. Copyright Office

www.marcschonbrun.com
Author's site

www.macosxaudio.com
Everything Mac audio

Books

Anderton, Craig. *Multieffects for Musicians*. (New York: Music Sales Corp., 1995).

Anderton, Craig. *Craig Anderton's Home Recording for Musicians*. (New York: Music Sales Corp., 1996).

Anderton, Craig. *MIDI for Musicians*. (New York: Music Sales Corp., 1984).

Anderton, Craig. *Audio Mastering* (Quick Start). (Bremen, Germany: Wizoo., 2002).

Franz, David. *Producing in the Home Studio with Pro Tools*. (Boston: Berklee Press, 2003).

Moulton, Dave. *Golden Ears Audio Eartraining Program*, 4 vol. (8 CDs and manual). (Sherman Oaks, CA: KIQ Productions, 1994).

Woran, John M., and Alan P. Kefauver. *The New Recording Studio Handbook*. (Plainview, NY: ELAR Publishing, 1989).

APPENDIX C

Glossary

algorithm

A computer's set of instruction. In the case of reverb, the algorithm is a computer-generated model of a real reverberant space.

ambience

The sound of the room in which you record.

amplitude

Loudness.

audio loop

Any piece of digital audio that has been recorded and edited to facilitate looping without any additional help.

aux inputs

Where you plug in an effect that requires a blend of effected and non-effected signals.

baffle

Any object that blocks sound, also referred to as a gobo.

bass drums

The lowest frequency in the drum set; also referred to as kick drum.

binary code

The pattern of zeroes and ones that makes up digital media.

bus

A path that audio can take.

cardiod microphone

A device that records sounds directly in front of it.

chorus

An effect that mimics the sound of multiple players.

click track

A steady metronome-like pulse that keeps the band from speeding up or slowing down.

clipping

The result of overloading the input, which causes distortion.

close-miking
Placing a microphone close to a sound source.

compression
An effect that boosts the volume of quieter notes and reduces that of louder ones, evening out the sound.

cross fade
An automatic volume change.

decay
The amount of time it takes for a sound to disappear.

decibel
The measure of the level of sound pressure.

decoding
The conversion of digital representation to analog signals.

delay
A simple effect that copies your signal and re-creates it at a specified interval after you play.

diffusion
A feature that allows you to mimic a room's reflectivity.

digital audio mix
Several audio files read at the same time.

direct input
An instrument that plugs directly into the recorder.

distortion
An effect that changes the tone quality.

editing
The ability to cut, copy, and rearrange recorded music.

effects
Adding signal processing such as reverb, delay, and compression in order to achieve a polished sound.

encoding
The conversion of analog signals to digital representation.

engineering
The art of setting up and placing microphones for optimum sound, getting proper recording levels, running the mixing board, and operating the recording device.

equalization
Boosting or lowering of certain frequencies in a mix.

expander
An effect that increases the range of volume.

figure eight microphone
A recording device that hears sound on two distinct sides.

frequency
The pitch of a sound.

frequency response
The sensitivity of a microphone to certain frequencies of sound.

gain
The volume or loudness of a signal.

gain stage
Any device, such as a mixer or preamplifier, that changes the volume.

humanize
A MIDI effect that inserts intentioned errors to make the sequence feel more human.

insert effect
An effect that can be plugged into only one channel.

keyboard controller
A device that sends MIDI signals to your computer for virtual instruments or sequencing.

latency
The time it takes for your computer to translate the audio (analog) signal of your music to a digital form it can understand and send the signal back to you to hear.

loop
A piece of prerecorded information, one that can repeat over and over again.

mastering
The final stage in the recording process; the process of taking all of the separate songs on an album and putting them together so they sound good together.

microphone
A device that converts acoustic sound pressure to electrical information that can be recorded.

MIDI
Musical instrument digital interface; a standard language that allows electronic instruments and computers to communicate.

mix down
Mixing all the tracks into a single stereo pair suitable for distribution or mastering.

mixing
The art of setting the loudness and sound color of each instrument that you record.

mixing board
A device that allows several sources of sound to be mixed together into any number of outputs.

monophonic signal
A recording signal that can be reproduced using only one speaker.

multitracking
The ability to record one track at a time and build up an arrangement rather than playing all the parts simultaneously.

omnidirectional microphone
A recording device that picks up sounds all around it.

overdubbing
The ability to rerecord certain sections of your performance to perfect the final result.

panning
Side-to-side placement of instruments and voices in the mix.

PCI-E
Peripheral component interconnect express; a standard card that sits inside a desktop computer and adds audio functionality.

phonograph
An invention by Thomas Edison that allowed people to play recorded music on disks in their own homes.

plosives
Certain parts of speech that make certain letters of the alphabet come out with much greater force than others.

pop filter
A screen placed between the microphone and the singer's mouth to stop the plosive from popping the microphone.

postproduction
Anything that happens after the recording sessions; most often, mixing the tracks to a polished, uniform sound.

preamplifier
A device that raises the output of a microphone; used to strengthen and clarify a signal.

preproduction
Everything that happens before the actual recording session.

processor
The brain of the computer, also referred to as the central processing unit or CPU.

production
The actual recording sessions.

proximity effect
When using a microphone, the closer you stand to it, the more bass frequencies come through.

quantize
To place all MIDI notes and events on a rhythmic grid.

RAM
Random access memory; a specialized area where data is stored temporarily while the computer is on.

recording
The transmittal of sound waves onto a device capable of preserving and reproducing that sound.

reverb
A natural occurrence when sound waves reflect and bounce of surfaces; also an effect that mimics this echo.

sound
A combination of frequency and amplitude.

stereophonic signal
A recording signal that uses two speakers: left and right.

sum
To combine many signals.

track levels
Loudness of each track

unidirectional microphone
A recording device that only hears what's directly in front of it.

unity gain
In recording, nothing is added and nothing is subtracted.

USB

Universal serial bus; a means to connect peripherals such as mice and joysticks to computers.

virtual instrument

A synthesizer on your computer.

XY technique

A recording technique that uses two microphones crossing at their heads, pointed in opposite directions, usually at a 90-degree angle from each other.

Index

The EVERYTHING Series!

BUSINESS & PERSONAL FINANCE

Everything® Accounting Book
Everything® Budgeting Book, 2nd Ed.
Everything® Business Planning Book
Everything® Coaching and Mentoring Book, 2nd Ed.
Everything® Fundraising Book
Everything® Get Out of Debt Book
Everything® Grant Writing Book, 2nd Ed.
Everything® Guide to Buying Foreclosures
Everything® Guide to Fundraising, $15.95
Everything® Guide to Mortgages
Everything® Guide to Personal Finance for Single Mothers
Everything® Home-Based Business Book, 2nd Ed.
Everything® Homebuying Book, 3rd Ed., $15.95
Everything® Homeselling Book, 2nd Ed.
Everything® Human Resource Management Book
Everything® Improve Your Credit Book
Everything® Investing Book, 2nd Ed.
Everything® Landlording Book
Everything® Leadership Book, 2nd Ed.
Everything® Managing People Book, 2nd Ed.
Everything® Negotiating Book
Everything® Online Auctions Book
Everything® Online Business Book
Everything® Personal Finance Book
Everything® Personal Finance in Your 20s & 30s Book, 2nd Ed.
Everything® Personal Finance in Your 40s & 50s Book, $15.95
Everything® Project Management Book, 2nd Ed.
Everything® Real Estate Investing Book
Everything® Retirement Planning Book
Everything® Robert's Rules Book, $7.95
Everything® Selling Book
Everything® Start Your Own Business Book, 2nd Ed.
Everything® Wills & Estate Planning Book

COOKING

Everything® Barbecue Cookbook
Everything® Bartender's Book, 2nd Ed., $9.95
Everything® Calorie Counting Cookbook
Everything® Cheese Book
Everything® Chinese Cookbook
Everything® Classic Recipes Book
Everything® Cocktail Parties & Drinks Book
Everything® College Cookbook
Everything® Cooking for Baby and Toddler Book
Everything® Diabetes Cookbook
Everything® Easy Gourmet Cookbook
Everything® Fondue Cookbook
Everything® Food Allergy Cookbook, $15.95
Everything® Fondue Party Book
Everything® Gluten-Free Cookbook
Everything® Glycemic Index Cookbook
Everything® Grilling Cookbook
Everything® Healthy Cooking for Parties Book, $15.95
Everything® Holiday Cookbook
Everything® Indian Cookbook
Everything® Lactose-Free Cookbook
Everything® Low-Cholesterol Cookbook

Everything® Low-Fat High-Flavor Cookbook, 2nd Ed., $15.95
Everything® Low-Salt Cookbook
Everything® Meals for a Month Cookbook
Everything® Meals on a Budget Cookbook
Everything® Mediterranean Cookbook
Everything® Mexican Cookbook
Everything® No Trans Fat Cookbook
Everything® One-Pot Cookbook, 2nd Ed., $15.95
Everything® Organic Cooking for Baby & Toddler Book, $15.95
Everything® Pizza Cookbook
Everything® Quick Meals Cookbook, 2nd Ed., $15.95
Everything® Slow Cooker Cookbook
Everything® Slow Cooking for a Crowd Cookbook
Everything® Soup Cookbook
Everything® Stir-Fry Cookbook
Everything® Sugar-Free Cookbook
Everything® Tapas and Small Plates Cookbook
Everything® Tex-Mex Cookbook
Everything® Thai Cookbook
Everything® Vegetarian Cookbook
Everything® Whole-Grain, High-Fiber Cookbook
Everything® Wild Game Cookbook
Everything® Wine Book, 2nd Ed.

GAMES

Everything® 15-Minute Sudoku Book, $9.95
Everything® 30-Minute Sudoku Book, $9.95
Everything® Bible Crosswords Book, $9.95
Everything® Blackjack Strategy Book
Everything® Brain Strain Book, $9.95
Everything® Bridge Book
Everything® Card Games Book
Everything® Card Tricks Book, $9.95
Everything® Casino Gambling Book, 2nd Ed.
Everything® Chess Basics Book
Everything® Christmas Crosswords Book, $9.95
Everything® Craps Strategy Book
Everything® Crossword and Puzzle Book
Everything® Crosswords and Puzzles for Quote Lovers Book, $9.95
Everything® Crossword Challenge Book
Everything® Crosswords for the Beach Book, $9.95
Everything® Cryptic Crosswords Book, $9.95
Everything® Cryptograms Book, $9.95
Everything® Easy Crosswords Book
Everything® Easy Kakuro Book, $9.95
Everything® Easy Large-Print Crosswords Book
Everything® Games Book, 2nd Ed.
Everything® Giant Book of Crosswords
Everything® Giant Sudoku Book, $9.95
Everything® Giant Word Search Book
Everything® Kakuro Challenge Book, $9.95
Everything® Large-Print Crossword Challenge Book
Everything® Large-Print Crosswords Book
Everything® Large-Print Travel Crosswords Book
Everything® Lateral Thinking Puzzles Book, $9.95
Everything® Literary Crosswords Book, $9.95
Everything® Mazes Book
Everything® Memory Booster Puzzles Book, $9.95

Everything® Movie Crosswords Book, $9.95
Everything® Music Crosswords Book, $9.95
Everything® Online Poker Book
Everything® Pencil Puzzles Book, $9.95
Everything® Poker Strategy Book
Everything® Pool & Billiards Book
Everything® Puzzles for Commuters Book, $9.95
Everything® Puzzles for Dog Lovers Book, $9.95
Everything® Sports Crosswords Book, $9.95
Everything® Test Your IQ Book, $9.95
Everything® Texas Hold 'Em Book, $9.95
Everything® Travel Crosswords Book, $9.95
Everything® Travel Mazes Book, $9.95
Everything® Travel Word Search Book, $9.95
Everything® TV Crosswords Book, $9.95
Everything® Word Games Challenge Book
Everything® Word Scramble Book
Everything® Word Search Book

HEALTH

Everything® Alzheimer's Book
Everything® Diabetes Book
Everything® First Aid Book, $9.95
Everything® Green Living Book
Everything® Health Guide to Addiction and Recovery
Everything® Health Guide to Adult Bipolar Disorder
Everything® Health Guide to Arthritis
Everything® Health Guide to Controlling Anxiety
Everything® Health Guide to Depression
Everything® Health Guide to Diabetes, 2nd Ed.
Everything® Health Guide to Fibromyalgia
Everything® Health Guide to Menopause, 2nd Ed.
Everything® Health Guide to Migraines
Everything® Health Guide to Multiple Sclerosis
Everything® Health Guide to OCD
Everything® Health Guide to PMS
Everything® Health Guide to Postpartum Care
Everything® Health Guide to Thyroid Disease
Everything® Hypnosis Book
Everything® Low Cholesterol Book
Everything® Menopause Book
Everything® Nutrition Book
Everything® Reflexology Book
Everything® Stress Management Book
Everything® Superfoods Book, $15.95

HISTORY

Everything® American Government Book
Everything® American History Book, 2nd Ed.
Everything® American Revolution Book, $15.95
Everything® Civil War Book
Everything® Freemasons Book
Everything® Irish History & Heritage Book
Everything® World War II Book, 2nd Ed.

HOBBIES

Everything® Candlemaking Book
Everything® Cartooning Book
Everything® Coin Collecting Book
Everything® Digital Photography Book, 2nd Ed.

Everything® Drawing Book
Everything® Family Tree Book, 2nd Ed.
Everything® Guide to Online Genealogy, $15.95
Everything® Knitting Book
Everything® Knots Book
Everything® Photography Book
Everything® Quilting Book
Everything® Sewing Book
Everything® Soapmaking Book, 2nd Ed.
Everything® Woodworking Book

HOME IMPROVEMENT

Everything® Feng Shui Book
Everything® Feng Shui Decluttering Book, $9.95
Everything® Fix-It Book
Everything® Green Living Book
Everything® Home Decorating Book
Everything® Home Storage Solutions Book
Everything® Homebuilding Book
Everything® Organize Your Home Book, 2nd Ed.

KIDS' BOOKS

All titles are $7.95
Everything® Fairy Tales Book, $14.95
Everything® Kids' Animal Puzzle & Activity Book
Everything® Kids' Astronomy Book
Everything® Kids' Baseball Book, 5th Ed.
Everything® Kids' Bible Trivia Book
Everything® Kids' Bugs Book
Everything® Kids' Cars and Trucks Puzzle and Activity Book
Everything® Kids' Christmas Puzzle & Activity Book
Everything® Kids' Connect the Dots
    Puzzle and Activity Book
Everything® Kids' Cookbook, 2nd Ed.
Everything® Kids' Crazy Puzzles Book
Everything® Kids' Dinosaurs Book
Everything® Kids' Dragons Puzzle and Activity Book
Everything® Kids' Environment Book $7.95
Everything® Kids' Fairies Puzzle and Activity Book
Everything® Kids' First Spanish Puzzle and Activity Book
Everything® Kids' Football Book
Everything® Kids' Geography Book
Everything® Kids' Gross Cookbook
Everything® Kids' Gross Hidden Pictures Book
Everything® Kids' Gross Jokes Book
Everything® Kids' Gross Mazes Book
Everything® Kids' Gross Puzzle & Activity Book
Everything® Kids' Halloween Puzzle & Activity Book
Everything® Kids' Hanukkah Puzzle and Activity Book
Everything® Kids' Hidden Pictures Book
Everything® Kids' Horses Book
Everything® Kids' Joke Book
Everything® Kids' Knock Knock Book
Everything® Kids' Learning French Book
Everything® Kids' Learning Spanish Book
Everything® Kids' Magical Science Experiments Book
Everything® Kids' Math Puzzles Book
Everything® Kids' Mazes Book
Everything® Kids' Money Book, 2nd Ed.
Everything® Kids' Mummies, Pharaoh's, and Pyramids
    Puzzle and Activity Book
Everything® Kids' Nature Book
Everything® Kids' Pirates Puzzle and Activity Book
Everything® Kids' Presidents Book
Everything® Kids' Princess Puzzle and Activity Book
Everything® Kids' Puzzle Book

Everything® Kids' Racecars Puzzle and Activity Book
Everything® Kids' Riddles & Brain Teasers Book
Everything® Kids' Science Experiments Book
Everything® Kids' Sharks Book
Everything® Kids' Soccer Book
Everything® Kids' Spelling Book
Everything® Kids' Spies Puzzle and Activity Book
Everything® Kids' States Book
Everything® Kids' Travel Activity Book
Everything® Kids' Word Search Puzzle and Activity Book

LANGUAGE

Everything® Conversational Japanese Book with CD, $19.95
Everything® French Grammar Book
Everything® French Phrase Book, $9.95
Everything® French Verb Book, $9.95
Everything® German Phrase Book, $9.95
Everything® German Practice Book with CD, $19.95
Everything® Inglés Book
Everything® Intermediate Spanish Book with CD, $19.95
Everything® Italian Phrase Book, $9.95
Everything® Italian Practice Book with CD, $19.95
Everything® Learning Brazilian Portuguese Book with CD, $19.95
Everything® Learning French Book with CD, 2nd Ed., $19.95
Everything® Learning German Book
Everything® Learning Italian Book
Everything® Learning Latin Book
Everything® Learning Russian Book with CD, $19.95
Everything® Learning Spanish Book
Everything® Learning Spanish Book with CD, 2nd Ed., $19.95
Everything® Russian Practice Book with CD, $19.95
Everything® Sign Language Book, $15.95
Everything® Spanish Grammar Book
Everything® Spanish Phrase Book, $9.95
Everything® Spanish Practice Book with CD, $19.95
Everything® Spanish Verb Book, $9.95
Everything® Speaking Mandarin Chinese Book with CD, $19.95

MUSIC

Everything® Bass Guitar Book with CD, $19.95
Everything® Drums Book with CD, $19.95
Everything® Guitar Book with CD, 2nd Ed., $19.95
Everything® Guitar Chords Book with CD, $19.95
Everything® Guitar Scales Book with CD, $19.95
Everything® Harmonica Book with CD, $15.95
Everything® Home Recording Book
Everything® Music Theory Book with CD, $19.95
Everything® Reading Music Book with CD, $19.95
Everything® Rock & Blues Guitar Book with CD, $19.95
Everything® Rock & Blues Piano Book with CD, $19.95
Everything® Rock Drums Book with CD, $19.95
Everything® Singing Book with CD, $19.95
Everything® Songwriting Book

NEW AGE

Everything® Astrology Book, 2nd Ed.
Everything® Birthday Personology Book
Everything® Celtic Wisdom Book, $15.95
Everything® Dreams Book, 2nd Ed.
Everything® Law of Attraction Book, $15.95
Everything® Love Signs Book, $9.95
Everything® Love Spells Book, $9.95
Everything® Palmistry Book
Everything® Psychic Book
Everything® Reiki Book

Everything® Sex Signs Book, $9.95
Everything® Spells & Charms Book, 2nd Ed.
Everything® Tarot Book, 2nd Ed.
Everything® Toltec Wisdom Book
Everything® Wicca & Witchcraft Book, 2nd Ed.

PARENTING

Everything® Baby Names Book, 2nd Ed.
Everything® Baby Shower Book, 2nd Ed.
Everything® Baby Sign Language Book with DVD
Everything® Baby's First Year Book
Everything® Birthing Book
Everything® Breastfeeding Book
Everything® Father-to-Be Book
Everything® Father's First Year Book
Everything® Get Ready for Baby Book, 2nd Ed.
Everything® Get Your Baby to Sleep Book, $9.95
Everything® Getting Pregnant Book
Everything® Guide to Pregnancy Over 35
Everything® Guide to Raising a One-Year-Old
Everything® Guide to Raising a Two-Year-Old
Everything® Guide to Raising Adolescent Boys
Everything® Guide to Raising Adolescent Girls
Everything® Mother's First Year Book
Everything® Parent's Guide to Childhood Illnesses
Everything® Parent's Guide to Children and Divorce
Everything® Parent's Guide to Children with ADD/ADHD
Everything® Parent's Guide to Children with Asperger's
    Syndrome
Everything® Parent's Guide to Children with Anxiety
Everything® Parent's Guide to Children with Asthma
Everything® Parent's Guide to Children with Autism
Everything® Parent's Guide to Children with Bipolar Disorder
Everything® Parent's Guide to Children with Depression
Everything® Parent's Guide to Children with Dyslexia
Everything® Parent's Guide to Children with Juvenile Diabetes
Everything® Parent's Guide to Children with OCD
Everything® Parent's Guide to Positive Discipline
Everything® Parent's Guide to Raising Boys
Everything® Parent's Guide to Raising Girls
Everything® Parent's Guide to Raising Siblings
Everything® Parent's Guide to Raising Your
    Adopted Child
Everything® Parent's Guide to Sensory Integration Disorder
Everything® Parent's Guide to Tantrums
Everything® Parent's Guide to the Strong-Willed Child
Everything® Parenting a Teenager Book
Everything® Potty Training Book, $9.95
Everything® Pregnancy Book, 3rd Ed.
Everything® Pregnancy Fitness Book
Everything® Pregnancy Nutrition Book
Everything® Pregnancy Organizer, 2nd Ed., $16.95
Everything® Toddler Activities Book
Everything® Toddler Book
Everything® Tween Book
Everything® Twins, Triplets, and More Book

PETS

Everything® Aquarium Book
Everything® Boxer Book
Everything® Cat Book, 2nd Ed.
Everything® Chihuahua Book
Everything® Cooking for Dogs Book
Everything® Dachshund Book
Everything® Dog Book, 2nd Ed.
Everything® Dog Grooming Book

Everything® Dog Obedience Book
Everything® Dog Owner's Organizer, $16.95
Everything® Dog Training and Tricks Book
Everything® German Shepherd Book
Everything® Golden Retriever Book
Everything® Horse Book, 2nd Ed., $15.95
Everything® Horse Care Book
Everything® Horseback Riding Book
Everything® Labrador Retriever Book
Everything® Poodle Book
Everything® Pug Book
Everything® Puppy Book
Everything® Small Dogs Book
Everything® Tropical Fish Book
Everything® Yorkshire Terrier Book

REFERENCE

Everything® American Presidents Book
Everything® Blogging Book
Everything® Build Your Vocabulary Book, $9.95
Everything® Car Care Book
Everything® Classical Mythology Book
Everything® Da Vinci Book
Everything® Einstein Book
Everything® Enneagram Book
Everything® Etiquette Book, 2nd Ed.
Everything® Family Christmas Book, $15.95
Everything® Guide to C. S. Lewis & Narnia
Everything® Guide to Divorce, 2nd Ed., $15.95
Everything® Guide to Edgar Allan Poe
Everything® Guide to Understanding Philosophy
Everything® Inventions and Patents Book
Everything® Jacqueline Kennedy Onassis Book
Everything® John F. Kennedy Book
Everything® Mafia Book
Everything® Martin Luther King Jr. Book
Everything® Pirates Book
Everything® Private Investigation Book
Everything® Psychology Book
Everything® Public Speaking Book, $9.95
Everything® Shakespeare Book, 2nd Ed.

RELIGION

Everything® Angels Book
Everything® Bible Book
Everything® Bible Study Book with CD, $19.95
Everything® Buddhism Book
Everything® Catholicism Book
Everything® Christianity Book
Everything® Gnostic Gospels Book
Everything® Hinduism Book, $15.95
Everything® History of the Bible Book
Everything® Jesus Book
Everything® Jewish History & Heritage Book
Everything® Judaism Book
Everything® Kabbalah Book
Everything® Koran Book
Everything® Mary Book
Everything® Mary Magdalene Book
Everything® Prayer Book

Everything® Saints Book, 2nd Ed.
Everything® Torah Book
Everything® Understanding Islam Book
Everything® Women of the Bible Book
Everything® World's Religions Book

SCHOOL & CAREERS

Everything® Career Tests Book
Everything® College Major Test Book
Everything® College Survival Book, 2nd Ed.
Everything® Cover Letter Book, 2nd Ed.
Everything® Filmmaking Book
Everything® Get-a-Job Book, 2nd Ed.
Everything® Guide to Being a Paralegal
Everything® Guide to Being a Personal Trainer
Everything® Guide to Being a Real Estate Agent
Everything® Guide to Being a Sales Rep
Everything® Guide to Being an Event Planner
Everything® Guide to Careers in Health Care
Everything® Guide to Careers in Law Enforcement
Everything® Guide to Government Jobs
Everything® Guide to Starting and Running a Catering Business
Everything® Guide to Starting and Running a Retail Store
Everything® Job Interview Book, 2nd Ed.
Everything® New Nurse Book
Everything® New Teacher Book
Everything® Paying for College Book
Everything® Practice Interview Book
Everything® Resume Book, 3rd Ed.
Everything® Study Book

SELF-HELP

Everything® Body Language Book
Everything® Dating Book, 2nd Ed.
Everything® Great Sex Book
Everything® Guide to Caring for Aging Parents, $15.95
Everything® Self-Esteem Book
Everything® Self-Hypnosis Book, $9.95
Everything® Tantric Sex Book

SPORTS & FITNESS

Everything® Easy Fitness Book
Everything® Fishing Book
Everything® Guide to Weight Training, $15.95
Everything® Krav Maga for Fitness Book
Everything® Running Book, 2nd Ed.
Everything® Triathlon Training Book, $15.95

TRAVEL

Everything® Family Guide to Coastal Florida
Everything® Family Guide to Cruise Vacations
Everything® Family Guide to Hawaii
Everything® Family Guide to Las Vegas, 2nd Ed.
Everything® Family Guide to Mexico
Everything® Family Guide to New England, 2nd Ed.

Everything® Family Guide to New York City, 3rd Ed.
Everything® Family Guide to Northern California and Lake Tahoe
Everything® Family Guide to RV Travel & Campgrounds
Everything® Family Guide to the Caribbean
Everything® Family Guide to the Disneyland® Resort, California Adventure®, Universal Studios®, and the Anaheim Area, 2nd Ed.
Everything® Family Guide to the Walt Disney World Resort®, Universal Studios®, and Greater Orlando, 5th Ed.
Everything® Family Guide to Timeshares
Everything® Family Guide to Washington D.C., 2nd Ed.

WEDDINGS

Everything® Bachelorette Party Book, $9.95
Everything® Bridesmaid Book, $9.95
Everything® Destination Wedding Book
Everything® Father of the Bride Book, $9.95
Everything® Green Wedding Book, $15.95
Everything® Groom Book, $9.95
Everything® Jewish Wedding Book, 2nd Ed., $15.95
Everything® Mother of the Bride Book, $9.95
Everything® Outdoor Wedding Book
Everything® Wedding Book, 3rd Ed.
Everything® Wedding Checklist, $9.95
Everything® Wedding Etiquette Book, $9.95
Everything® Wedding Organizer, 2nd Ed., $16.95
Everything® Wedding Shower Book, $9.95
Everything® Wedding Vows Book, 3rd Ed., $9.95
Everything® Wedding Workout Book
Everything® Weddings on a Budget Book, 2nd Ed., $9.95

WRITING

Everything® Creative Writing Book
Everything® Get Published Book, 2nd Ed.
Everything® Grammar and Style Book, 2nd Ed.
Everything® Guide to Magazine Writing
Everything® Guide to Writing a Book Proposal
Everything® Guide to Writing a Novel
Everything® Guide to Writing Children's Books
Everything® Guide to Writing Copy
Everything® Guide to Writing Graphic Novels
Everything® Guide to Writing Research Papers
Everything® Guide to Writing a Romance Novel, $15.95
Everything® Improve Your Writing Book, 2nd Ed.
Everything® Writing Poetry Book